ALL GLORY TO ŚRĪ GURU AND GAURĀṄGA

ŚRĪMAD BHĀGAVATAM

of

KṚṢṆA-DVAIPĀYANA VYĀSA

नामसंकीर्तनं यस्य सर्वपापप्रणाशनम् ।
प्रणामो दुःखशमनस्तं नमामि हरिं परम् ॥२३॥

nāma-saṅkīrtanaṁ yasya
sarva-pāpa-praṇāśanam
praṇāmo duḥkha-śamanas
taṁ namāmi hariṁ param

(p. 209)

BOOKS by
His Divine Grace
A. C. Bhaktivedanta Swami Prabhupāda

Bhagavad-gītā As It Is
Śrīmad-Bhāgavatam, Cantos 1–10 (30 volumes)
Śrī Caitanya-caritāmṛta (17 vols.)
Teachings of Lord Caitanya
The Nectar of Devotion
The Nectar of Instruction
Śrī Īśopaniṣad
Easy Journey to Other Planets
Kṛṣṇa Consciousness: The Topmost Yoga System
Kṛṣṇa, the Supreme Personality of Godhead (3 vols.)
Perfect Questions, Perfect Answers
Teachings of Lord Kapila, the Son of Devahūti
Transcendental Teachings of Prahlāda Mahārāja
Teachings of Queen Kuntī
Kṛṣṇa, the Reservoir of Pleasure
The Science of Self-Realization
The Path of Perfection
Search for Liberation
Life Comes From Life
The Perfection of Yoga
Beyond Birth and Death
On the Way to Kṛṣṇa
Geetār-gān (Bengali)
Vairāgya-vidyā (Bengali)
Buddhi-yoga (Bengali)
Bhakti-ratna-bolī (Bengali)
Rāja-vidyā: The King of Knowledge
Elevation to Kṛṣṇa Consciousness
Kṛṣṇa Consciousness: The Matchless Gift
Back to Godhead magazine (founder)

A complete catalog is available upon request.

Bhaktivedanta Book Trust
Mail Order Division
3764 Watseka Avenue
Los Angeles, California 90034

ŚRĪMAD BHĀGAVATAM

Twelfth Canto

"The Age of Deterioration"

(Part Two—Chapters 7-13)

With the Original Sanskrit Text, Its Roman Transliteration, Synonyms, Translation and Elaborate Purports

The Great Work of

His Divine Grace

A. C. Bhaktivedanta Swami Prabhupāda

Founder-*Ācārya* of the International Society for Krishna Consciousness

Continued by

His Divine Grace

Hridayananda dāsa Goswami Ācāryadeva

Sanskrit Editing by

Gopīparāṇadhana dāsa Adhikārī

THE BHAKTIVEDANTA BOOK TRUST

Los Angeles • London • Paris • Bombay • Sydney • Hong Kong

Readers interested in the subject matter of this book are invited by the International Society for Krishna Consciousness to correspond with its Secretary:

International Society for Krishna Consciousness
3764 Watseka Avenue
Los Angeles, California 90034

First Printing, 1984: 5,000 copies

Printed in the United States of America

Library of Congress Cataloging in Publication Data (Revised)

Purāṇas. Bhāgavatapurāṇa. English & Sanskrit.
Śrīmad-Bhāgavatam.

Includes bibliographical references and indexes.
Contents: Canto 1. Creation (3 v)— Canto 2. The cosmic manifestation (2 v)— Canto 3. The status quo (4 v)— Canto 4. The creation of the fourth order (4 v)— Canto 5. The creative impetus (2 v)— Canto 6. Prescribed duties for mankind (3 v)— Canto 7. The science of God (3 v)— Canto 8. Withdrawal of the cosmic creations (3 v)— Canto 9. Liberation (3 v)— Canto 10. The summum bonum (3 v)— Canto 11. General history (5 v)
Canto 12- by Hridayananda Goswami Ācāryadeva, completing the great work of His Divine Grace A. C. Bhaktivedanta Swami Prabhupāda; Sanskrit editing by Gopīparāṇadhana Dāsa Adhikārī.
1. Purāṇas. Bhāgavatapurāṇa—Criticism, interpretation, etc. 2. Chaitanya, 1486-1534. 3. Vaishnavites—India—Biography.
I. Bhaktivedanta Swami, A. C., 1896-1977.
II. Hridayananda Goswami, 1948-
III. Gopīparāṇadhana Dāsa Adhikārī.
IV. Title.
BL1140.4.B432E5 1972 294.5'925 73-169353
ISBN 0-89213-126-8 (Canto 12, v.2) AACR2

Table of Contents

Preface *ix*
Foreword *xiii*
Introduction *xvii*

CHAPTER SEVEN
The Purāṇic Literatures

Chapter Summary 1
Ancient Scholars of the *Atharva Veda* 3
The Purāṇic Wisdom Is Passed from *Guru* to Disciple 5
Characteristics of a *Purāṇa* 7
Primary and Secondary Creation 9
The Six Kinds of Incarnations of the Lord 12
Why the Lord is the Unlimited, Unique Shelter 15
The Eighteen Major *Purāṇas* 18

CHAPTER EIGHT
Mārkaṇḍeya's Prayers to Nara-Nārāyaṇa Ṛṣi

Chapter Summary 21
Some Puzzling Facts about Mārkaṇḍeya Ṛṣi 24
How Mārkaṇḍeya Conquered Death 27
Indra Sends Cupid to Break Mārkaṇḍeya's Vows 31
Heavenly Singers and Dancers Try to Seduce Mārkaṇḍeya 35
Mārkaṇḍeya Defeats the Mischief-makers 38
The Appearance of Nara-Nārāyaṇa Ṛṣi 40
An Ecstatic Mārkaṇḍeya Greets the Lords 42
The Sage Offers Prayers to Nara-Nārāyaṇa Ṛṣi 45
The Lord's Lotus Feet: the Only Relief from Fear 47
Empirical Means are Futile for Understanding the Lord 53

CHAPTER NINE
Mārkaṇḍeya Ṛṣi Sees the Illusory Potency of the Lord

Chapter Summary 55
Lord Nārāyaṇa Offers Mārkaṇḍeya a Benediction 57
Mārkaṇḍeya Asks to See the Lord's Illusory Potency 60
A Terrible Storm Overwhelms the Sage in His Hermitage 63
Wandering Alone in the Universal Inundation 66
Mārkaṇḍeya Comes Upon an Island in the Vast Sea 69
Description of the Lord as an Infant Lying on a Banyan Leaf 71
The Sage Beholds the Creation Within the Lord's Body 73
The Lord and His Illusory Potency Disappear 77

CHAPTER TEN
Lord Śiva and Umā Glorify Mārkaṇḍeya Ṛṣi

Chapter Summary 79
Lord Śiva and Umā Come Upon Mārkaṇḍeya in Trance 82
Lord Śiva Enters Within the Sage's Heart 86
Mārkaṇḍeya Worships Lord Śiva and Umā 88
Even Lord Brahmā, Lord Viṣṇu and Lord Śiva Honor Saintly *Brāhmaṇas* 92
Why Great Souls Show Humility Before Their Subordinates 98
Mārkaṇḍeya's Benedictions 103
Benediction for the Readers 107

CHAPTER ELEVEN
Summary Description of the Mahāpuruṣa

Chapter Summary 109
How to Attain Immortality 111

The Universal Form of the Lord 114
Service to the Lord Eradicates All Sin 119
Three Infallible Entities 123
Four Personal Expansions of the Lord 125
The Benefits of Singing the Lord's Glories 127
The Sun Is the Creator, Regulator and Soul of All the Worlds 130
Enumeration of Twelve Sets of the Sun-god's Associates 132
Value of Remembering the Sun-god and His Associates 143

CHAPTER TWELVE
The Topics of Śrīmad-Bhāgavatam Summarized

Chapter Summary 145
To Be a Human Being, One Must Hear *Śrīmad-Bhāgavatam* 147
The Mystery of the Absolute Truth and Devotional Service 149
Creation of the Universal Egg 152
The Continents, the Celestial Sphere and Hell 156
Incarnations of the Lord 158
The Appearance and Pastimes of Lord Śrī Kṛṣṇa 162
The Chaos of the Age of Kali 171
Lord Kṛṣṇa Enters and Cleanses the Hearts of His Glorifiers 174
Words Glorifying Lord Kṛṣṇa Are a Perpetual Festival for the Mind 176
Remembrance of the Lord's Lotus Feet Destroys Everything Inauspicious 180
Benefits of Hearing *Śrīmad-Bhāgavatam* 183
Lord Hari is Abundantly and Constantly Glorified Only in *Śrīmad-Bhāgavatam* 187
Śrī Sūta Gosvāmī Praises Śukadeva Gosvāmī 190

CHAPTER THIRTEEN
The Glories of Śrīmad-Bhāgavatam

Chapter Summary 191

Glorification of Lord Kūrma 193

Verse Length of the Eighteen Major *Purāṇas* 196

Lord Brahmā First Heard the *Bhāgavatam* from the Supreme Lord 198

The *Bhāgavatam* Is Full of the Lord's Nectarean Pastimes 200

Śrīmad-Bhāgavatam: the Essence of All Vedānta Philosophy 203

Śrīmad-Bhāgavatam: the Spotless *Purāṇa* 205

Conclusion 209

Appendixes

The Author 213

His Divine Grace A. C. Bhaktivedanta Swami Prabhupāda 215

References 219

Glossary 221

Sanskrit Pronunciation Guide 227

Index of Sanskrit Verses 231

General Index 239

Preface

nama oṁ viṣṇu-pādāya kṛṣṇa-preṣṭhāya bhū-tale
śrīmate bhaktivedānta-svāmin iti nāmine

I offer my most respectful obeisances at the lotus feet of His Divine Grace A. C. Bhaktivedanta Swami Prabhupāda, who is very dear to Lord Kṛṣṇa on this earth, having taken shelter at His lotus feet.

namas te sārasvate deve gaura-vāṇī-pracāriṇe
nirviśeṣa-śūnyavādi-pāścātya-deśa-tāriṇe

I offer my most respectful obeisances unto the lotus feet of His Divine Grace A. C. Bhaktivedanta Swami Prabhupāda, who is the disciple of Śrīla Bhaktisiddhānta Sarasvatī Ṭhākura and who is powerfully distributing the message of Caitanya Mahāprabhu and thus saving the fallen Western countries from impersonalism and voidism.

Śrīmad-Bhāgavatam, with authorized translation and elaborate purports in the English language, is the great work of His Divine Grace Oṁ Viṣṇupāda Paramahaṁsa Parivrājakācārya Aṣṭottara-śata Śrī Śrīmad A. C. Bhaktivedanta Swami Prabhupāda, our beloved spiritual master. Our present publication is a humble attempt by his servants to complete his most cherished work of *Śrīmad-Bhāgavatam.* Just as one may worship the holy Ganges River by offering Ganges water unto the Ganges, similarly, in our attempt to serve our spiritual master, we are offering to him that which he has given to us.

Śrīla Prabhupāda came to America in 1965 at a critical moment in the history of America and the world in general. The story of Śrīla Prabhupāda's arrival and his specific impact on world civilization, and especially

Western civilization, has been brilliantly documented by His Divine Grace Satsvarūpa dāsa Goswami. From Śrīla Satsvarūpa's authorized biography of Śrīla Prabhupāda, called *Śrīla Prabhupāda-līlāmṛta*, the reader can fully understand Śrīla Prabhupāda's purpose, desire and mission in presenting *Śrīmad-Bhāgavatam*. Further, in Śrīla Prabhupāda's own preface to the *Bhāgavatam* (reprinted as the Foreword in this volume), he clearly states that this transcendental literature will provoke a cultural revolution in the world, and that is now underway. I do not wish to be redundant in repeating what Śrīla Prabhupāda has so eloquently stated in his preface, nor that which has been so abundantly documented by Śrīla Satsvarūpa in his authorized biography.

It is necessary to mention, however, that *Śrīmad-Bhāgavatam* is a completely transcendental, liberated sound vibration coming from the spiritual world. And, being absolute, it is not different from the Absolute Truth Himself, Lord Śrī Kṛṣṇa. By understanding *Śrīmad-Bhāgavatam*, consisting of twelve cantos, the reader acquires perfect knowledge, by which he or she may live peacefully and progressively on the earth, attending to all material necessities and simultaneously achieving supreme spiritual liberation. As we have worked to prepare this and other volumes of *Śrīmad-Bhāgavatam*, our intention has been always to serve faithfully the lotus feet of our spiritual master, carefully trying to translate and comment exactly as he would have, thus preserving the unity and spiritual potency of this edition of *Śrīmad-Bhāgavatam*. In other words, by strictly following the disciplic succession, called in Sanskrit *guru-paramparā*, this edition of the *Bhāgavatam* will continue to be throughout its volumes a liberated work, free from material contamination and capable of elevating the reader to the kingdom of God.

The purport is that we have faithfully followed the commentaries of previous *ācāryas* and exercised a calculated selectivity of material based on the example and mood of Śrīla Prabhupāda. One may write transcendental literature only by the mercy of the Supreme Personality of Godhead, Śrī Kṛṣṇa, and the authorized, liberated spiritual masters coming in disciplic succession. Thus, we humbly fall at the lotus feet of the previous *ācāryas*, offering special gratitude to the great commentators on the *Bhāgavatam*, namely Śrīla Śrīdhara Svāmī, Śrīla Jīva Gosvāmī, Śrīla Viśvanātha Cakravartī Ṭhākura and Śrīla Bhaktisiddhānta Sarasvatī Gosvāmī, the spiritual master of Śrīla Prabhupāda. We also offer our obeisances at the lotus feet of Śrīla Vīrarāghavācārya, Śrīla Vijayadhvaja Ṭhākura and Śrīla Vaṁśīdhara Ṭhākura, whose commentaries have also helped in this work. Additionally, we offer our humble obeisances at the lotus feet of the great *ācārya* Śrīla Madhva, who has made innumerable learned comments on *Śrīmad-Bhāgavatam*. We further offer our humble obeisances at the lotus feet of the Supreme Personality of Godhead, Śrī Kṛṣṇa Caitanya Mahāprabhu, and to all of His eternally liberated followers, headed by Śrīla Nityānanda Prabhu, Advaita Prabhu, Gadādhara Prabhu and Śrīvāsa Ṭhākura, and to the six Gosvāmīs, Śrīla Rūpa Gosvāmī, Śrīla Sanātana Gosvāmī, Śrīla Raghunātha dāsa Gosvāmī, Śrīla Raghunātha Bhaṭṭa Gosvāmī, Śrīla Jīva Gosvāmī and Śrīla Gopāla Bhaṭṭa Gosvāmī. Finally we offer our most respectful obeisances at the lotus feet of the Absolute Truth, Śrī Śrī Rādhā and Kṛṣṇa, and humbly beg for Their mercy so that this great work of *Śrīmad-Bhāgavatam* can be quickly finished. *Śrīmad-Bhāgavatam* is undoubtedly the most important book within the universe, and the sincere readers of *Śrīmad-Bhāgavatam* will undoubtedly achieve the highest perfection of life, Kṛṣṇa consciousness.

In conclusion, I again remind the reader that *Śrīmad-Bhāgavatam* is the great work of His Divine Grace A. C. Bhaktivedanta Swami Prabhupāda, and that the present volume is the humble attempt of his devoted servants.

Hare Kṛṣṇa

Hridayananda dāsa Goswami

Foreword

We must know the present need of human society. And what is that need? Human society is no longer bounded by geographical limits to particular countries or communities. Human society is broader than in the Middle Ages, and the world tendency is toward one state or one human society. The ideals of spiritual communism, according to *Śrīmad-Bhāgavatam,* are based more or less on the oneness of the entire human society, nay, of the entire energy of living beings. The need is felt by great thinkers to make this a successful ideology. *Śrīmad-Bhāgavatam* will fill this need in human society. It begins, therefore, with an aphorism of Vedānta philosophy, *janmādy asya yataḥ,* to establish the ideal of a common cause.

Human society, at the present moment, is not in the darkness of oblivion. It has made rapid progress in the fields of material comforts, education and economic development throughout the entire world. But there is a pinprick somewhere in the social body at large, and therefore there are large-scale quarrels, even over less important issues. There is need of a clue as to how humanity can become one in peace, friendship and prosperity with a common cause. *Śrīmad-Bhāgavatam* will fill this need, for it is a cultural presentation for the respiritualization of the entire human society.

Śrīmad-Bhāgavatam should be introduced also in the schools and colleges, for it is recommended by the great student-devotee Prahlāda Mahārāja in order to change the demoniac face of society.

kaumāra ācaret prājño
dharmān bhāgavatān iha
durlabhaṁ mānuṣaṁ janma
tad apy adhruvam artha-dam
(*Bhāg.* 7.6.1)

Disparity in human society is due to lack of principles in a godless civilization. There is God, or the Almighty One, from whom everything emanates, by whom everything is maintained and in whom everything is merged to rest. Material science has tried to find the ultimate source of creation very insufficiently, but it is a fact that there is one ultimate source of everything that be. This ultimate source is explained rationally and authoritatively in the beautiful *Bhāgavatam*, or *Śrīmad-Bhāgavatam*.

Śrīmad-Bhāgavatam is the transcendental science not only for knowing the ultimate source of everything but also for knowing our relation with Him and our duty toward perfection of the human society on the basis of this perfect knowledge. It is powerful reading matter in the Sanskrit language, and it is now rendered into English elaborately so that simply by a careful reading one will know God perfectly well, so much so that the reader will be sufficiently educated to defend himself from the onslaught of atheists. Over and above this, the reader will be able to convert others to accepting God as a concrete principle.

Śrīmad-Bhāgavatam begins with the definition of the ultimate source. It is a bona fide commentary on the *Vedānta-sūtra* by the same author, Śrīla Vyāsadeva, and gradually it develops into nine cantos up to the highest state of God realization. The only qualification one needs to study this great book of transcendental knowledge is to proceed step by step cautiously and not jump forward haphazardly like with an ordinary book. It should be gone through chapter by chapter, one after another. The reading matter is so arranged with its original Sanskrit text, its English transliteration, synonyms, translation and purports so that one is sure to become a God-realized soul at the end of finishing the first nine cantos.

The Tenth Canto is distinct from the first nine cantos because it deals directly with the transcendental activities of the Personality of Godhead Śrī Kṛṣṇa. One will be unable to capture the effects of the Tenth Canto without going through the first nine cantos. The book is complete in twelve cantos, each independent, but it is good for all to read them in small installments one after another.

I must admit my frailties in presenting *Śrīmad-Bhāgavatam*, but still I am hopeful of its good reception by the thinkers and leaders of society on the strength of the following statement of *Śrīmad-Bhāgavatam* (1.5.11):

tad-vāg-visargo janatāgha-viplavo
yasmin prati-ślokam abaddhavaty api

nāmāny anantasya yaśo 'ṅkitāni yac
chṛṇvanti gāyanti gṛṇanti sādhavaḥ

"On the other hand, that literature which is full of descriptions of the transcendental glories of the name, fame, form and pastimes of the unlimited Supreme Lord is a transcendental creation meant for bringing about a revolution in the impious life of a misdirected civilization. Such transcendental literature, even though irregularly composed, is heard, sung and accepted by purified men who are thoroughly honest."

Oṁ tat sat

A. C. Bhaktivedanta Swami

Introduction

"This *Bhāgavata Purāṇa* is as brilliant as the sun, and it has arisen just after the departure of Lord Kṛṣṇa to His own abode, accompanied by religion, knowledge, etc. Persons who have lost their vision due to the dense darkness of ignorance in the age of Kali shall get light from this *Purāṇa*." (*Śrīmad-Bhāgavatam* 1.3.43)

The timeless wisdom of India is expressed in the *Vedas*, ancient Sanskrit texts that touch upon all fields of human knowledge. Originally preserved through oral tradition, the *Vedas*, were first put into writing five thousand years ago by Śrīla Vyāsadeva, the "literary incarnation of God." After compiling the *Vedas*, Vyāsadeva set forth their essence in the aphorisms known as *Vedānta-sūtras*. *Śrīmad-Bhāgavatam* (*Bhāgavata Purāṇa*) is Vyāsadeva's commentary on his own *Vedānta-sūtras*. It was written in the maturity of his spiritual life under the direction of Nārada Muni, his spiritual master. Referred to as "the ripened fruit of the tree of Vedic literature," *Śrīmad-Bhāgavatam* is the most complete and authoritative exposition of Vedic knowledge.

After compiling the *Bhāgavatam*, Vyāsa imparted the synopsis of it to his son, the sage Śukadeva Gosvāmī. Śukadeva Gosvāmī subsequently recited the entire *Bhāgavatam* to Mahārāja Parīkṣit in an assembly of learned saints on the bank of the Ganges at Hastināpura (now Delhi). Mahārāja Parīkṣit was the emperor of the world and was a great *rājarṣi* (saintly king). Having received a warning that he would die within a week, he renounced his entire kingdom and retired to the bank of the Ganges to fast until death and receive spiritual enlightenment. The *Bhāgavatam* begins with Emperor Parīkṣit's sober inquiry to Śukadeva Gosvāmī: "You are the spiritual master of great saints and devotees. I am therefore begging you to show the way of perfection for all persons, and especially for one who is about to die. Please let me know what a man should hear, chant, remember and worship, and also what he should not do. Please explain all this to me."

Śukadeva Gosvāmī's answer to this question, and numerous other questions posed by Mahārāja Parīkṣit, concerning everything from the nature of the self to the origin of the universe, held the assembled sages in rapt attention continuously for the seven days leading up to the king's death. The sage Sūta Gosvāmī, who was present in that assembly when Śukadeva Gosvāmī first recited *Śrīmad-Bhāgavatam,* later repeated the *Bhāgavatam* before a gathering of sages in the forest of Naimiṣāraṇya. Those sages, concerned about the spiritual welfare of the people in general, had gathered to perform a long, continuous chain of sacrifices to counteract the degrading influence of the incipient age of Kali. In response to the sages' request that he speak the essence of Vedic wisdom, Sūta Gosvāmī repeated from memory the entire eighteen thousand verses of *Śrīmad-Bhāgavatam,* as spoken by Śukadeva Gosvāmī to Mahārāja Parīkṣit.

The reader of *Śrīmad-Bhāgavatam* hears Sūta Gosvāmī relate the questions of Mahārāja Parīkṣit and the answers of Śukadeva Gosvāmī. Also, Sūta Gosvāmī sometimes responds directly to questions put by Śaunaka Ṛṣi, the spokesman for the sages gathered at Naimiṣāraṇya. One therefore simultaneously hears two dialogues: one between Mahārāja Parīkṣit and Śukadeva Gosvāmī on the bank of the Ganges, and another at Naimiṣāraṇya between Sūta Gosvāmī and the sages at Naimiṣāraṇya Forest, headed by Śaunaka Ṛṣi. Furthermore, while instructing King Parīkṣit, Śukadeva Gosvāmī often relates historical episodes and gives accounts of lengthy philosophical discussions between such great souls as Nārada Muni and Vasudeva. With this understanding of the history of the *Bhāgavatam,* the reader will easily be able to follow its intermingling of dialogues and events from various sources. Since philosophical wisdom, not chronological order, is most important in the text, one need only be attentive to the subject matter of *Śrīmad-Bhāgavatam* to appreciate fully its profound message.

The translators of this edition compare the *Bhāgavatam* to sugar candy—wherever you taste it, you will find it equally sweet and relishable. Therefore, to taste the sweetness of the *Bhāgavatam,* one may begin by reading any of its volumes. After such an introductory taste, however, the serious reader is best advised to go back to Volume One of the First Canto and then proceed through the *Bhāgavatam*, volume after volume, in its natural order.

This edition of the *Bhāgavatam* is the first complete English translation of this important text with an elaborate commentary, and it is the first widely available to the English-speaking public. The first thirty volumes (Canto One through Canto Ten, Volume Three) are the product of the scholarly and devotional effort of His Divine Grace A. C. Bhaktivedanta Swami Prabhupāda, the world's most distinguished teacher of Indian religious and philosophical thought. His consummate Sanskrit scholarship and intimate familiarity with Vedic culture and thought as well as the modern way of life combine to reveal to the West a magnificent exposition of this important classic. After the departure of Śrīla Prabhupāda from this world in 1977, his monumental work of translating *Śrīmad-Bhāgavatam* is being continued by his disciple His Divine Grace Hridayananda dāsa Goswami Ācāryadeva.

Readers will find this work of value for many reasons. For those interested in the classical roots of Indian civilization, it serves as a vast reservoir of detailed information on virtually every one of its aspects. For students of comparative philosophy and religion, the *Bhāgavatam* offers a penetrating view into the meaning of India's profound spiritual heritage. To sociologists and anthropologists, the *Bhāgavatam* reveals the practical workings of a peaceful and scientifically organized Vedic culture, whose institutions were integrated on the basis of a highly developed spiritual world view. Students of literature will discover the *Bhāgavatam* to be a masterpiece of majestic poetry. For students of psychology, the text provides important perspectives on the nature of consciousness, human behavior and the philosophical study of identity. Finally, to those seeking spiritual insight, the *Bhāgavatam* offers simple and practical guidance for attainment of the highest self-knowledge and realization of the Absolute Truth. The entire multivolume text, presented by the Bhaktivedanta Book Trust, promises to occupy a significant place in the intellectual, cultural and spiritual life of modern man for a long time to come.

—The Publishers

CHAPTER SEVEN

The Purāṇic Literatures

In this chapter Śrī Sūta Gosvāmī describes the expansion of the branches of the *Atharva Veda,* enumerates the compilers of the *Purāṇas* and explains the characteristics of a *Purāṇa.* He then lists the eighteen major *Purāṇas* and finishes his account by stating that any person who hears about these matters from someone in a proper disciplic succession will acquire spiritual potency.

TEXT 1

सूत उवाच
अथर्ववित् सुमन्तुश्च शिष्यमध्यापयत् स्वकाम् ।
संहितां सोऽपि पथ्याय वेददर्शाय चोक्तवान् ॥१॥

sūta uvāca
atharva-vit sumantuś ca
śiṣyam adhyāpayat svakām
saṁhitāṁ so 'pi pathyāya
vedadarśāya coktavān

sūtaḥ uvāca—Sūta Gosvāmī said; *atharva-vit*—the expert knower of the *Atharva Veda; sumantuḥ*—Sumantu; *ca*—and; *śiṣyam*—to his disciple; *adhyāpayat*—instructed; *svakām*—his own; *saṁhitām*—collection; *saḥ*—he, the disciple of Sumantu; *api*—also; *pathyāya*—to Pathya; *vedadarśāya*—to Vedadarśa; *ca*—and; *uktavān*—spoke.

TRANSLATION

Sūta Gosvāmī said: Sumantu Ṛṣi, the authority on the *Atharva Veda,* taught his *saṁhitā* to his disciple Kabandha, who in turn spoke it to Pathya and Vedadarśa.

PURPORT

As confirmed in the *Viṣṇu Purāṇa:*

atharva-vedaṁ sa muniḥ
sumantur amita-dyutiḥ
śiṣyam adhyāpayām āsa
kabandhaṁ so 'pi ca dvidhā
kṛtvā tu vedadarśāya
tathā pathyāya dattavān

"That sage Sumantu, whose brilliance was immeasurable, taught the *Atharva Veda* to his disciple Kabandha. Kabandha in turn divided it into two parts and passed them down to Vedadarśa and Pathya."

TEXT 2

शौक्लायनिर्ब्रह्मबलिर्मोदोषः पिप्पलायनिः ।
वेददर्शस्य शिष्यास्ते पथ्यशिष्यानथो शृणु ।
कुमुदः शुनको ब्रह्मन् जाजलिश्चाप्यथर्ववित् ॥२॥

śauklāyanir brahmabalir
modoṣaḥ pippalāyaniḥ
vedadarśasya śiṣyās te
pathya-śiṣyān atho śṛṇu
kumudaḥ śunako brahman
jājaliś cāpy atharva-vit

śauklāyaniḥ brahmabaliḥ—Śauklāyani and Brahmabali; *modoṣaḥ pippalāyaniḥ*—Modoṣa and Pippalāyani; *vedadarśasya*—of Vedadarśa; *śiṣyāḥ*—the disciples; *te*—they; *pathya-śiṣyān*—the disciples of Pathya; *atho*—furthermore; *śṛṇu*—please hear; *kumudaḥ śunakaḥ*—Kumuda and Śunaka; *brahman*—O *brāhmaṇa*, Śaunaka; *jājaliḥ*—Jājali; *ca*—and; *api*—also; *atharva-vit*—full in knowledge of the *Atharva Veda.*

TRANSLATION

Śauklāyani, Brahmabali, Modoṣa and Pippalāyani were disciples of Vedadarśa. Hear from me also the names of the disciples of Pathya. My dear *brāhmaṇa,* they are Kumuda, Śunaka and Jājali, all of whom knew the *Atharva Veda* very well.

PURPORT

According to Śrīla Śrīdhara Svāmī, Vedadarśa divided his edition of the *Atharva Veda* into four parts and instructed them to his four disciples. Pathya divided his edition into three parts and instructed it to the three disciples mentioned here.

TEXT 3

बभ्रुः शिष्योऽथाङ्गिरसः सैन्धवायन एव च ।
अधीयेतां संहिते द्वे सावर्णाद्यास्तथापरे ॥३॥

babhruḥ śiṣyo 'thāṅgirasaḥ
saindhavāyana eva ca
adhīyetāṁ saṁhite dve
sāvarṇādyās tathāpare

babhruḥ—Babhru; *śiṣyaḥ*—the disciple; *atha*—then; *aṅgirasaḥ*—of Śunaka (also known as Aṅgirā); *saindhavāyanaḥ*—Saindhavāyana; *eva*—indeed; *ca*—also; *adhīyetām*—they learned; *saṁhite*—collections; *dve*—two; *sāvarṇa*—Sāvarṇa; *ādyāḥ*—headed by; *tathā*—similarly; *apare*—other disciples.

TRANSLATION

Babhru and Saindhavāyana, disciples of Śunaka, studied the two divisions of their spiritual master's compilation of the *Atharva Veda.* Saindhavāyana's disciple Sāvarṇa and disciples of other great sages also studied this edition of the *Atharva Veda.*

TEXT 4

नक्षत्रकल्पः शान्तिश्च कश्यपाङ्गिरसादयः ।
एते आथर्वणाचार्याः शृणु पौराणिकान्मुने ॥४॥

nakṣatrakalpaḥ śāntiś ca
kaśyapāṅgirasādayaḥ
ete ātharvaṇācāryāḥ
śṛṇu paurāṇikān mune

nakṣatrakalpaḥ—Nakṣatrakalpa; *śāntiḥ*—Sāntikalpa; *ca*—also; *kaśyapa-āṅgirasa-ādayaḥ*—Kaśyapa, Āṅgirasa and others; *ete*—these; *ātharvaṇa-ācāryāḥ*—spiritual masters of the *Atharva Veda; śṛṇu*—now hear; *paurāṇikān*—the authorities of the *Purāṇas; mune*—O sage, Śaunaka.

TRANSLATION

Nakṣatrakalpa, Śāntikalpa, Kaśyapa, Āṅgirasa and others were also among the *ācāryas* of the *Atharva Veda*. Now, O sage, listen as I name the authorities on Purāṇic literature.

TEXT 5

त्रय्यारुणिः कश्यपश्च सावर्णिरकृतव्रणः ।
वैशम्पायनहारीतौ षड् वै पौराणिका इमे ॥५॥

trayyāruṇiḥ kaśyapaś ca
sāvarṇir akṛtavraṇaḥ
vaiśampāyana-hārītau
ṣaḍ vai paurāṇikā ime

trayyāruṇiḥ kaśyapaḥ ca—Trayyāruṇi and Kaśyapa; *sāvarṇiḥ akṛta-vraṇaḥ*—Sāvarṇi and Akṛtavraṇa; *vaiśampāyana-hārītau*—Vaiśampāyana and Hārīta; *ṣaṭ*—six; *vai*—indeed; *paurāṇikāḥ*—spiritual masters of the *Purāṇas; ime*—these.

TRANSLATION

Trayyāruṇi, Kaśyapa, Sāvarṇi, Akṛtavraṇa, Vaiśampāyana and Hārīta are the six masters of the *Purāṇas*.

TEXT 6

अधीयन्त व्यासशिष्यात् संहितां मत्पितुर्मुखात् ।
एकैकामहमेतेषां शिष्यः सर्वाः समध्यगाम् ॥६॥

adhīyanta vyāsa-śiṣyāt
saṁhitāṁ mat-pitur mukhāt
ekaikām aham eteṣāṁ
śiṣyaḥ sarvāḥ samadhyagām

adhīyanta—they have learned; *vyāsa-śiṣyāt*—from the disciple of Vyāsadeva (Romaharṣaṇa); *saṁhitām*—the collection of the *Purāṇas; mat-pituḥ*—of my father; *mukhāt*—from the mouth; *eka-ekām*—each learning one portion; *aham*—I; *eteṣām*—of these; *śiṣyaḥ*—the disciple; *sarvāḥ*—all the collections; *samadhyagām*—I have thoroughly learned.

TRANSLATION

Each of them studied one of the six anthologies of the *Purāṇas* from my father, Romaharṣaṇa, who was a disciple of Śrīla Vyāsadeva. I became the disciple of these six authorities and thoroughly learned all their presentations of Purāṇic wisdom.

TEXT 7

कश्यपोऽहं च सावर्णी रामशिष्योऽकृतव्रणः ।
अधीमहि व्यासशिष्याच्चत्वारो मूलसंहिताः ॥७॥

kaśyapo 'haṁ ca sāvarṇī
rāma-śiṣyo 'kṛtavraṇaḥ
adhīmahi vyāsa-śiṣyāc
catvāro mūla-saṁhitāḥ

kaśyapaḥ—Kaśyapa; *aham*—I; *ca*—and; *sāvarṇiḥ*—Sāvarṇi; *rāma-śiṣyaḥ*—a disciple of Rāma; *akṛtvraṇaḥ*—namely Akṛtavraṇa; *adhīmahi*—we have assimilated; *vyāsa-śiṣyāt*—from the disciple of Vyāsa (Romaharṣaṇa); *catvāraḥ*—four; *mūla-saṁhitāḥ*—basic collections.

TRANSLATION

Romaharṣaṇa, a disciple of Vedavyāsa, divided the *Purāṇas* into four basic compilations. The sage Kaśyapa and I, along with Sāvarṇi and Akṛtavraṇa, a disciple of Rāma, learned these four divisions.

TEXT 8

पुराणलक्षणं ब्रह्मन् ब्रह्मर्षिभिर्निरूपितम् ।
शृणुष्व बुद्धिमाश्रित्य वेदशास्त्रानुसारतः ॥८॥

purāṇa-lakṣaṇaṁ brahman
brahmarṣibhir nirūpitam
śṛṇuṣva buddhim āśritya
veda-śāstrānusārataḥ

purāṇa-lakṣaṇam—the characteristics of a *Purāṇa; brahman*—O *brāhmaṇa,* Śaunaka; *brahma-ṛṣibhiḥ*—by great learned *brāhmaṇas; nirūpitam*—ascertained; *śṛṇuṣva*—please hear; *buddhim*—intelligence; *āśritya*—resorting to; *veda-śāstra*—the Vedic scriptures; *anusārataḥ*—in accordance with.

TRANSLATION

O Śaunaka, please hear with attention the characteristics of a *Purāṇa,* which have been defined by the most eminent learned *brāhmaṇas* in accordance with Vedic literature.

TEXTS 9–10

सर्गोऽस्याथ विसर्गश्च वृत्तिरक्षान्तराणि च ।
वंशो वंशानुचरितं संस्था हेतुरपाश्रयः ॥९॥

दशभिर्लक्षणैर्युक्तं पुराणं तद्विदो विदुः ।
केचित् पञ्चविधं ब्रह्मन्महदल्पव्यवस्थया ॥१०॥

sargo 'syātha visargaś ca
vṛtti-rakṣāntarāṇi ca
vaṁśo vaṁśānucaritaṁ
saṁsthā hetur apāśrayaḥ

daśabhir lakṣaṇair yuktaṁ
purāṇaṁ tad-vido viduḥ
kecit pañca-vidhaṁ brahman
mahad-alpa-vyavasthayā

sargaḥ—the creation; *asya*—of this universe; *atha*—then; *visargaḥ*—the secondary creation; *ca*—and; *vṛtti*—maintenance; *rakṣā*—protection by sustenance; *antarāṇi*—the reigns of the Manus; *ca*—and; *vaṁśaḥ*—the dynasties of great kings; *vaṁśa-anucaritam*—the narrations of their activities; *saṁsthā*—the annihilation; *hetuḥ*—the motivation (for the living entities' involvement in material activities); *apāśrayaḥ*—the supreme shelter; *daśabhiḥ*—with the ten; *lakṣaṇaiḥ*—characteristics; *yuktam*—endowed; *purāṇam*—a *Purāṇa; tat*—of this matter; *vidaḥ*—those who know; *viduḥ*—they know; *kecit*—some authorities; *pañca-vidham*—fivefold; *brahman*—O *brāhmaṇa; mahat*—of great; *alpa*—and lesser; *vyavasthayā*—according to the distinction.

TRANSLATION

O *brāhmaṇa*, authorities on the matter understand a *Purāṇa* to contain ten characteristic topics: the creation of this universe, the subsequent creation of worlds and beings, the maintenance of all living beings, their sustenance, the rule of various Manus, the dynasties of great kings, the activities of such kings, annihilation, motivation and the supreme shelter. Other scholars state that the great *Purāṇas* deal with these ten topics, while lesser *Purāṇas* may deal with five.

PURPORT

The ten subjects of a great *Purāṇa* are also described in the Second Canto of *Śrīmad-Bhāgavatam* (2.10.1):

śrī-śuka uvāca
atra sargo visargaś ca
sthānaṁ poṣaṇam ūtayaḥ
manvantareśānukathā
nirodho muktir āśrayaḥ

"Śrī Śukadeva Gosvāmī said: In the *Śrīmad-Bhāgavatam* there are ten divisions of statements regarding the following: the creation of the universe, subcreation, planetary systems, protection by the Lord, the creative impetus, the change of Manus, the science of God, returning home (back to Godhead), liberation and the *summum bonum*."

According to Śrīla Jīva Gosvāmī, *Purāṇas* such as *Śrīmad-Bhāgavatam* deal with these ten topics, whereas lesser *Purāṇas* deal with only five. As stated in Vedic literature:

sargaś ca pratisargaś ca
vaṁśo manvantarāṇi ca
vaṁśānucaritaṁ ceti
purāṇaṁ pañca-lakṣaṇam

"Creation, secondary creation, the dynasties of kings, the reigns of Manus and the activities of various dynasties are the five characteristics of a *Purāṇa*." *Purāṇas* covering five categories of knowledge are understood to be secondary Purāṇic literature.

Śrīla Jīva Gosvāmī has explained that the ten principal topics of *Śrīmad-Bhāgavatam* are found within each of the twelve cantos. One should not try to assign each of the ten topics to a particular canto. Nor should the *Śrīmad-Bhāgavatam* be artificially interpreted to show that it deals with the topics successively. The simple fact is that all aspects of knowledge important to human beings, summarized in the ten categories mentioned above, are described with various degrees of emphasis and analysis throughout the *Śrīmad-Bhāgavatam*.

TEXT 11

अव्याकृतगुणक्षोभान्महतस्त्रिवृतोऽहमः ।
भूतसूक्ष्मेन्द्रियार्थानां सम्भवः सर्ग उच्यते ॥११॥

avyākṛta-guṇa-kṣobhān
mahatas tri-vṛto 'hamaḥ
bhūta-sūkṣmendriyārthānāṁ
sambhavaḥ sarga ucyate

avyākṛta—of the unmanifest stage of nature; *guṇa-kṣobhāt*—by the agitation of the modes; *mahataḥ*—from the basic *mahat-tattva; tri-vṛtaḥ*—threefold; *ahamaḥ*—from the false ego; *bhūta-sūkṣma*—of the subtle forms of perception; *indriya*—of the senses; *arthānām*—and the objects of sense perception; *sambhavaḥ*—the generation; *sargaḥ*—creation; *ucyate*—is called.

TRANSLATION

From the agitation of the original modes within the unmanifest material nature, the *mahat-tattva* arises. From the *mahat-tattva* comes the element false ego, which divides into three aspects. This threefold false ego further manifests as the subtle forms of perception, as the senses and as the gross sense objects. The generation of all these is called creation.

TEXT 12

पुरुषानुगृहीतानामेतेषां वासनामयः ।
विसर्गोऽयं समाहारो बीजाद् बीजं चराचरम् ॥१२॥

puruṣānugṛhītānām
eteṣāṁ vāsanā-mayaḥ
visargo 'yaṁ samāhāro
bījād bījaṁ carācaram

puruṣa—of the Supreme Personality of Godhead in His pastime role of creation; *anugṛhītānām*—which have received the mercy; *eteṣām*—of these elements; *vāsanā-mayaḥ*—consisting predominantly of the remnants of past desires of the living entities; *visargaḥ*—the secondary creation; *ayam*—this; *samāhāraḥ*—manifest amalgamation; *bījāt*—from a seed; *bījam*—another seed; *cara*—moving beings; *acaram*—and nonmoving beings.

TRANSLATION

The secondary creation, which exists by the mercy of the Lord, is the manifest amalgamation of the desires of the living entities. Just as a seed produces additional seeds, activities that promote material desires in the performer produce moving and nonmoving life forms.

PURPORT

Just as a seed grows into a tree that produces thousands of new seeds, material desire develops into fruitive activity that stimulates thousands of new desires within the heart of the conditioned soul. The word *puruṣānugṛhītānām* indicates that by the mercy of the Supreme Lord one is allowed to desire and act in this world.

TEXT 13

वृत्तिर्भूतानि भूतानां चराणामचराणि च ।
कृता स्वेन नृणां तत्र कामाच्चोदनयापि वा ॥१३॥

vṛttir bhūtāni bhūtānāṁ
carāṇām acarāṇi ca
kṛtā svena nṛṇāṁ tatra
kāmāc codanayāpi vā

vṛttiḥ—the sustenance; *bhūtāni*—living beings; *bhūtānām*—of living beings; *carāṇām*—of those that move; *acarāṇi*—those that do not move; *ca*—and; *kṛtā*—executed; *svena*—by one's own conditioned nature; *nṛṇām*—for human beings; *tatra*—therein; *kāmāt*—out of lust; *codanayā*—in pursuit of Vedic injunction; *api*—indeed; *vā*—or.

TRANSLATION

***Vṛtti* means the process of sustenance, by which the moving beings live upon the nonmoving. For a human, *vṛtti* specifically means acting for one's livelihood in a manner suited to his personal nature. Such action may be carried out either in pursuit of selfish desire or in accordance with the law of God.**

TEXT 14

रक्षाच्युतावतारेहा विश्वस्यानु युगे युगे ।
तिर्यङ्मर्त्यर्षिदेवेषु हन्यन्ते यैस्त्रयीद्विषः ॥१४॥

rakṣācyutāvatārehā
viśvasyānu yuge yuge
tiryaṅ-martyarṣi-deveṣu
hanyante yais trayī-dviṣaḥ

rakṣā—protection; *acyuta-avatāra*—of the incarnations of Lord Acyuta; *īhā*—the activities; *viśvasya*—of this universe; *anu yuge yuge*—in each age; *tiryak*—among the animals; *martya*—human beings; *ṛṣi*—sages; *deveṣu*—and demigods; *hanyante*—are killed; *yaiḥ*—by which incarnations; *trayī-dviṣaḥ*—the Daityas, who are enemies of Vedic culture.

TRANSLATION

In each age, the infallible Lord appears in this world among the animals, human beings, sages and demigods. By His activities in these incarnations He protects the universe and kills the enemies of Vedic culture.

PURPORT

The protective activities of the Lord, indicated by the word *rakṣā,* constitute one of the ten fundamental topics of a *Mahā-purāṇa,* or a great Purāṇic literature.

TEXT 15

मन्वन्तरं मनुर्देवा मनुपुत्राः सुरेश्वराः ।
ऋषयोऽशांवताराश्च हरेः षड्विधमुच्यते ॥१५॥

manvantaraṁ manur devā
manu-putrāḥ sureśvarāḥ
ṛṣayo 'ṁśāvatārāś ca
hareḥ ṣaḍ-vidham ucyate

manu-antaram—the reign of each Manu; *manuḥ*—the Manu; *devāḥ*—the demigods; *manu-putrāḥ*—the sons of Manu; *sura-īśvarāḥ*—the different Indras; *ṛṣayaḥ*—the chief sages; *aṁśa-avatārāḥ*—the incarnations of portions of the Supreme Lord; *ca*—and; *hareḥ*—of Lord Hari; *ṣaṭ-vidham*—sixfold; *ucyate*—is said.

TRANSLATION

In each reign of Manu, six types of personalities appear as manifestations of Lord Hari: the ruling Manu, the chief demigods, the sons of Manu, Indra, the great sages and the partial incarnations of the Supreme Personality of Godhead.

TEXT 16

राज्ञां ब्रह्मप्रसूतानां वंशस्त्रैकालिकोऽन्वयः ।
वंशानुचरितं तेषां वृत्तं वंशधराश्च ये ॥१६॥

rājñāṁ brahma-prasūtānām
vaṁśas trai-kāliko 'nvayaḥ
vaṁśānucaritaṁ teṣāṁ
vṛttaṁ vaṁśa-dharāś ca ye

rājñām—of the kings; *brahma-prasūtānām*—born originally from Brahmā; *vaṁśaḥ*—dynasty; *trai-kālikaḥ*—extending into the three phases of time (past, present and future); *anvayaḥ*—the series; *vaṁśa-anucaritam*—histories of the dynasties; *teṣām*—of these dynasties; *vṛttam*—the activities; *vaṁśa-dharāḥ*—the prominent members of the dynasties; *ca*—and; *ye*—which.

TRANSLATION

Dynasties are lines of kings originating with Lord Brahmā and extending continuously through past, present and future. The accounts of such dynasties, especially of their most prominent members, constitute the subject of dynastic history.

TEXT 17

नैमित्तिकः प्राकृतिको नित्य आत्यन्तिको लयः ।
संस्थेति कविभिः प्रोक्तश्चतुर्धास्य स्वभावतः ॥१७॥

naimittikaḥ prākṛtiko
nitya ātyantiko layaḥ
saṁstheti kavibhiḥ proktaś
caturdhāsya svabhāvataḥ

naimittikaḥ—occasional; *prākṛtikaḥ*—elemental; *nityaḥ*—continuous; *ātyantikaḥ*—ultimate; *layaḥ*—annihilation; *saṁsthā*—the dissolution; *iti*—thus; *kavibhiḥ*—by learned scholars; *proktaḥ*—described; *caturdhā*—in four aspects; *asya*—of this universe; *svabhāvataḥ*—by the inherent energy of the Supreme Personality of Godhead.

TRANSLATION

There are four types of cosmic annihilation—occasional, elemental, continuous and ultimate—all of which are effected by the inherent potency of the Supreme Lord. Learned scholars have designated this topic dissolution.

TEXT 18

हेतुर्जीवोऽस्य सर्गादेरविद्याकर्मकारकः ।
यं चानुशायिनं प्राहुरव्याकृतमुतापरे ॥१८॥

hetur jīvo 'sya sargāder
avidyā-karma-kārakaḥ
yaṁ cānuśāyinaṁ prāhur
avyākṛtam utāpare

hetuḥ—the cause; *jīvaḥ*—the living being; *asya*—of this universe; *sarga-ādeḥ*—of the creation, maintenance and destruction; *avidyā*—out of ignorance; *karma-kārakaḥ*—the performer of material activities; *yam*—whom; *ca*—and; *anuśāyinam*—the underlying personality; *prāhuḥ*—they call; *avyākṛtam*—the unmanifest; *uta*—indeed; *apare*—others.

TRANSLATION

Out of ignorance the living being performs material activities and thereby becomes in one sense the cause of the creation, maintenance and destruction of the universe. Some authorities call the living being the personality underlying the material creation, while others say he is the unmanifest self.

PURPORT

The Supreme Lord Himself creates, maintains and annihilates the cosmos. However, such activities are performed in response to the desires of conditioned souls, who are described herein as *hetu,* or the cause of cosmic activity. The Lord creates this world to facilitate the conditioned soul's attempt to exploit nature and ultimately to facilitate his self-realization.

Since conditioned souls cannot perceive their own constitutional identity, they are described here as *avyākṛtam,* or unmanifest. In other words, the living entity cannot perceive his real form unless he is completely Kṛṣṇa conscious.

TEXT 19

व्यतिरेकान्वयो यस्य जाग्रत्स्वप्नसुषुप्तिषु ।
मायामयेषु तद् ब्रह्म जीववृत्तिष्वपाश्रयः ॥१९॥

vyatirekānvayo yasya
jāgrat-svapna-suṣuptiṣu
māyā-mayeṣu tad brahma
jīva-vṛttiṣv apāśrayaḥ

vyatireka—the presence as separate; *anvayaḥ*—and as conjoint; *yasya*—of which; *jāgrat*—within waking consciousness; *svapna*—sleep;

suṣuptiṣu—and deep sleep; *māyā-mayeṣu*—within the products of the illusory energy; *tat*—that; *brahma*—the Absolute Truth; *jīva-vṛttiṣu*—within the functions of the living entities; *apāśrayaḥ*—the unique shelter.

TRANSLATION

The Supreme Absolute Truth is present throughout all the stages of awareness—waking consciousness, sleep and deep sleep—throughout all the phenomena manifested by the illusory energy, and within the functions of all living entities, and He also exists separate from all these. Thus situated in His own transcendence, He is the ultimate and unique shelter.

TEXT 20

पदार्थेषु यथा द्रव्यं सन्मात्रं रूपनामसु ।
बीजादिपञ्चतान्तासु ह्यवस्थासु युतायुतम् ॥२०॥

padārtheṣu yathā dravyaṁ
san-mātraṁ rūpa-nāmasu
bījādi-pañcatāntāsu
hy avasthāsu yutāyutam

pada-artheṣu—within material objects; *yathā*—just as; *dravyam*—the basic substance; *sat-mātram*—the sheer existence of things; *rūpa-nāmasu*—among their forms and names; *bīja-ādi*—beginning from the seed (i.e., from the time of conception); *pañcatā-antāsu*—ending with death; *hi*—indeed; *avasthāsu*—throughout the various phases of bodily existence; *yuta-ayutam*—both conjoined and separate.

TRANSLATION

Although a material object may assume various forms and names, its essential ingredient is always present as the basis of its existence. Similarly, both conjointly and separately, the Supreme Absolute Truth is always present with the created material body throughout its phases of existence, beginning with conception and ending with death.

PURPORT

Moist clay can be molded into various shapes and named "waterpot," "flowerpot" or "storage pot." Despite the various names and forms, the essential ingredient, earth, is constantly present. Similarly, the Supreme Lord is present throughout a material body's stages of bodily existence. The Lord is identical with material nature, being its ultimate generating source. At the same time, the unique Supreme Being exists separately, aloof in His own abode.

TEXT 21

विरमेत यदा चित्तं हित्वा वृत्तित्रयं स्वयम् ।
योगेन वा तदात्मानं वेदेहाया निवर्तते ॥२१॥

virameta yadā cittaṁ
hitvā vṛtti-trayaṁ svayam
yogena vā tadātmānaṁ
vedehāyā nivartate

virameta—desists; *yadā*—when; *cittam*—the mind; *hitvā*—giving up; *vṛtti-trayam*—the functions of material life in the three phases of waking, sleep and deep sleep; *svayam*—automatically; *yogena*—by regulated spiritual practice; *vā*—or; *tadā*—then; *ātmānam*—the Supreme Soul; *veda*—he knows; *īhāyāḥ*—from material endeavor; *nivartate*—he ceases.

TRANSLATION

Either automatically or because of one's regulated spiritual practice, one's mind may stop functioning on the material platform of waking consciousness, sleep and deep sleep. Then one understands the Supreme Soul and withdraws from material endeavor.

PURPORT

As stated in *Śrīmad-Bhāgavatam* (3.25.33), *jarayaty āśu yā kośaṁ nigīrṇam analo yathā:* "*Bhakti*, devotional service, dissolves the subtle body of the living entity without separate endeavor, just as fire in the stomach digests all that we eat." The subtle material body is inclined to exploit nature through sex, greed, false pride and madness. Loving service to the Lord, however, dissolves the stubborn false ego and lifts one to pure blissful consciousness, Kṛṣṇa consciousness, the sublime perfection of existence.

TEXT 22

एवं लक्षणलक्ष्याणि पुराणानि पुराविदः ।
मुनयोऽष्टादश प्राहुः क्षुल्लकानि महान्ति च ॥२२॥

evaṁ lakṣaṇa-lakṣyāṇi
purāṇāni purā-vidaḥ
munayo 'ṣṭādaśa prāhuḥ
kṣullakāni mahānti ca

evam—in this way; *lakṣaṇa-lakṣyāṇi*—symptomized by their characteristics; *purāṇāni*—the *Purāṇas; purā-vidaḥ*—those who are expert in such ancient histories; *munayaḥ*—the sages; *aṣṭādaśa*—eighteen; *prāhuḥ*—say; *kṣullakāni*—minor; *mahānti*—great; *ca*—also.

TRANSLATION

Sages expert in ancient histories have declared that the *Purāṇas*, according to their various characteristics, can be divided into eighteen major *Purāṇas* and eighteen secondary *Purāṇas*.

TEXTS 23–24

ब्राह्मं पाद्मं वैष्णवं च शैवं लैंगं सगारुडं ।
नारदीयं भागवतमाग्नेयं स्कान्दसंज्ञितम् ॥२३॥
भविष्यं ब्रह्मवैवर्तं मार्कण्डेयं सवामनम् ।
वाराहं मात्स्यं कौर्मं च ब्रह्माण्डाख्यमिति त्रिषट् ॥२४॥

brāhmaṁ pādmaṁ vaiṣṇavaṁ ca
śaivaṁ laiṅgaṁ sa-gāruḍaṁ
nāradīyaṁ bhāgavatam
āgneyaṁ skānda-saṁjñitam

bhaviṣyaṁ brahma-vaivartaṁ
mārkaṇḍeyaṁ sa-vāmanam
vārāhaṁ mātsyaṁ kaurmaṁ ca
brahmāṇḍākhyam iti tri-ṣaṭ

brāhmam—the *Brahmā Purāṇa; pādmam*—the *Padma Purāṇa; vaiṣṇavam*—the *Viṣṇu Purāṇa; ca*—and; *śaivam*—the *Śiva Purāṇa; laiṅgam*—the *Liṅga Purāṇa; sa-gāruḍam*—along with the *Garuḍa Purāṇa; nāradīyam*—the *Nārada Purāṇa; bhāgavatam*—the *Bhāgavata Purāṇa; āgneyam*—the *Agni Purāṇa; skānda*—the *Skanda Purāṇa; saṁjñitam*—known as; *bhaviṣyam*—the *Bhaviṣya Purāṇa; brahma-vaivartam*—the *Brahma-vaivarta Purāṇa; mārkaṇḍeyam*—the *Mārkaṇḍeya Purāṇa; sa-vāmanam*—together with the *Vāmana Purāṇa; vārāham*—the *Varāha Purāṇa; mātsyam*—the *Matsya Purāṇa; kaurmam*—the *Kūrma Purāṇa; ca*—and; *brahmāṇḍa-ākhyam*—known as the *Brahmāṇḍa Purāṇa; iti*—thus; *tri-ṣaṭ*—three times six.

TRANSLATION

The eighteen major *Purāṇas* are the *Brahmā, Padma, Viṣṇu, Śiva, Liṅga, Garuḍa, Nārada, Bhāgavata, Agni, Skanda, Bhaviṣya, Brahma-vaivarta, Mārkaṇḍeya, Vāmana, Varāha, Matsya, Kūrma* and *Brahmāṇḍa Purāṇas.*

PURPORT

Śrīla Jīva Gosvāmī has quoted from the *Varāha Purāṇa, Śiva Purāṇa* and *Matsya Purāṇa* in confirmation of the above two verses.

TEXT 25

ब्रह्मन्निदं समाख्यातं शाखाप्रणयनं मुनेः ।
शिष्यशिष्यप्रशिष्याणां ब्रह्मतेजोविवर्धनम् ॥२५॥

brahmann idaṁ samākhyātaṁ
śākhā-praṇayanaṁ muneḥ
śiṣya-śiṣya-praśiṣyāṇāṁ
brahma-tejo-vivardhanam

brahman—O *brāhmaṇa; idam*—this; *samākhyātam*—thoroughly described; *śākhā-praṇayanam*—the expansion of the branches; *muneḥ*—of the sage (Śrīla Vyāsadeva); *śiṣya*—of the disciples; *śiṣya-praśiṣyāṇām*—and the subsequent disciples of his disciples; *brahma-tejaḥ*—spiritual potency; *vivardhanam*—which increases.

TRANSLATION

I have thoroughly described to you, O *brāhmaṇa*, the expansion of the branches of the *Vedas* by the great sage Vyāsadeva, his disciples and the disciples of his disciples. One who listens to this narration will increase in spiritual strength.

Thus end the purports of the humble servant of His Divine Grace A. C. Bhaktivedanta Swami Prabhupāda to the Twelfth Canto, Seventh Chapter, of the Śrīmad-Bhāgavatam, *entitled "The Purāṇic Literatures."*

CHAPTER EIGHT

Mārkaṇḍeya's Prayers to Nara-Nārāyaṇa Ṛṣi

This chapter describes how Mārkaṇḍeya Ṛṣi performed austerities, defeated by his potency Cupid and all his associates, and offered prayers to Lord Śrī Hari in His forms of Nara and Nārāyaṇa.

Śrī Śaunaka was confused about the extraordinarily long life span of Śrī Mārkaṇḍeya, who had taken birth in Śaunaka's own dynasty yet who had moved about alone in the ocean of devastation millions of years previously and seen a wonderful young child lying upon a banyan leaf. It seemed to Śaunaka that Mārkaṇḍeya had lived through two days of Brahmā, and he asked Śrī Sūta Gosvāmī to explain this.

Sūta Gosvāmī replied that the sage Mārkaṇḍeya, after receiving the purificatory ritual of brahminical initiation from his father, had fixed himself in the vow of lifelong celibacy. He then worshiped the Supreme Lord Hari for six lifetimes of Manu. In the seventh *manvantara*, Lord Indra sent Kāmadeva (Cupid) and his associates to interrupt the sage's austerities. But Mārkaṇḍeya Ṛṣi defeated them by the potency generated from his penance.

Then, to show mercy to Mārkaṇḍeya, Lord Śrī Hari appeared before him in the form of Nara-Nārāyaṇa. Śrī Mārkaṇḍeya prostrated himself in obeisance and then worshiped the Lords by offering Them comfortable seats, water for washing Their feet, and other respectful presentations. He then prayed, "O Almighty Lord, You bring to life the vital air of all creatures, and You also protect the three worlds, vanquish distress and award liberation. You never allow those who have taken shelter of You to be defeated by any kind of misery. Attaining Your lotus feet is the only auspicious goal for the conditioned souls, and service to You fulfills all their desires. Your pastimes, enacted in the mode of pure goodness, can award everyone salvation from material life. Therefore those who are intelligent worship Your personal form of pure goodness named Śrī Nārāyaṇa, along with Nara, who represents Your unalloyed devotee.

"The living entity bewildered by illusion can directly understand You if he receives the knowledge presented in the *Vedas* and promulgated by

You, the spiritual master of the entire universe. Even great thinkers like Brahmā are simply bewildered when they try to understand Your identity by struggling on the path of *sāṅkhya-yoga.* You Yourself manifest the proponents of Sāṅkhya and other philosophies, and thus Your true personal identity remains hidden beneath the designative covering of the *jīva* soul. I offer my homage to You, the Mahāpuruṣa."

TEXT 1

श्रीशौनक उवाच
सूत जीव चिरं साधो वद नो वदतां वर ।
तमस्यपारे भ्रमतां नृणां त्वं पारदर्शनः ॥१॥

śrī-śaunaka uvāca
sūta jīva ciraṁ sādho
vada no vadatāṁ vara
tamasy apāre bhramatāṁ
nṛṇāṁ tvaṁ pāra-darśanaḥ

śrī-śaunakaḥ uvāca—Śrī Śaunaka said; *sūta*—O Sūta Gosvāmī; *jīva*—may you live; *ciram*—for a long time; *sādho*—O saint; *vada*—please speak; *naḥ*—to us; *vadatām*—of speakers; *vara*—O you who are the best; *tamasi*—in darkness; *apāre*—unbounded; *bhramatām*—who are wandering; *nṛṇām*—for men; *tvam*—you; *pāra-darśanaḥ*—the seer of the opposite shore.

TRANSLATION

Śrī Śaunaka said: O Sūta, may you live a long life! O saintly one, best of speakers, please continue speaking to us. Indeed, only you can show men the path out of the ignorance in which they are wandering.

PURPORT

According to Śrīla Jīva Gosvāmī, the sages saw that Sūta Gosvāmī was about to end his narration of *Śrīmad-Bhāgavatam*, and thus they urged him to first tell the story of Mārkaṇḍeya Ṛṣi.

TEXTS 2–5

आहुश्चिरायुषमृषिं मृकण्डुतनयं जनाः ।
यः कल्पान्ते ह्युर्वरितो येन ग्रस्तमिदं जगत् ॥२॥
स वा अस्मत्कुलोत्पन्नः कल्पेऽस्मिन् भार्गवर्षभः ।
नैवाधुनापि भूतानां सम्प्लवः कोऽपि जायते ॥३॥
एक एवार्णवे भ्राम्यन् ददर्श पुरुषं किल ।
वटपत्रपुटे तोकं शयानं त्वेकमद्भुतम् ॥४॥
एष नः संशयो भूयान् सूत कौतूहलं यतः ।
तं नश्छिन्धि महायोगिन् पुराणेष्वपि सम्मतः ॥५॥

āhuś cirāyuṣam ṛṣiṁ
mṛkaṇḍu-tanayaṁ janāḥ
yaḥ kalpānte hy urvarito
yena grastam idaṁ jagat

sa vā asmat-kulotpannaḥ
kalpe 'smin bhārgavarṣabhaḥ
naivādhunāpi bhūtānāṁ
samplavaḥ ko 'pi jāyate

eka evārṇave bhrāmyan
dadarśa puruṣaṁ kila
vaṭa-patra-puṭe tokaṁ
śayānaṁ tv ekam adbhutam

eṣa naḥ saṁśayo bhūyān
sūta kautūhalaṁ yataḥ
taṁ naś chindhi mahā-yogin
purāṇeṣv api sammataḥ

āhuḥ—they say; *cira-āyuṣam*—having an extraordinarily long life span; *ṛṣim*—the sage; *mṛkaṇḍu-tanayam*—the son of Mṛkaṇḍu; *janāḥ*—people; *yaḥ*—who; *kalpa-ante*—at the end of the day of Lord Brahmā;

hi—indeed; *urvaritaḥ*—remaining alone; *yena*—by which (annihilation); *grastam*—seized; *idam*—this; *jagat*—entire universe; *saḥ*—he, Mārkaṇḍeya; *vai*—indeed; *asmat-kula*—in my own family; *utpannaḥ*—born; *kalpe*—in the day of Brahmā; *asmin*—this; *bhārgava-ṛṣabhaḥ*—the most eminent descendant of Bhṛgu Muni; *na*—not; *eva*—certainly; *adhunā*—in our age; *api*—even; *bhūtānām*—of all creation; *samplavaḥ*—annihilation by flood; *kaḥ*—any; *api*—at all; *jāyate*—has arisen; *ekaḥ*—alone; *eva*—indeed; *arṇave*—in the great ocean; *bhrāmyan*—wandering; *dadarśa*—he saw; *puruṣam*—a personality; *kila*—it is said; *vaṭa-patra*—of a banyan leaf; *puṭe*—within the fold; *tokam*—an infant boy; *śayānam*—lying; *tu*—but; *ekam*—one; *adbhutam*—wonderful; *eṣaḥ*—this; *naḥ*—our; *saṁśayaḥ*—doubt; *bhūyān*—great; *sūta*—O Sūta Gosvāmī; *kautūhalam*—curiosity; *yataḥ*—due to which; *tam*—that; *naḥ*—for us; *chindhi*—please cut; *mahā-yogin*—O great *yogī; purāṇeṣu*—of the *Purāṇas; api*—indeed; *sammataḥ*—universally accepted (as the expert knower).

TRANSLATION

Authorities say that Mārkaṇḍeya Ṛṣi, the son of Mṛkaṇḍu, was an exceptionally long-lived sage who was the only survivor at the end of Brahmā's day, when the entire universe was merged in the flood of annihilation. But this same Mārkaṇḍeya Ṛṣi, the foremost descendant of Bhṛgu, took birth in my own family during the current day of Brahmā, and we have not yet seen any total annihilation in this day of Brahmā. Also, it is well known that Mārkaṇḍeya, while wandering helplessly in the great ocean of annihilation, saw in those fearful waters a wonderful personality—an infant boy lying alone within the fold of a banyan leaf. O Sūta, I am most bewildered and curious about this great sage, Mārkaṇḍeya Ṛṣi. O great *yogī*, you are universally accepted as the authority on all the *Purāṇas*. Therefore kindly dispel my confusion.

PURPORT

Lord Brahmā's day, consisting of his 12 hours, lasts 4 billion 320 million years, and his night is of the same duration. Apparently Mārkaṇḍeya lived throughout one such day and night and in the following day of Brahmā continued living as the same Mārkaṇḍeya. It seems that when annihilation occurred during Brahmā's night, the sage wandered throughout the fearful waters of destruction and saw within those waters an extraordinary personality lying on a banyan leaf. All of these mysteries concerning Mārkaṇḍeya will be clarified by Sūta Gosvāmī at the request of the great sages.

TEXT 6

सूत उवाच
प्रश्नस्त्वया महर्षेऽयं कृतो लोकभ्रमापहः ।
नारायणकथा यत्र गीता कलिमलापहा ॥६॥

sūta uvāca
praśnas tvayā maharṣe 'yaṁ
kṛto loka-bhramāpahaḥ
nārāyaṇa-kathā yatra
gītā kali-malāpahā

sūtaḥ uvāca—Sūta Gosvāmī said; *praśnaḥ*—question; *tvayā*—by you; *mahā-ṛṣe*—O great sage, Śaunaka; *ayam*—this; *kṛtaḥ*—made; *loka*—of the entire world; *bhrama*—the delusion; *apahaḥ*—which takes away; *nārāyaṇa-kathā*—discussion of the Supreme Lord, Nārāyaṇa; *yatra*—in which; *gītā*—is sung; *kali-mala*—the contamination of the present age of Kali; *apahā*—removing.

TRANSLATION

Sūta Gosvāmī said: O great sage Śaunaka, your very question will help remove everyone's illusion, for it leads to the topics of Lord Nārāyaṇa, which cleanse away the contamination of this Kali age.

TEXTS 7–11

प्राप्तद्विजातिसंस्कारो मार्कण्डेयः पितुः क्रमात् ।
छन्दांस्यधीत्य धर्मेण तपःस्वाध्यायसंयुतः ॥७॥

बृहद्व्रतधरः शान्तो जटिलो वल्कलाम्बरः ।
बिभ्रत्कमण्डलुं दण्डमुपवीतं समेखलम् ॥८॥
कृष्णाजिनं साक्षसूत्रं कुशांश्च नियमर्द्धये ।
अग्न्यर्कगुरुविप्रात्मस्वर्चयन् सन्ध्ययोर्हरिम् ॥९॥
सायं प्रातः स गुरवे भैक्ष्यमाहृत्य वाग्यतः ।
बुभुजे गुर्वनुज्ञातः सकृन्नो चेदुपोषितः ॥१०॥
एवं तपःस्वाध्यायपरो वर्षाणामयुतायुतम् ।
आराधयन् हृषीकेशं जिग्ये मृत्युं सुदुर्जयम् ॥११॥

prāpta-dvijāti-saṁskāro
mārkaṇḍeyaḥ pituḥ kramāt
chandāṁsy adhītya dharmeṇa
tapaḥ-svādhyāya-saṁyutaḥ

bṛhad-vrata-dharaḥ śānto
jaṭilo valkalāmbaraḥ
bibhrat kamaṇḍaluṁ daṇḍam
upavītaṁ sa-mekhalam

kṛṣṇājinaṁ sākṣa-sūtraṁ
kuśāṁś ca niyamarddhaye
agny-arka-guru-viprātmasv
arcayan sandhyayor harim

sāyaṁ prātaḥ sa gurave
bhaikṣyam āhṛtya vāg-yataḥ
bubhuje gurv-anujñātaḥ
sakṛn no ced upoṣitaḥ

evaṁ tapaḥ-svādhyāya-paro
varṣāṇām ayutāyutam
ārādhayan hṛṣīkeśaṁ
jigye mṛtyuṁ su-durjayam

prāpta—having received; *dvi-jāti*—of second birth; *saṁskāraḥ*—the purificatory rituals; *mārkaṇḍeyaḥ*—Mārkaṇḍeya; *pituḥ*—from his father; *kramāt*—by proper sequence; *chandāṁsi*—the Vedic hymns; *adhītya*—studying; *dharmeṇa*—along with regulative principles; *tapaḥ*—in austerities; *svādhyāya*—and study; *saṁyutaḥ*—full; *bṛhat-vrata*—the great vow of lifelong celibacy; *dharaḥ*—maintaining; *śāntaḥ*—peaceful; *jaṭilaḥ*—with matted hair; *valkala-ambaraḥ*—wearing bark as his clothing; *bibhrat*—carrying; *kamaṇḍalum*—a waterpot; *daṇḍam*—a mendicant's staff; *upavītam*—the sacred thread; *sa-mekhalam*—along with the ritual belt of a *brahmacārī; kṛṣṇa-ajinam*—the skin of a black deer; *sa-akṣa-sūtram*—and prayer beads made of lotus seeds; *kuśān*—*kuśa* grass; *ca*—also; *niyama-ṛddhaye*—to facilitate his spiritual progress; *agni*—in the form of fire; *arka*—the sun; *guru*—the spiritual master; *vipra*—the *brāhmaṇas; ātmasu*—and the Supersoul; *arcayan*—worshiping; *sandhyayoḥ*—at the beginning and the end of the day; *harim*—the Supreme Personality of Godhead; *sāyam*—in the evening; *prātaḥ*—in the early morning; *saḥ*—he; *gurave*—unto his spiritual master; *bhaikṣyam*—alms obtained by begging; *āhṛtya*—bringing; *vāk-yataḥ*—with controlled speech; *bubhuje*—he partook; *guru-anujñātaḥ*—invited by his spiritual master; *sakṛt*—once; *na*—not (invited); *u*—indeed; *cet*—if; *upoṣitaḥ*—fasting; *evam*—in this way; *tapaḥ-svādhyāya-paraḥ*—dedicated to austerities and study of the Vedic literature; *varṣāṇām*—years; *ayuta-ayutam*—ten thousand times ten thousand; *ārādhayan*—worshiping; *hṛṣīka-īśam*—the supreme master of the senses, Lord Viṣṇu; *jigye*—he conquered; *mṛtyum*—death; *su-durjayam*—impossible to conquer.

TRANSLATION

After being purified by his father's performance of the prescribed rituals leading to Mārkaṇḍeya's brahminical initiation, Mārkaṇḍeya studied the Vedic hymns and strictly observed the regulative principles. He became advanced in austerity and Vedic knowledge and remained a lifelong celibate. Appearing most peaceful with his matted hair and his clothing made of bark, he furthered his spiritual progress by carrying the mendicant's

waterpot, staff, sacred thread, *brahmacārī* belt, black deerskin, lotus-seed prayer beads and bundles of *kuśa* grass. At the sacred junctures of the day he regularly worshiped the Supreme Personality of Godhead in five forms—the sacrificial fire, the sun, his spiritual master, the *brāhmaṇas* and the Supersoul within his heart. Morning and evening he would go out begging, and upon returning he would present all the food he had collected to his spiritual master. Only when his spiritual master invited him would he silently take his one meal of the day; otherwise he would fast. Thus devoted to austerity and Vedic study, Mārkaṇḍeya Ṛṣi worshiped the supreme master of the senses, the Personality of Godhead, for countless millions of years, and in this way he conquered unconquerable death.

TEXT 12

ब्रह्मा भृगुर्भवो दक्षो ब्रह्मपुत्राश्च येऽपरे ।
नृदेवपितृभूतानि तेनासन्नतिविस्मिताः ॥१२॥

brahmā bhṛgur bhavo dakṣo
brahma-putrāś ca ye 'pare
nṛ-deva-pitṛ-bhūtāni
tenāsann ati-vismitāḥ

brahmā—Lord Brahmā; *bhṛguḥ*—Bhṛgu Muni; *bhavaḥ*—Lord Śiva; *dakṣaḥ*—Prajāpati Dakṣa; *brahma-putrāḥ*—the great sons of Brahmā; *ca*—and; *ye*—who; *apare*—others; *nṛ*—human beings; *deva*—demigods; *pitṛ*—forefathers; *bhūtāni*—and ghostly spirits; *tena*—with that (conquest of death); *āsan*—they all became; *ati-vismitāḥ*—extremely amazed.

TRANSLATION

Lord Brahmā, Bhṛgu Muni, Lord Śiva, Prajāpati Dakṣa, the great sons of Brahmā, and many others among the human beings, demigods, forefathers and ghostly spirits—all were astonished by the achievement of Mārkaṇḍeya Ṛṣi.

TEXT 13

इत्थं बृहद्व्रतधरस्तपःस्वाध्यायसंयमैः ।
दध्यावधोक्षजं योगी ध्वस्तक्लेशान्तरात्मना ॥१३॥

ittham bṛhad-vrata-dharas
tapaḥ-svādhyāya-saṁyamaiḥ
dadhyāv adhokṣajaṁ yogī
dhvasta-kleśāntarātmanā

ittham—in this manner; *bṛhat-vrata-dharaḥ*—maintaining the vow of celibacy, *brahmacarya; tapaḥ-svādhyāya-saṁyamaiḥ*—by his austerities, study of the *Vedas* and regulative principles; *dadhyau*—he meditated; *adhokṣajam*—upon the transcendental Lord; *yogī*—the *yogī; dhvasta*—destroyed; *kleśa*—all troubles; *antaḥ-ātmanā*—with his introspective mind.

TRANSLATION

In this way the devotional mystic Mārkaṇḍeya maintained rigid celibacy through penance, study of the *Vedas* and self-discipline. With his mind thus free of all disturbances, he turned it inward and meditated on the Supreme Personality of Godhead, who lies beyond the material senses.

TEXT 14

तस्यैवं युञ्जतश्चित्तं महायोगेन योगिनः ।
व्यतीयाय महान् कालो मन्वन्तरषडात्मकः ॥१४॥

tasyaivaṁ yuñjataś cittaṁ
mahā-yogena yoginaḥ
vyatīyāya mahān kālo
manvantara-ṣaḍ-ātmakaḥ

tasya—he; *evam*—thus; *yuñjataḥ*—while fixing; *cittam*—his mind; *mahā-yogena*—by powerful practice of *yoga; yoginaḥ*—the mystic sage;

vyatīyāya—passed by; *mahān*—a great; *kālaḥ*—period of time; *manu-antara*—lifetimes of Manu; *ṣaṭ*—six; *ātmakaḥ*—consisting of.

TRANSLATION

While the mystic sage thus concentrated his mind by powerful *yoga* practice, the tremendous period of six lifetimes of Manu passed by.

TEXT 15

एतत् पुरन्दरो ज्ञात्वा सप्तमेऽस्मिन् किलान्तरे ।
तपोविशङ्कितो ब्रह्मन्नारेभे तद्विघातनम् ॥१५॥

etat purandaro jñātvā
saptame 'smin kilāntare
tapo-viśaṅkito brahmann
ārebhe tad-vighātanam

etat—this; *purandaraḥ*—Lord Indra; *jñātvā*—learning; *saptame*—in the seventh; *asmin*—this; *kila*—indeed; *antare*—reign of Manu; *tapaḥ*—of the austerities; *viśaṅkitaḥ*—becoming fearful; *brahman*—O *brāhmaṇa* Śaunaka; *ārebhe*—he set into motion; *tat*—of that austerity; *vighātanam*—obstruction.

TRANSLATION

O *brāhmaṇa*, during the seventh reign of Manu, the current age, Lord Indra came to know of Mārkaṇḍeya's austerities and became fearful of his growing mystic potency. Thus he tried to impede the sage's penance.

TEXT 16

गन्धर्वाप्सरसः कामं वसन्तमलयानिलौ ।
मुनये प्रेषयामास रजस्तोकमदौ तथा ॥१६॥

gandharvāpsarasaḥ kāmaṁ
vasanta-malayānilau
munaye preṣayām āsa
rajas-toka-madau tathā

gandharva-apsarasaḥ—the celestial singers and dancing girls; *kāmam*—Cupid; *vasanta*—the spring season; *malaya-anilau*—and the refreshing breeze from the Malaya Hills; *munaye*—to the sage; *preṣayām āsa*—he sent; *rajaḥ-toka*—the child of passion, greed; *madau*—and intoxication; *tathā*—also.

TRANSLATION

To ruin the sage's spiritual practice, Lord Indra sent Cupid, beautiful celestial singers, dancing girls, the season of spring and the sandalwood-scented breeze from the Malaya Hills, along with greed and intoxication personified.

TEXT 17

ते वै तदाश्रमं जग्मुर्हिमाद्रेः पार्श्व उत्तरे ।
पुष्पभद्रा नदी यत्र चित्राख्या च शिला विभो ॥१७॥

te vai tad-āśramaṁ jagmur
himādreḥ pārśva uttare
puṣpabhadrā nadī yatra
citrākhyā ca śilā vibho

te—they; *vai*—indeed; *tat*—of Mārkaṇḍeya Ṛṣi; *āśramam*—to the hermitage; *jagmuḥ*—went; *hima-adreḥ*—of the Himālaya Mountains; *pārśve*—to the side; *uttare*—on the north; *puṣpabhadrā nadī*—the Puṣpabhadrā River; *yatra*—where; *citrā-ākhyā*—named Citrā; *ca*—and; *śilā*—the peak; *vibho*—O powerful Śaunaka.

TRANSLATION

O most powerful Śaunaka, they went to Mārkaṇḍeya's hermitage, on the northern side of the Himālaya Mountains where the Puṣpabhadrā River passes by the famous peak Citrā.

TEXTS 18–20

तदाश्रमपदं पुण्यं पुण्यद्रुमलताञ्चितम् ।
पुण्यद्विजकुलाकीर्णं पुण्यामलजलाशयम् ॥१८॥
मत्तभ्रमरसंगीतं मत्तकोकिलकूजितम् ।
मत्तबर्हिनटाटोपं मत्तद्विजकुलाकुलम् ॥१९॥
वायुः प्रविष्ट आदाय हिमनिर्झरशीकरान् ।
सुमनोभिः परिष्वक्तो ववावुत्तम्भयन् स्मरम् ॥२०॥

tad-āśrama-padaṁ puṇyaṁ
puṇya-druma-latāñcitam
puṇya-dvija-kulākīrṇaṁ
puṇyāmala-jalāśayam

matta-bhramara-saṅgītaṁ
matta-kokila-kūjitam
matta-barhi-naṭāṭopaṁ
matta-dvija-kulākulam

vāyuḥ praviṣṭa ādāya
hima-nirjhara-śīkarān
sumanobhiḥ pariṣvakto
vavāv uttambhayan smaram

tat—his; *āśrama-padam*—place of hermitage; *puṇyam*—pious; *puṇya*—pious; *druma*—with trees; *latā*—and creepers; *añcitam*—specially marked; *puṇya*—pious; *dvija*—of *brāhmaṇa* sages; *kula*—with the groups; *ākīrṇam*—brimming; *puṇya*—pious; *amala*—spotless; *jala-āśayam*—having reservoirs of water; *matta*—maddened; *bhramara*—of bees; *saṅgītam*—with singing; *matta*—maddened; *kokila*—of cuckoos; *kūjitam*—with cooing; *matta*—maddened; *barhi*—of peacocks; *naṭa-āṭopam*—with the frenzy of dancing; *matta*—maddened; *dvija*—of birds; *kula*—with the families; *ākulam*—filled; *vāyuḥ*—the wind of the Malaya Hills; *praviṣṭaḥ*—entering; *ādāya*—taking up; *hima*—chilling; *nirjhara*—of the waterfalls; *śīkarān*—the drops of mist; *sumanobhiḥ*—by the flowers; *pariṣvaktaḥ*—being embraced; *vavau*—blew; *uttambhayan*—evoking; *smaram*—Cupid.

TRANSLATION

Groves of pious trees decorated the holy *āśrama* of Mārkaṇḍeya Ṛṣi, and many saintly *brāhmaṇas* lived there, enjoying the abundant pure, sacred ponds. The *āśrama* resounded with the buzzing of intoxicated bees and the cooing of excited cuckoos, while jubilant peacocks danced about. Indeed, many families of maddened birds crowded that hermitage. The springtime breeze sent by Lord Indra entered there, carrying cooling drops of spray from nearby waterfalls. Fragrant from the embrace of forest flowers, that breeze entered the hermitage and began evoking the lusty spirit of Cupid.

TEXT 21

उद्यच्चन्द्रनिशावक्त्रः प्रवालस्तबकालिभिः ।
गोपद्रुमलताजालैस्तत्रासीत् कुसुमाकरः ॥२१॥

udyac-candra-niśā-vaktraḥ
pravāla-stabakālibhiḥ
gopa-druma-latā-jālais
tatrāsīt kusumākaraḥ

udyat—rising; *candra*—with the moon; *niśā*—nighttime; *vaktraḥ*—whose face; *pravāla*—of new sprouts; *stabaka*—and blossoms; *āli-bhiḥ*—with rows; *gopa*—being hidden; *druma*—of the trees; *latā*—and creepers; *jālaiḥ*—along with the multitude; *tatra*—there; *āsīt*—appeared; *kusuma-ākaraḥ*—the spring season.

TRANSLATION

Springtime then appeared in Mārkaṇḍeya's *āśrama.* Indeed, the evening sky, glowing with the light of the rising moon, became the very face of spring, and sprouts and fresh blossoms virtually covered the multitude of trees and creepers.

TEXT 22

अन्वीयमानो गन्धर्वैर्गीतवादित्रयूथकैः ।
अदृश्यतात्तचापेषुः स्वःस्त्रीयूथपतिः स्मरः ॥२२॥

anvīyamāno gandharvair
gīta-vāditra-yūthakaiḥ
adṛśyatātta-cāpeṣuḥ
svaḥ-strī-yūtha-patiḥ smaraḥ

anvīyamānaḥ—being followed; *gandharvaiḥ*—by Gandharvas; *gīta*—of singers; *vāditra*—and players of musical instruments; *yūthakaiḥ*—by companies; *adṛśyata*—was seen; *ātta*—holding up; *cāpa-iṣuḥ*—his bow and arrows; *svaḥ-strī-yūtha*—of hoardes of heavenly women; *patiḥ*—the master; *smaraḥ*—Cupid.

TRANSLATION

Cupid, the master of many heavenly women, then came there holding his bow and arrows. He was followed by groups of Gandharvas playing musical instruments and singing.

TEXT 23

हुत्वाग्निं समुपासीनं ददृशुः शक्रकिंकराः ।
मीलिताक्षं दुराधर्षं मूर्तिमन्तमिवानलम् ॥२३॥

hutvāgniṁ samupāsīnaṁ
dadṛśuḥ śakra-kiṅkarāḥ
mīlitākṣaṁ durādharṣaṁ
mūrtimantam ivānalam

hutvā—having offered oblations; *agnim*—to the sacrificial fire; *samupāsīnam*—sitting in yogic meditation; *dadṛśuḥ*—they saw; *śakra*—of Indra; *kiṅkarāḥ*—the servants; *mīlita*—closed; *akṣam*—his eyes; *durādharṣam*—invincible; *mūrti-mantam*—personified; *iva*—as if; *analam*—fire.

TRANSLATION

These servants of Indra found the sage sitting in meditation, having just offered his prescribed oblations into the sacrificial fire. His eyes closed in trance, he seemed invincible, like fire personified.

TEXT 24

ननृतुस्तस्य पुरतः स्त्रियोऽथो गायका जगुः ।
मृदंगवीणापणवैर्वाद्यं चक्रुर्मनोरमम् ॥२४॥

nanṛtus tasya purataḥ
striyo 'tho gāyakā jaguḥ
mṛdaṅga-vīṇā-paṇavair
vādyaṁ cakrur mano-ramam

nanṛtuḥ—danced; *tasya*—of him; *purataḥ*—in front; *striyaḥ*—women; *atha u*—and furthermore; *gāyakāḥ*—singers; *jaguḥ*—sang; *mṛdaṅga*—with drums; *vīṇā*—stringed instruments; *paṇavaiḥ*—and cymbals; *vādyam*—instrumental music; *cakruḥ*—they made; *manaḥ-ramam*—charming.

TRANSLATION

The women danced before the sage, and the celestial singers sang to the charming accompaniment of drums, cymbals and *vīṇās*.

TEXT 25

सन्दधेऽस्त्रं स्वधनुषि कामः पञ्चमुखं तदा ।
मधुर्मनो रजस्तोक इन्द्रभृत्या व्यकम्पयन् ॥२५॥

sandadhe 'straṁ sva-dhanuṣi
kāmaḥ pañca-mukhaṁ tadā
madhur mano rajas-toka
indra-bhṛtyā vyakampayan

sandadhe—he fixed; *astram*—the weapon; *sva-dhanuṣi*—upon his bow; *kāmaḥ*—Cupid; *pañca-mukham*—having five heads (sight, sound, smell, touch and taste); *tadā*—then; *madhuḥ*—spring; *manaḥ*—the mind of the sage; *rajaḥ-tokaḥ*—the child of passion, greed; *indra-bhṛtyāḥ*—the servants of Indra; *vyakampayan*—attempted to agitate.

TRANSLATION

While the son of passion [greed personified], spring and the other servants of Indra all tried to agitate Mārkaṇḍeya's mind, Cupid drew his five-headed arrow and fixed it upon his bow.

TEXTS 26–27

क्रीडन्त्याः पुञ्जिकस्थल्याः कन्दुकैः स्तनगौरवात् ।
भृशमुद्विग्नमध्यायाः केशविस्रंसितस्रजः ॥२६॥
इतस्ततो भ्रमद्दृष्टेश्चलन्त्या अनु कन्दुकम् ।
वायुर्जहार तद्वासः सूक्ष्मं त्रुटितमेखलम् ॥२७॥

krīḍantyāḥ puñjikasthalyāḥ
kandukaiḥ stana-gauravāt
bhṛśam udvigna-madhyāyāḥ
keśa-visraṁsita-srajaḥ

itas tato bhramad-dṛṣṭeś
calantyā anu kandukam
vāyur jahāra tad-vāsaḥ
sūkṣmaṁ truṭita-mekhalam

krīḍantyāḥ—who was playing; *puñjikasthalyāḥ*—of the Apsarā named Puñjikasthalī; *kandukaiḥ*—with a number of balls; *stana*—of her breasts; *gauravāt*—because of the great weight; *bhṛśam*—very much; *udvigna*—overburdened; *madhyāyāḥ*—whose waist; *keśa*—from her hair; *visraṁsita*—falling; *srajaḥ*—the flower garland; *itaḥ tataḥ*—here and there; *bhramat*—wandering; *dṛṣṭeḥ*—whose eyes; *calantyāḥ*—who was running about; *anu kandukam*—after her ball; *vāyuḥ*—the wind; *jahāra*—stole away; *tat-vāsaḥ*—her garment; *sūkṣmam*—fine; *truṭita*—loosened; *mekhalam*—the belt.

TRANSLATION

The Apsarā Puñjikasthalī made a show of playing with a number of toy balls. Her waist seemed weighed down by her heavy

breasts, and the wreath of flowers in her hair became disheveled. As she ran about after the balls, glancing here and there, the belt of her thin garment loosened, and suddenly the wind blew her clothes away.

TEXT 28

विससर्ज तदा बाणं मत्वा तं स्वजितं स्मरः ।
सर्वं तत्राभवन्मोघमनीशस्य यथोद्यमः ॥२८॥

visasarja tadā bāṇaṁ
matvā taṁ sva-jitaṁ smaraḥ
sarvaṁ tatrābhavan mogham
anīśasya yathodyamaḥ

visasarja—shot; *tadā*—then; *bāṇam*—the arrow; *matvā*—thinking; *tam*—him; *sva*—by himself; *jitam*—conquered; *smaraḥ*—Cupid; *sarvam*—all this; *tatra*—directed at the sage; *abhavat*—became; *mogham*—futile; *anīśasya*—of an atheist disbeliever; *yathā*—just as; *udyamaḥ*—the endeavors.

TRANSLATION

Cupid, thinking he had conquered the sage, then shot his arrow. But all these attempts to seduce Mārkaṇḍeya proved futile, just like the useless endeavors of an atheist.

TEXT 29

त इत्थमपकुर्वन्तो मुनेस्तत्तेजसा मुने ।
दह्यमाना निववृतुः प्रबोध्याहिमिवार्भकाः ॥२९॥

ta ittham apakurvanto
munes tat-tejasā mune
dahyamānā nivavṛtuḥ
prabodhyāhim ivārbhakāḥ

te—they; *ittham*—in this way; *apakurvantaḥ*—trying to do harm; *muneḥ*—to the sage; *tat*—his; *tejasā*—by the potency; *mune*—O sage (Śaunaka); *dahyamānāḥ*—feeling burned; *nivavṛtuḥ*—they desisted; *prabodhya*—having awakened; *ahim*—a snake; *iva*—as if; *arbhakāḥ*—children.

TRANSLATION

O learned Śaunaka, while Cupid and his followers tried to harm the sage, they felt themselves being burned alive by his potency. Thus they stopped their mischief, just like children who have aroused a sleeping snake.

TEXT 30

इतीन्द्रानुचरैर्ब्रहमन् धर्षितोऽपि महामुनिः ।
यन्नागादहमो भावं न तच्चित्रं महत्सु हि ॥३०॥

itīndrānucarair brahman
dharṣito 'pi mahā-muniḥ
yan nāgād ahamo bhāvaṁ
na tac citraṁ mahatsu hi

iti—thus; *indra-anucaraiḥ*—by the followers of Indra; *brahman*—O *brāhmaṇa; dharṣitaḥ*—impudently attacked; *api*—although; *mahā-muniḥ*—the elevated sage; *yat*—that; *na agāt*—he did not succumb; *ahamaḥ*—of false ego; *bhāvam*—to the transformation; *na*—not; *tat*—that; *citram*—surprising; *mahatsu*—for great souls; *hi*—indeed.

TRANSLATION

O *brāhmaṇa*, the followers of Lord Indra had impudently attacked the saintly Mārkaṇḍeya, yet he did not succumb to any influence of false ego. For great souls such tolerance is not at all surprising.

TEXT 31

दृष्ट्वा निस्तेजसं कामं सगणं भगवान् स्वराट् ।
श्रुत्वानुभावं ब्रह्मर्षेर्विस्मयं समगात्परम् ॥३१॥

dṛṣṭvā nistejasaṁ kāmaṁ
sa-gaṇaṁ bhagavān svarāṭ
śrutvānubhāvaṁ brahmarṣer
vismayaṁ samagāt param

dṛṣṭvā—seeing; *nistejasam*—deprived of his power; *kāmam*—Cupid; *sa-gaṇam*—along with his associates; *bhagavān*—the powerful lord; *sva-rāṭ*—King Indra; *śrutvā*—and hearing; *anubhāvam*—the influence; *brahma-ṛṣeḥ*—of the sage among the *brāhmaṇas; vismayam*—astonishment; *samagāt*—he attained; *param*—great.

TRANSLATION

The mighty King Indra was most astonished when he heard of the mystic prowess of the exalted sage Mārkaṇḍeya and saw how Cupid and his associates had become powerless in his presence.

TEXT 32

तस्यैवं युञ्जतश्चित्तं तपःस्वाध्यायसंयमैः ।
अनुग्रहायाविरासीन्नरनारायणो हरिः ॥३२॥

tasyaivaṁ yuñjataś cittaṁ
tapaḥ-svādhyāya-saṁyamaiḥ
anugrahāyāvirāsīn
nara-nārāyaṇo hariḥ

tasya—while he, Mārkaṇḍeya; *evam*—in this way; *yuñjataḥ*—was fixing; *cittam*—his mind; *tapaḥ*—by austerity; *svādhyāya*—study of the *Vedas; saṁyamaiḥ*—and regulative principles; *anugrahāya*—for showing mercy; *āvirāsīt*—made Himself manifest; *nara-nārāyaṇaḥ*—exhibiting the forms of Nara and Nārāyaṇa; *hariḥ*—the Supreme Personality of Godhead.

TRANSLATION

Desiring to bestow His mercy upon the saintly Mārkaṇḍeya, who had perfectly fixed his mind in self-realization through penance, Vedic study and observance of regulative principles, the Supreme Personality of Godhead personally appeared before the sage in the forms of Nara and Nārāyaṇa.

TEXTS 33–34

तौ शुक्लकृष्णौ नवकञ्जलोचनौ
चतुर्भुजौ रौरववल्कलाम्बरौ ।
पवित्रपाणी उपवीतकं त्रिवृत्
कमण्डलुं दण्डमृजुं च वैणवम् ॥३३॥
पद्माक्षमालामुत जन्तुमार्जनं
वेदं च साक्षात्तप एव रूपिणौ ।
तपत्तडिद्वर्णपिशंगरोचिषा
प्रांशू दधानौ विबुधर्षभार्चितौ ॥३४॥

tau śukla-kṛṣṇau nava-kañja-locanau
catur-bhujau raurava-valkalāmbarau
pavitra-pāṇī upavītakaṁ tri-vṛt
kamaṇḍaluṁ daṇḍam ṛjuṁ ca vaiṇavam

padmākṣa-mālām uta jantu-mārjanaṁ
vedaṁ ca sākṣāt tapa eva rūpiṇau
tapat-taḍid-varṇa-piśaṅga-rociṣā
prāṁśū dadhānau vibudharṣabhārcitau

tau—the two of Them; *śukla-kṛṣṇau*—one white and the other black; *nava-kañja*—like blooming lotus flowers; *locanau*—Their eyes; *catuḥ-bhujau*—having four arms; *raurava*—black deerskin; *valkala*—and bark;

ambarau—as Their clothing; *pavitra*—most purifying; *pāṇī*—Their hands; *upavītakam*—sacred thread; *tri-vṛt*—threefold; *kamaṇḍalum*—waterpot; *daṇḍam*—staff; *ṛjum*—straight; *ca*—and; *vaiṇavam*—made of bamboo; *padma-akṣa*—of lotus seeds; *mālām*—prayer beads; *uta*—and; *jantu-mārjanam*—which purifies all living beings; *vedam*—the *Vedas* (represented by bundles of *darbha* grass); *ca*—and; *sākṣāt*—directly; *tapaḥ*—austerity; *eva*—indeed; *rūpiṇau*—personified; *tapat*—blazing; *taḍit*—lightning; *varṇa*—the color; *piśaṅga*—yellowish; *rociṣā*—with Their effulgence; *prāṁśū*—very tall; *dadhānau*—bearing; *vibudha-ṛṣabha*—by the chief of the demigods; *arcitau*—worshiped.

TRANSLATION

One of Them was of a whitish complexion, the other blackish, and They both had four arms. Their eyes resembled the petals of blooming lotuses, and They wore garments of black deerskin and bark, along with the three-stranded sacred thread. In Their hands, which were most purifying, They carried the mendicant's waterpot, straight bamboo staff and lotus-seed prayer beads, as well as the all-purifying *Vedas* in the symbolic form of bundles of *darbha* grass. Their bearing was tall and Their yellow effulgence the color of radiant lightning. Appearing as austerity personified, They were being worshiped by the foremost demigods.

TEXT 35

ते वै भगवतो रूपे नरनारायणावृषी ।
दृष्ट्वोत्थायादरेणोच्चैर्ननामांगेन दण्डवत् ॥३५॥

te vai bhagavato rūpe
nara-nārāyaṇāv ṛṣī
dṛṣṭvotthāyādareṇoccair
nanāmāṅgena daṇḍa-vat

te—They; *vai*—indeed; *bhagavataḥ*—of the Personality of Godhead; *rūpe*—the personal manifestations; *nara-nārāyaṇau*—Nara and Nārāyaṇa; *ṛṣī*—the two sages; *dṛṣṭvā*—seeing; *utthāya*—standing up; *ādareṇa*—with respect; *uccaiḥ*—great; *nanāma*—bowed down; *aṅgena*—with his entire body; *daṇḍa-vat*—just like a stick.

TRANSLATION

These two sages, Nara and Nārāyaṇa, were the direct personal forms of the Supreme Lord. When Mārkaṇḍeya Ṛṣi saw Them, he immediately stood up and then with great respect offered Them obeisances by falling down flat on the ground like a stick.

TEXT 36

स तत्सन्दर्शनानन्दनिर्वृतात्मेन्द्रियाशयः ।
हृष्टरोमाश्रुपूर्णाक्षो न सेहे तावुदीक्षितुम् ॥३६॥

sa tat-sandarśanānanda-
nirvṛtātmendriyāśayaḥ
hṛṣṭa-romāśru-pūrṇākṣo
na sehe tāv udīkṣitum

saḥ—he, Mārkaṇḍeya; *tat*—of Them; *sandarśana*—because of seeing; *ānanda*—by the ecstasy; *nirvṛta*—pleased; *ātma*—whose body; *indriya*—senses; *āśayaḥ*—and mind; *hṛṣṭa*—standing on end; *romā*—his bodily hairs; *aśru*—with tears; *pūrṇa*—filled; *akṣaḥ*—his eyes; *na sehe*—he was unable; *tau*—upon them; *udīkṣitum*—to glance.

TRANSLATION

The ecstasy of seeing Them completely satisfied Mārkaṇḍeya's body, mind and senses and caused the hairs on his body to stand on end and his eyes to fill with tears. Overwhelmed, Mārkaṇḍeya found it difficult to look at Them.

TEXT 37

उत्थाय प्राञ्जलिः प्रह्व औत्सुक्यादाश्लिषन्निव ।
नमो नम इतीशानौ बभाषे गद्गदाक्षरम् ॥३७॥

utthāya prāñjaliḥ prahva
autsukyād āśliṣann iva
namo nama itīśānau
babhāṣe gadgadākṣaram

utthāya—standing up; *prāñjaliḥ*—with folded hands; *prahvaḥ*—humble; *autsukyāt*—out of eagerness; *āśliṣan*—embracing; *iva*—as if; *namaḥ*—obeisances; *namaḥ*—obeisances; *iti*—thus; *īśānau*—to the two Lords; *babhāṣe*—he spoke; *gadgada*—choking with ecstasy; *akṣaram*—the syllables.

TRANSLATION

Standing with his hands folded in supplication and his head bowed in humility, Mārkaṇḍeya felt such eagerness that he imagined he was embracing the two Lords. In a voice choked with ecstasy, he repeatedly said, "I offer You my humble obeisances."

TEXT 38

तयोरासनमादाय पादयोरवनिज्य च ।
अर्हणेनानुलेपेन धूपमाल्यैरपूजयत् ॥३८॥

tayor āsanam ādāya
pādayor avanijya ca
arhaṇenānulepena
dhūpa-mālyair apūjayat

tayoḥ—to Them; *āsanam*—sitting places; *ādāya*—offering; *pādayoḥ*—Their feet; *avanijya*—bathing; *ca*—and; *arhaṇena*—with suitable respectful offerings; *anulepena*—by anointing Them with sandalwood pulp and other fragrant substances; *dhūpa*—with incense; *mālyaiḥ*—and flower garlands; *apūjayat*—he worshiped.

TRANSLATION

He gave Them sitting places and washed Their feet, and then he worshiped Them with presentations of *arghya*, sandalwood pulp, fragrant oils, incense and flower garlands.

TEXT 39

सुखमासनमासीनौ प्रसादाभिमुखौ मुनी ।
पुनरानम्य पादाभ्यां गरिष्ठाविदमब्रवीत् ॥३९॥

sukham āsanam āsīnau
prasādābhimukhau munī
punar ānamya pādābhyāṁ
gariṣṭhāv idam abravīt

sukham—comfortably; *āsanam*—on sitting places; *āsīnau*—seated; *prasāda*—mercy; *abhimukhau*—ready to give; *munī*—to the Lord's incarnation as the two sages; *punaḥ*—again; *ānamya*—bowing down; *pādābhyām*—at Their feet; *gariṣṭhau*—to the supremely worshipable; *idam*—this; *abravīt*—he spoke.

TRANSLATION

Mārkaṇḍeya Ṛṣi once again bowed down at the lotus feet of those two most worshipable sages, who were sitting at ease, ready to bestow all mercy upon him. He then addressed Them as follows.

TEXT 40

श्रीमार्कण्डेय उवाच
किं वर्णये तव विभो यदुदीरितोऽसुः
संस्पन्दते तमनु वाङ्मनइन्द्रियाणि ।
स्पन्दन्ति वै तनुभृतामजशर्वयोश्च
स्वस्याप्यथापि भजतामसि भावबन्धुः ॥४०॥

śrī-mārkaṇḍeya uvāca
kiṁ varṇaye tava vibho yad-udīrito 'suḥ
saṁspandate tam anu vāṅ-mana-indriyāṇi
spandanti vai tanu-bhṛtām aja-śarvayoś ca
svasyāpy athāpi bhajatām asi bhāva-bandhuḥ

śrī-mārkaṇḍeyaḥ uvāca—Śrī Mārkaṇḍeya said; *kim*—what; *varṇaye*—shall I describe; *tava*—about You; *vibho*—O Almighty Lord; *yat*—by whom; *udīritaḥ*—moved; *asuḥ*—the vital air; *saṁspandate*—comes to life; *tam anu*—following it; *vāk*—the power of speech; *manaḥ*—the mind; *indriyāṇi*—and the senses; *spandanti*—begin to act; *vai*—indeed;

tanu-bhṛtām—of all embodied living beings; *aja-śarvayoḥ*—of Lord Brahmā and Lord Śiva; *ca*—as well; *svasya*—of myself; *api*—also; *atha api*—nevertheless; *bhajatām*—for those who are worshiping; *asi*—You become; *bhāva-bandhuḥ*—the intimate loving friend.

TRANSLATION

Śrī Mārkaṇḍeya said: O Almighty Lord, how can I possibly describe You? You awaken the vital air, which then impels the mind, senses and power of speech to act. This is true for all ordinary conditioned souls and even for great demigods like Brahmā and Śiva. So it is certainly true for me. Nevertheless, You become the intimate friend of those who worship You.

TEXT 41

मूर्ती इमे भगवतो भगवंस्त्रिलोक्याः
क्षेमाय तापविरमाय च मृत्युजित्यै ।
नाना बिभर्ष्यवितुमन्यतनूर्यथेदं
सृष्ट्वा पुनर्ग्रससि सर्वमिवोर्णनाभिः ॥४१॥

mūrtī ime bhagavato bhagavaṁs tri-lokyāḥ
kṣemāya tāpa-viramāya ca mṛtyu-jityai
nānā bibharṣy avitum anya-tanūr yathedaṁ
sṛṣṭvā punar grasasi sarvam ivorṇanābhiḥ

mūrtī—the two personal forms; *ime*—these; *bhagavataḥ*—of the Supreme Personality of Godhead; *bhagavan*—O Lord; *tri-lokyāḥ*—of all the three worlds; *kṣemāya*—for the ultimate benefit; *tāpa*—of material misery; *viramāya*—for the cessation; *ca*—and; *mṛtyu*—of death; *jityai*—for the conquest; *nānā*—various; *bibharṣi*—You manifest; *avitum*—for the purpose of protecting; *anya*—other; *tanūḥ*—transcendental bodies; *yathā*—just as; *idam*—this universe; *sṛṣṭvā*—having created; *punaḥ*—once again; *grasasi*—You swallow up; *sarvam*—entirely; *iva*—just like; *ūrṇa-nābhiḥ*—a spider.

TRANSLATION

O Supreme Personality of Godhead, these two personal forms of Yours have appeared to bestow the ultimate benefit for the three worlds—the cessation of material misery and the conquest of death. My Lord, although You create this universe and then assume many transcendental forms to protect it, You also swallow it up, just like a spider who spins and later withdraws its web.

TEXT 42

तस्यावितुः स्थिरचरेशितुरङ्घ्रिमूलं
यत्स्थं न कर्मगुणकालरजः स्पृशन्ति ।
यद्वै स्तुवन्ति निनमन्ति यजन्त्यभीक्ष्णं
ध्यायन्ति वेदहृदया मुनयस्तदाप्त्यै ॥४२॥

tasyāvituḥ sthira-careśitur aṅghri-mūlaṁ
yat-sthaṁ na karma-guṇa-kāla-rajaḥ spṛśanti
yad vai stuvanti ninamanti yajanty abhīkṣṇaṁ
dhyāyanti veda-hṛdayā munayas tad-āptyai

tasya—of Him; *avituḥ*—the protector; *sthira-cara*—of the stationary and moving living beings; *īśituḥ*—the supreme controller; *aṅghri-mūlam*—the soles of His lotus feet; *yat-stham*—one who is situated at which; *na*—do not; *karma-guṇa-kāla*—of material work, material qualities and time; *rajaḥ*—the contamination; *spṛśanti*—touch; *yat*—whom; *vai*—indeed; *stuvanti*—praise; *ninamanti*—bow down to; *yajanti*—worship; *abhīkṣṇam*—at every moment; *dhyāyanti*—meditate upon; *veda-hṛdayāḥ*—who have assimilated the essence of the *Vedas;* *munayaḥ*—sages; *tat-āptyai*—for the purpose of achieving Him.

TRANSLATION

Because You are the protector and the supreme controller of all moving and nonmoving beings, anyone who takes shelter of Your lotus feet can never be touched by the contamination of material

work, material qualities or time. Great sages who have assimilated the essential meaning of the *Vedas* offer their prayers to You. To gain Your association, they bow down to You at every opportunity and constantly worship You and meditate upon You.

TEXT 43

नान्यं तवाङ्घ्र्युपनयादपवर्गमूर्तेः
क्षेमं जनस्य परितोभिय ईश विद्मः ।
ब्रह्मा बिभेत्यलमतो द्विपरार्धधिष्ण्यः
कालस्य ते किमुत तत्कृतभौतिकानाम् ॥४३॥

nānyaṁ tavāṅghry-upanayād apavarga-mūrteḥ
kṣemaṁ janasya parito-bhiya īśa vidmaḥ
brahmā bibhety alam ato dvi-parārdha-dhiṣṇyaḥ
kālasya te kim uta tat-kṛta-bhautikānām

na anyam—no other; *tava*—Your; *aṅghri*—of the lotus feet; *upanayāt*—than the attainment; *apavarga-mūrteḥ*—who are liberation personified; *kṣemam*—benefit; *janasya*—for the person; *paritaḥ*—on all sides; *bhiyaḥ*—who is fearful; *īśa*—O Lord; *vidmaḥ*—do we know; *brahmā*—Lord Brahmā; *bibheti*—is afraid; *alam*—very much; *ataḥ*—on account of this; *dvi-parārdha*—the entire duration of the universe; *dhiṣṇyaḥ*—the period of whose reign; *kālasya*—because of time; *te*—Your feature; *kim uta*—then what to speak; *tat-kṛta*—created by him, Brahmā; *bhautikānām*—of the mundane creatures.

TRANSLATION

My dear Lord, even Lord Brahmā, who enjoys his exalted position for the entire duration of the universe, fears the passage of time. Then what to speak of those whom Brahmā creates, the conditioned souls. They encounter fearful dangers at every step of their lives. I do not know of any relief from this fear except shelter at Your lotus feet, which are the very form of liberation.

TEXT 44

तद्वै भजाम्यृतधियस्तव पादमूलं
हित्वेदमात्मच्छदि चात्मगुरोः परस्य ।
देहाद्यपार्थमसदन्त्यमभिज्ञमात्रं
विन्देत ते तर्हि सर्वमनीषितार्थम् ॥४४॥

tad vai bhajāmy ṛta-dhiyas tava pāda-mūlaṁ
hitvedam ātma-cchadi cātma-guroḥ parasya
dehādy apārtham asad antyam abhijña-mātraṁ
vindeta te tarhi sarva-manīṣitārtham

tat—therefore; *vai*—indeed; *bhajāmi*—I worship; *ṛta-dhiyaḥ*—of Him whose intelligence always perceives the truth; *tava*—of You; *pāda-mūlam*—the soles of the lotus feet; *hitvā*—giving up; *idam*—this; *ātma-chadi*—covering of the self; *ca*—and; *ātma-guroḥ*—of the master of the soul; *parasya*—who is the Supreme Truth; *deha-ādi*—the material body and other false designations; *apārtham*—useless; *asat*—insubstantial; *antyam*—temporary; *abhijña-mātram*—only imagined to have a separate existence; *vindeta*—one obtains; *te*—from You; *tarhi*—then; *sarva*—all; *manīṣita*—desired; *artham*—objects.

TRANSLATION

Therefore I worship Your lotus feet, having renounced my identification with the material body and everything else that covers my true self. These useless, insubstantial and temporary coverings are merely presumed to be separate from You, whose intelligence encompasses all truth. By attaining You—the Supreme Godhead and the master of the soul—one attains everything desirable.

PURPORT

One who falsely identifies himself as the material body or mind automatically feels entitled to exploit the material world. But when we realize our eternal spiritual nature and Lord Kṛṣṇa's supreme proprietorship over all that be, we renounce our false enjoying propensity by the strength of spiritual knowledge.

TEXT 45

सत्त्वं रजस्तम इतीश तवात्मबन्धो
मायामयाः स्थितिलयोदयहेतवोऽस्य ।
लीला धृता यदपि सत्त्वमयी प्रशान्त्यै
नान्ये नृणां व्यसनमोहभियश्च याभ्याम् ॥४५॥

sattvaṁ rajas tama itīśa tavātma-bandho
māyā-mayāḥ sthiti-layodaya-hetavo 'sya
līlā dhṛtā yad api sattva-mayī praśāntyai
nānye nṛṇāṁ vyasana-moha-bhiyaś ca yābhyām

sattvam—goodness; *rajaḥ*—passion; *tamaḥ*—ignorance; *iti*—the modes of nature thus termed; *īśa*—O Lord; *tava*—Your; *ātma-bandho*—O supreme friend of the soul; *māyā-mayāḥ*—produced from Your personal energy; *sthiti-laya-udaya*—of maintenance, destruction and creation; *hetavaḥ*—the causes; *asya*—of this universe; *līlāḥ*—as pastimes; *dhṛtāḥ*—assumed; *yat api*—although; *sattva-mayī*—that which is in the mode of goodness; *praśāntyai*—for liberation; *na*—not; *anye*—the other two; *nṛṇām*—for persons; *vyasana*—danger; *moha*—bewilderment; *bhiyaḥ*—and fear; *ca*—also; *yābhyām*—from which.

TRANSLATION

O my Lord, O supreme friend of the conditioned soul, although for the creation, maintenance and annihilation of this world You accept the modes of goodness, passion and ignorance, which constitute Your illusory potency, You specifically employ the mode of goodness to liberate the conditioned souls. The other two modes simply bring them suffering, illusion and fear.

PURPORT

The words *līlā dhṛtāḥ* indicate that the creative activities of Lord Brahmā, the destructive activities of Lord Śiva and the sustaining functions of Lord Viṣṇu are all pastimes of the Absolute Truth, Lord Kṛṣṇa. But ultimately only Lord Viṣṇu can award liberation from the clutches of material illusion, as indicated by the words *sattva-mayī praśāntyai.*

Our passionate and ignorant activities cause great suffering, illusion and fear for us and others; therefore they should be given up. One should become firmly situated in the mode of goodness and live peacefully on the spiritual platform. The essence of goodness is to renounce selfish interest in all one's activities and thus dedicate one's entire being to the Supreme Being, Lord Kṛṣṇa, who is the source of our existence.

TEXT 46

तस्मात्तवेह भगवन्नथ तावकानां
शुक्लां तनुं स्वदयितां कुशला भजन्ति ।
यत्सात्वताः पुरुषरूपमुशन्ति सत्त्वं
लोको यतोऽभयमुतात्मसुखं न चान्यत् ॥४६॥

tasmāt taveha bhagavann atha tāvakānāṁ
śuklāṁ tanuṁ sva-dayitāṁ kuśalā bhajanti
yat sātvatāḥ puruṣa-rūpam uśanti sattvaṁ
loko yato 'bhayam utātma-sukhaṁ na cānyat

tasmāt—therefore; *tava*—Your; *iha*—in this world; *bhagavan*—O Supreme Lord; *atha*—and; *tāvakānām*—of Your devotees; *śuklām*—transcendental; *tanum*—the personal form; *sva-dayitām*—most dear to them; *kuśalāḥ*—those who are expert in spiritual knowledge; *bhajanti*—worship; *yat*—because; *sātvatāḥ*—the great devotees; *puruṣa*—of the original Personality of Godhead; *rūpam*—the form; *uśanti*—consider; *sattvam*—the mode of goodness; *lokaḥ*—the spiritual world; *yataḥ*—from which; *abhayam*—fearlessness; *uta*—and; *ātma-sukham*—the happiness of the soul; *na*—not; *ca*—and; *anyat*—any other.

TRANSLATION

O Lord, because fearlessness, spiritual happiness and the kingdom of God are all achieved through the mode of pure goodness, Your devotees consider this mode, but never passion and

ignorance, to be a direct manifestation of You, the Supreme Personality of Godhead. Intelligent persons thus worship Your beloved transcendental form, composed of pure goodness, along with the spiritual forms of Your pure devotees.

PURPORT

Intelligent persons do not worship the demigods, who represent the modes of passion and ignorance. Lord Brahmā represents passion, Lord Śiva represents ignorance, and demigods such as Indra also represent the modes of material nature. But Lord Viṣṇu, or Nārāyaṇa, represents pure spiritual goodness, which brings one realization of the spiritual world, freedom from fear, and spiritual bliss. Such benefits can never be derived from impure, material goodness, for it is always mixed with the modes of passion and ignorance. As clearly indicated in this verse, the transcendental form of God is fully constituted of eternal spiritual goodness and thus has no tinge of the material mode of goodness, passion or ignorance.

TEXT 47

तस्मै नमो भगवते पुरुषाय भूम्ने
विश्वाय विश्वगुरवे परदैवताय ।
नारायणाय ऋषये च नरोत्तमाय
हंसाय संयतगिरे निगमेश्वराय ॥४७॥

tasmai namo bhagavate puruṣāya bhūmne
viśvāya viśva-gurave para-daivatāya
nārāyaṇāya ṛṣaye ca narottamāya
haṁsāya saṁyata-gire nigameśvarāya

tasmai—to Him; *namaḥ*—my obeisances; *bhagavate*—to the Godhead; *puruṣāya*—the Supreme Person; *bhūmne*—the all-pervading one; *viśvāya*—the all-inclusive manifestation of the universe; *viśva-gurave*—the spiritual master of the universe; *para-daivatāya*—the supremely worshipable Deity; *nārāyaṇāya*—to Lord Nārāyaṇa; *ṛṣaye*—the sage; *ca*—and; *nara-uttamāya*—to the best of human beings; *haṁsāya*—situated in perfect purity; *saṁyata-gire*—who has controlled his speech; *nigama-īśvarāya*—the master of the Vedic scriptures.

TRANSLATION

I offer my humble obeisances to Him, the Supreme Personality of Godhead. He is the all-pervading and all-inclusive form of the universe, as well as its spiritual master. I bow down to Lord Nārāyaṇa, the supremely worshipable Deity appearing as a sage, and also to the saintly Nara, the best of human beings, who is fixed in perfect goodness, fully in control of his speech, and the propagator of the Vedic literatures.

TEXT 48

यं वै न वेद वितथाक्षपथैर्भ्रमद्धीः
सन्तं स्वकेष्वसुषु हृद्यपि दृक्पथेषु ।
तन्माययावृतमतिः स उ एव साक्षाद्
आद्यस्तवाखिलगुरोरुपसाद्य वेदम् ॥४८॥

yaṁ vai na veda vitathākṣa-pathair bhramad-dhīḥ
santaṁ svakeṣv asuṣu hṛdy api dṛk-patheṣu
tan-māyayāvṛta-matiḥ sa u eva sākṣād
ādyas tavākhila-guror upasādya vedam

yam—whom; *vai*—indeed; *na veda*—does not recognize; *vitatha*—deceptive; *akṣa-pathaiḥ*—by methods of empirical perception; *bhramat*—becoming diverted; *dhīḥ*—whose intelligence; *santam*—present; *svakeṣu*—within one's own; *asuṣu*—senses; *hṛdi*—within the heart; *api*—even; *dṛk-patheṣu*—among perceived objects of the external world; *tat-māyayā*—by His illusory potency; *āvṛta*—covered over; *matiḥ*—his understanding; *saḥ*—he; *u*—even; *eva*—indeed; *sākṣāt*—directly; *ādyaḥ*—originally (in ignorance); *tava*—of You; *akhila-guroḥ*—the spiritual master of all living beings; *upasādya*—obtaining; *vedam*—the knowledge of the *Vedas*.

TRANSLATION

A materialist, his intelligence perverted by the action of his deceptive senses, cannot recognize You at all, although You are always present within his own senses and heart and also among

the objects of his perception. Yet even though one's understanding has been covered by Your illusory potency, if one obtains Vedic knowledge from You, the supreme spiritual master of all, he can directly understand You.

TEXT 49

यद्दर्शनं निगम आत्मरहःप्रकाशं
मुह्यन्ति यत्र कवयोऽजपरा यतन्तः ।
तं सर्ववादविषयप्रतिरूपशीलं
वन्दे महापुरुषमात्मनिगूढबोधम् ॥४९॥

yad-darśanaṁ nigama ātma-rahaḥ-prakāśaṁ
muhyanti yatra kavayo 'ja-parā yatantaḥ
taṁ sarva-vāda-viṣaya-pratirūpa-śīlaṁ
vande mahā-puruṣam ātma-nigūḍha-bodham

yat—of whom; *darśanam*—the vision; *nigame*—in the *Vedas; ātma*—of the Supreme Soul; *rahaḥ*—the mystery; *prakāśam*—which reveals; *muhyanti*—become bewildered; *yatra*—about which; *kavayaḥ*—great learned authorities; *aja-parāḥ*—headed by Brahmā; *yatantaḥ*—endeavoring; *tam*—to Him; *sarva-vāda*—of all different philosophies; *viṣaya*—the subject matter; *pratirūpa*—adjusting itself as suitable; *śīlam*—whose personal nature; *vande*—I offer my homage; *mahā-puruṣam*—to the Supreme Personality of Godhead; *ātma*—from the spirit soul; *nigūḍha*—hidden; *bodham*—understanding.

TRANSLATION

My dear Lord, the Vedic literatures alone reveal confidential knowledge of Your supreme personality, and thus even such great scholars as Lord Brahmā himself are bewildered in their attempt to understand You through empirical methods. Each philosopher understands You according to his particular speculative conclusions. I worship that Supreme Person, knowledge of whom is hidden by the bodily designations covering the conditioned soul's spiritual identity.

PURPORT

Even great demigods like Brahmā are bewildered in their speculative attempts to understand the Supreme Personality of Godhead. Each philosopher is covered by a unique combination of the modes of nature and thus describes the Supreme Truth according to his own material conditioning. Therefore even strenuous empirical endeavor will never bring one to the conclusion of all knowledge. The highest knowledge is Kṛṣṇa, the Supreme Personality of Godhead, and one can understand Him only by fully surrendering to Him and serving Him with love. This is why Mārkaṇḍeya Ṛṣi states here, *vande mahā-puruṣam:* "I simply worship that Supreme Personality." Those who try to worship God but at the same time continue speculating or acting fruitively will attain only mixed and bewildering results. To be pure a devotee must give up all fruitive activity and mental speculation; in that way his loving service to the Lord will yield perfect knowledge of the Supreme. Only this perfection can satisfy the eternal soul.

Thus end the purports of the humble servant of His Divine Grace A. C. Bhaktivedanta Swami Prabhupāda to the Twelfth Canto, Eighth Chapter, of the Śrīmad-Bhāgavatam, *entitled "Mārkaṇḍeya's Prayers to Nara-Nārāyaṇa Ṛṣi."*

CHAPTER NINE

Mārkaṇḍeya Ṛṣi Sees the Illusory Potency of the Lord

This chapter describes Mārkaṇḍeya Ṛṣi's vision of the Supreme Personality of Godhead's illusory energy.

Satisfied by the prayers Śrī Mārkaṇḍeya had offered, the Supreme Lord told him to ask for a benediction, and the sage said he wanted to see the Lord's illusory energy. The Supreme Lord Śrī Hari, present before Mārkaṇḍeya in the form of Nara-Nārāyaṇa, replied, "So be it," and then left for Badarikāśrama. One day, as Śrī Mārkaṇḍeya was offering his evening prayers, the water of devastation suddenly flooded the three worlds. With great difficulty Mārkaṇḍeya moved about all alone in this water for a long time, until he came upon a banyan tree. Lying upon a leaf of that tree was an infant boy glowing with a charming effulgence. As Mārkaṇḍeya moved toward the leaf, he was pulled by the boy's inhalation and, just like a mosquito, drawn within His body.

Inside the boy's body, Mārkaṇḍeya was amazed to see the entire universe just as it had been before the annihilation. After a moment the sage was carried out by the force of the child's exhalation and hurled back into the ocean of annihilation. Then, seeing that the child on the leaf was actually Śrī Hari, the transcendental Lord situated within his own heart, Śrī Mārkaṇḍeya tried to embrace Him. But at that moment Lord Hari, the master of all mystic power, disappeared. Then the waters of annihilation disappeared as well, and Śrī Mārkaṇḍeya found himself in his own *āśrama,* just as before.

TEXT 1

सूत उवाच
संस्तुतो भगवानित्थं मार्कण्डेयेन धीमता ।
नारायणो नरसखः प्रीत आह भृगूद्वहम् ॥१॥

sūta uvāca
saṁstuto bhagavān itthaṁ
mārkaṇḍeyena dhīmatā
nārāyaṇo nara-sakhaḥ
prīta āha bhṛgūdvaham

sūtaḥ uvāca—Sūta Gosvāmī said; *saṁstutaḥ*—properly glorified; *bhagavān*—the Supreme Lord; *ittham*—in this way; *mārkaṇḍeyena*—by Mārkaṇḍeya; *dhī-matā*—the intelligent sage; *nārāyaṇaḥ*—Lord Nārāyaṇa; *nara-sakhaḥ*—the friend of Nara; *prītaḥ*—satisfied; *āha*—spoke; *bhṛgu-udvaham*—to the most eminent descendant of Bhṛgu.

TRANSLATION

Sūta Gosvāmī said: The Supreme Lord Nārāyaṇa, the friend of Nara, was satisfied by the proper glorification offered by the intelligent sage Mārkaṇḍeya. Thus the Lord addressed that excellent descendant of Bhṛgu.

TEXT 2

श्रीभगवानुवाच
भो भो ब्रह्मर्षिवर्योऽसि सिद्ध आत्मसमाधिना ।
मयि भक्त्यानपायिन्या तपःस्वाध्यायसंयमैः ॥२॥

śrī-bhagavān uvāca
bho bho brahmarṣi-varyo 'si
siddha ātma-samādhinā
mayi bhaktyānapāyinyā
tapaḥ-svādhyāya-saṁyamaiḥ

śrī-bhagavān uvāca—the Supreme Personality of Godhead said; *bhoḥ bhoḥ*—dear sage; *brahma-ṛṣi*—of all learned *brāhmaṇas; varyaḥ*—the best; *asi*—you are; *siddhaḥ*—perfect; *ātma-samādhinā*—by fixed meditation upon the Self; *mayi*—directed toward Me; *bhaktyā*—by devotional service; *anapāyinyā*—undeviating; *tapaḥ*—by austerities; *svādhyāya*—study of the *Vedas; saṁyamaiḥ*—and regulative principles.

TRANSLATION

The Supreme Personality of Godhead said: My dear Mārkaṇḍeya, you are indeed the best of all learned *brāhmaṇas.* You have perfected your life by practicing fixed meditation upon the Supreme Soul, as well as by focusing upon Me your undeviating devotional service, your austerities, your study of the *Vedas* and your strict adherence to regulative principles.

TEXT 3

वयं ते परितुष्टाः स्म त्वद्बृहद्व्रतचर्यया ।
वरं प्रतीच्छ भद्रं ते वरदोऽस्मि त्वदीप्सितम् ॥३॥

vayaṁ te parituṣṭāḥ sma
tvad-bṛhad-vrata-caryayā
varaṁ pratīccha bhadraṁ te
vara-do 'smi tvad-īpsitam

vayam—We; *te*—with you; *parituṣṭāḥ*—perfectly satisfied; *sma*—have become; *tvat*—your; *bṛhat-vrata*—of the vow of lifelong celibacy; *caryayā*—by performance; *varam*—a benediction; *pratīccha*—please choose; *bhadram*—all good; *te*—unto you; *vara-daḥ*—the giver of benedictions; *asmi*—I am; *tvat-īpsitam*—desired by you.

TRANSLATION

We are perfectly satisfied with your practice of lifelong celibacy. Please choose whatever benediction you desire, since I can grant your wish. May you enjoy all good fortune.

PURPORT

Śrīla Viśvanātha Cakravartī Ṭhākura explains that the Lord used the plural form in the beginning of this verse—"We are satisfied"—because He was referring to Himself along with Śiva and Umā, who will later be glorified by Mārkaṇḍeya. The Lord then used the singular—"I am the bestower of benedictions"—because ultimately only Lord Nārāyaṇa

(Kṛṣṇa) can award the highest perfection of life, eternal Kṛṣṇa consciousness.

TEXT 4

श्रीऋषिरुवाच
जितं ते देवदेवेश प्रपन्नार्तिहराच्युत ।
वरेणैतावतालं नो यद् भवान् समदृश्यत ॥४॥

śrī-ṛṣir uvāca
jitaṁ te deva-deveśa
prapannārti-harācyuta
vareṇaitāvatālaṁ no
yad bhavān samadṛśyata

śrī-ṛṣiḥ uvāca—the sage said; *jitam*—are victorious; *te*—You; *deva-deva-īśa*—O Lord of lords; *prapanna*—of one who is surrendered; *ārti-hara*—O remover of all distress; *acyuta*—O infallible one; *vareṇa*—with the benediction; *etāvatā*—this much; *alam*—enough; *naḥ*—by us; *yat*—that; *bhavān*—Your good self; *samadṛśyata*—has been seen.

TRANSLATION

The sage said: O Lord of lords, all glories to You! O Lord Acyuta, You remove all distress for the devotees who surrender unto You. That you have allowed me to see You is all the benediction I want.

TEXT 5

गृहीत्वाजादयो यस्य श्रीमत्पादाब्जदर्शनम् ।
मनसा योगपक्वेन स भवान्मेऽक्षिगोचरः ॥५॥

gṛhītvājādayo yasya
śrīmat-pādābja-darśanam
manasā yoga-pakvena
sa bhavān me 'kṣi-gocaraḥ

gṛhītvā—receiving; *aja-ādayaḥ*—(became) Brahmā and others; *yasya*—whose; *śrīmat*—all-opulent; *pāda-abja*—of the lotus feet; *darśanam*—the sight; *manasā*—by the mind; *yoga-pakvena*—matured in *yoga* practice; *saḥ*—He; *bhavān*—Yourself; *me*—my; *akṣi*—to the eyes; *go-caraḥ*—perceptible.

TRANSLATION

Even such demigods as Lord Brahmā achieved their exalted positions simply by seeing Your beautiful lotus feet after their minds had become mature in *yoga* practice. Yet now, my Lord, You have personally appeared before me.

PURPORT

Mārkaṇḍeya Ṛṣi points out that exalted demigods like Lord Brahmā achieved their positions simply by glimpsing the Lord's lotus feet, and yet Mārkaṇḍeya Ṛṣi was now able to see Lord Kṛṣṇa's entire body. Thus he could not even imagine the extent of his good fortune.

TEXT 6

अथाप्यम्बुजपत्राक्ष पुण्यश्लोकशिखामणे ।
द्रक्ष्ये मायां यया लोकः सपालो वेद सद्भिदाम् ॥६॥

athāpy ambuja-patrākṣa
puṇya-śloka-śikhāmaṇe
drakṣye māyāṁ yayā lokaḥ
sa-pālo veda sad-bhidām

atha api—nonetheless; *ambuja-patra*—like the petals of a lotus; *akṣa*—O You whose eyes; *puṇya-śloka*—of famous personalities; *śikhā-maṇe*—O crest jewel; *drakṣye*—I desire to see; *māyām*—the illusory energy; *yayā*—by which; *lokaḥ*—the entire world; *sa-pālaḥ*—along with its ruling demigods; *veda*—considers; *sat*—of the absolute reality; *bhidām*—material differentiation.

TRANSLATION

O lotus-eyed Lord, O crest jewel of renowned personalities, although I am satisfied simply by seeing You, I do wish to see Your illusory potency, by whose influence the entire world, together with its ruling demigods, considers reality to be materially variegated.

PURPORT

A conditioned soul sees the material world to be constituted of independent, separate entities. Actually, all things are united, being potencies of the Supreme Lord. Mārkaṇḍeya Ṛṣi is curious to witness the exact process by which *māyā*, the Lord's bewildering potency, casts living beings into illusion.

TEXT 7

सूत उवाच
इतीडितोऽर्चितः काममृषिणा भगवान्मुने ।
तथेति स स्मयन् प्रागाद् बदर्याश्रममीश्वरः ॥७॥

sūta uvāca
itīḍito 'rcitaḥ kāmam
ṛṣiṇā bhagavān mune
tatheti sa smayan prāgād
badary-āśramam īśvaraḥ

sūtaḥ uvāca—Sūta Gosvāmī said; *iti*—in these words; *īḍitaḥ*—glorified; *arcitaḥ*—worshiped; *kāmam*—satisfactorily; *ṛṣiṇā*—by the sage Mārkaṇḍeya; *bhagavān*—the Personality of Godhead; *mune*—O wise Śaunaka; *tathā iti*—"so be it"; *saḥ*—He; *smayan*—smiling; *prāgāt*—departed; *badarī-āśramam*—for the hermitage Badarikāśrama; *īśvaraḥ*—the Supreme Lord.

TRANSLATION

Sūta Gosvāmī said: O wise Śaunaka, thus satisfied by Mārkaṇḍeya's praise and worship, the Supreme Personality of Godhead, smiling, replied, "So be it," and then departed for His hermitage at Badarikāśrama.

PURPORT

The words *bhagavān* and *īśvara* in this verse refer to the Supreme Lord in His incarnation as the twin sages Nara and Nārāyaṇa. According to Śrīla Viśvanātha Cakravartī Ṭhākura, the Supreme Lord smiled ruefully, because He prefers that His pure devotees stay away from His illusory energy. Curiosity to see the illusory energy of the Lord sometimes develops into sinful material desire. Nonetheless, to please His devotee Mārkaṇḍeya, thc Lord granted his request, just as a father who cannot convince his son to give up pursuing a harmful desire may let him experience some painful reaction so that he will then voluntarily desist. Thus, understanding what would soon happen to Mārkaṇḍeya, the Lord smiled as He prepared to display the illusory potency to him.

TEXTS 8–9

तमेव चिन्तयन्नर्थमृषिः स्वाश्रम एव सः ।
वसन्नग्न्यर्कसोमाम्बुभूवायुवियदात्मसु ॥८॥
ध्यायन् सर्वत्र च हरिं भावद्रव्यैरपूजयत् ।
क्वचित् पूजां विसस्मार प्रेमप्रसरसम्प्लुतः ॥९॥

tam eva cintayann artham
ṛṣiḥ svāśrama eva saḥ
vasann agny-arka-somāmbu-
bhū-vāyu-viyad-ātmasu

dhyāyan sarvatra ca hariṁ
bhāva-dravyair apūjayat
kvacit pūjāṁ visasmāra
prema-prasara-samplutaḥ

tam—that; *eva*—indeed; *cintayan*—thinking of; *artham*—the goal; *ṛṣiḥ*—the sage Mārkaṇḍeya; *sva-āśrame*—at his own hermitage; *eva*—indeed; *saḥ*—he; *vasan*—remaining; *agni*—in the fire; *arka*—the sun; *soma*—the moon; *ambu*—the water; *bhū*—the earth; *vāyu*—the wind; *viyat*—the lightning; *ātmasu*—and in his own heart; *dhyāyan*—meditating; *sarvatra*—in all circumstances; *ca*—and; *harim*—upon Lord Hari;

bhāva-dravyaiḥ—with paraphernalia conceived in his mind; *apūjayat*—he offered worship; *kvacit*—sometimes; *pūjām*—the worship; *visasmāra*—he forgot; *prema*—of pure love of God; *prasara*—in the flood; *samplutaḥ*—being drowned.

TRANSLATION

Thinking always of his desire to see the Lord's illusory energy, the sage remained in his *āśrama*, meditating constantly upon the Lord within fire, the sun, the moon, water, the earth, air, lightning and his own heart and worshiping Him with paraphernalia conceived in his mind. But sometimes, overwhelmed by waves of love for the Lord, Mārkaṇḍeya would forget to perform his regular worship.

PURPORT

It is apparent from these verses that Mārkaṇḍeya Ṛṣi was a great devotee of Lord Kṛṣṇa; therefore he wanted to see the illusory energy of the Lord not to fulfill some material ambition but to learn how His potency is working.

TEXT 10

तस्यैकदा भृगुश्रेष्ठ पुष्पभद्रातटे मुनेः ।
उपासीनस्य सन्ध्यायां ब्रह्मन् वायुरभून्महान् ॥१०॥

tasyaikadā bhṛgu-śreṣṭha
puṣpabhadrā-taṭe muneḥ
upāsīnasya sandhyāyām
brahman vāyur abhūn mahān

tasya—while he; *ekadā*—one day; *bhṛgu-śreṣṭha*—O best of the descendants of Bhṛgu; *puṣpabhadrā-taṭe*—on the bank of the river Puṣpabhadrā; *muneḥ*—the sage; *upāsīnasya*—was performing worship; *sandhyāyām*—at the juncture of the day; *brahman*—O *brāhmaṇa;* *vāyuḥ*—a wind; *abhūt*—arose; *mahān*—great.

TRANSLATION

O *brāhmaṇa* Śaunaka, best of the Bhṛgus, one day while Mārkaṇḍeya was performing his evening worship on the bank of the Puṣpabhadrā, a great wind suddenly arose.

TEXT 11

तं चण्डशब्दं समुदीरयन्तं
बलाहका अन्वभवन् करालाः ।
अक्षस्थविष्ठा मुमुचुस्तडिद्भिः
स्वनन्त उच्चैरभि वर्षधाराः ॥११॥

taṁ caṇḍa-śabdaṁ samudīrayantaṁ
balāhakā anv abhavan karālāḥ
akṣa-sthaviṣṭhā mumucus taḍidbhiḥ
svananta uccair abhi varṣa-dhārāḥ

tam—that wind; *caṇḍa-śabdam*—a terrible sound; *samudīrayantam*—which was creating; *balāhakāḥ*—clouds; *anu*—following it; *abhavan*—appeared; *karālāḥ*—fearful; *akṣa*—like wagon wheels; *sthaviṣṭhāḥ*—solid; *mumucuḥ*—they released; *taḍidbhiḥ*—along with lightning; *svanantaḥ*—resounding; *uccaiḥ*—greatly; *abhi*—in all directions; *varṣa*—of rain; *dhārāḥ*—torrents.

TRANSLATION

That wind created a terrible sound and brought in its wake fearsome clouds that were accompanied by lightning and roaring thunder and that poured down on all sides torrents of rain as heavy as wagon wheels.

TEXT 12

ततो व्यदृश्यन्त चतुः समुद्राः
समन्ततः क्ष्मातलमाग्रसन्तः ।
समीरवेगोर्मिभिरुग्रनक्र-
महाभयावर्तगभीरघोषाः ॥१२॥

tato vyadṛśyanta catuḥ samudrāḥ
samantataḥ kṣmā-talam āgrasantaḥ
samīra-vegormibhir ugra-nakra-
mahā-bhayāvarta-gabhīra-ghoṣāḥ

tataḥ—then; *vyadṛśyanta*—appeared; *catuḥ samudrāḥ*—the four oceans; *samantataḥ*—on all sides; *kṣmā-talam*—the surface of the earth; *āgrasantaḥ*—swallowing up; *samīra*—of the wind; *vega*—impelled by the force; *ūrmibhiḥ*—with their waves; *ugra*—terrible; *nakra*—with sea monsters; *mahā-bhaya*—very fearful; *āvarta*—with whirlpools; *gabhīra*—grave; *ghoṣāḥ*—with sounds.

TRANSLATION

Then the four great oceans appeared on all sides, swallowing up the surface of the earth with their wind-tossed waves. In these oceans were terrible sea monsters, fearful whirlpools and ominous rumblings.

TEXT 13

अन्तर्बहिश्चाद्भिरतिद्युभिः खरैः
शतह्रदाभिरुपतापितं जगत् ।
चतुर्विधं वीक्ष्य सहात्मना मुनिर्
जलाप्लुतां क्ष्मां विमनाः समत्रसत् ॥१३॥

antar bahiś cādbhir ati-dyubhiḥ kharaiḥ
śatahradābhir upatāpitaṁ jagat
catur-vidhaṁ vīkṣya sahātmanā munir
jalāplutāṁ kṣmāṁ vimanāḥ samatrasat

antaḥ—internally; *bahiḥ*—externally; *ca*—and; *adbhiḥ*—by the water; *ati-dyubhiḥ*—rising higher than the sky; *kharaiḥ*—by the fierce (winds); *śata-hradābhiḥ*—by lightning bolts; *upatāpitam*—greatly distressed; *jagat*—all the inhabitants of the universe; *catuḥ-vidham*—of four varieties (those who have taken birth from embryos, from eggs, from seeds and from perspiration); *vīkṣya*—seeing; *saha*—along with; *ātmanā*—himself;

muniḥ—the sage; *jala*—by the water; *āplutām*—flooded; *kṣmām*—the earth; *vimanāḥ*—perplexed; *samatrasat*—he became fearful.

TRANSLATION

The sage saw all the inhabitants of the universe, including himself, tormented within and without by the harsh winds, the bolts of lightning, and the great waves rising beyond the sky. As the whole earth flooded, he grew perplexed and fearful.

PURPORT

Here the word *catur-vidham* refers to the four sources of birth for conditioned souls: embryos, eggs, seeds and perspiration.

TEXT 14

तस्यैवमुद्वीक्षत ऊर्मिभीषणः
प्रभञ्जनाघूर्णितवार्महार्णवः ।
आपूर्यमाणो वरषद्भिरम्बुदैः
क्ष्मामप्यधाद् द्वीपवर्षाद्रिभिः समम् ॥१४॥

tasyaivam udvīkṣata ūrmi-bhīṣaṇaḥ
prabhañjanāghūrṇita-vār mahārṇavaḥ
āpūryamāṇo varaṣadbhir ambudaiḥ
kṣmām apyadhād dvīpa-varṣādribhiḥ samam

tasya—while he; *evam*—in this way; *udvīkṣataḥ*—was looking on; *ūrmi*—with its waves; *bhīṣaṇaḥ*—frightening; *prabhañjana*—by hurricane winds; *āghūrṇita*—swirled around; *vāḥ*—its water; *mahā-arṇavaḥ*—the great ocean; *āpūryamāṇaḥ*—becoming filled; *varaṣadbhiḥ*—with rain; *ambu-daiḥ*—by the clouds; *kṣmām*—the earth; *apyadhāt*—covered over; *dvīpa*—with its islands; *varṣa*—continents; *adribhiḥ*—and mountains; *samam*—together.

TRANSLATION

Even as Mārkaṇḍeya looked on, the rain pouring down from the clouds filled the ocean more and more until that great sea, its

waters violently whipped into terrifying waves by hurricanes, covered up all the earth's islands, mountains and continents.

TEXT 15

सक्ष्मान्तरिक्षं सदिवं सभागणं
त्रैलोक्यमासीत् सह दिग्भिराप्लुतम् ।
स एक एवोर्वरितो महामुनिर्
बभ्राम विक्षिप्य जटा जडान्धवत् ॥१५॥

sa-kṣmāntarikṣaṁ sa-divaṁ sa-bhā-gaṇaṁ
trai-lokyam āsīt saha digbhir āplutam
sa eka evorvarito mahā-munir
babhrāma vikṣipya jaṭā jaḍāndha-vat

sa—along with; *kṣmā*—the earth; *antarikṣam*—and outer space; *sa-divam*—along with the heavenly planets; *sa-bhā-gaṇam*—along with all the celestial bodies; *trai-lokyam*—the three worlds; *āsīt*—became; *saha*—along with; *digbhiḥ*—all the directions; *āplutam*—flooded; *saḥ*—he; *ekaḥ*—alone; *eva*—indeed; *urvaritaḥ*—remaining; *mahā-muniḥ*—the great sage; *babhrāma*—wandered about; *vikṣipya*—scattering; *jaṭāḥ*—his matted locks; *jaḍa*—a dumb person; *andha*—a blind person; *vat*—like.

TRANSLATION

The water inundated the earth, outer space, heaven and the celestial region. Indeed, the entire expanse of the universe was flooded in all directions, and out of all its inhabitants only Mārkaṇḍeya remained. His matted hair scattered, the great sage wandered about alone in the water as if dumb and blind.

TEXT 16

क्षुत्तृट्परीतो मकरैस्तिमिंगिलैर्
उपद्रुतो वीचिनभस्वताहतः ।
तमस्यपारे पतितो भ्रमन् दिशो
न वेद खं गां च परिश्रमेषितः ॥१६॥

kṣut-tṛṭ-parīto makarais timiṅgilair
upadruto vīci-nabhasvatāhataḥ
tamasy apāre patito bhraman diśo
na veda khaṁ gāṁ ca pariśrameṣitaḥ

kṣut—by hunger; *tṛṭ*—and thirst; *parītaḥ*—enveloped; *makaraiḥ*—by the *makaras,* a species of monster crocodile; *timiṅgilaiḥ*—and by the *timiṅgila,* a variety of huge fish that eats whales; *upadrutaḥ*—harassed; *vīci*—by the waves; *nabhasvatā*—and the wind; *āhataḥ*—tormented; *tamasi*—in the darkness; *apāre*—which was unlimited; *patitaḥ*—having fallen; *bhraman*—wandering; *diśaḥ*—the directions; *na veda*—did not recognize; *kham*—the sky; *gām*—the earth; *ca*—and; *pariśrama-iṣitaḥ*—overcome by exhaustion.

TRANSLATION

Tormented by hunger and thirst, attacked by monstrous *makaras* and *timiṅgila* fish and battered by the wind and waves, he moved aimlessly through the infinite darkness into which he had fallen. As he grew increasingly exhausted, he lost all sense of direction and could not tell the sky from the earth.

TEXTS 17–18

क्वचिन्मग्नो महावर्ते तरलैस्ताडितः क्वचित् ।
यादोभिर्भक्ष्यते क्वापि स्वयमन्योन्यघातिभिः ॥१७॥
क्वचिच्छोकं क्वचिन्मोहं क्वचिद्दुःखं सुखं भयम् ।
क्वचिन्मृत्युमवाप्नोति व्याध्यादिभिरुतार्दितः ॥१८॥

kvacin magno mahāvarte
taralais tāḍitaḥ kvacit
yādobhir bhakṣyate kvāpi
svayam anyonya-ghātibhiḥ

kvacic chokaṁ kvacin mohaṁ
kvacid duḥkhaṁ sukhaṁ bhayam
kvacin mṛtyum avāpnoti
vyādhy-ādibhir utārditaḥ

kvacit—sometimes; *magnaḥ*—drowning; *mahā-āvarte*—in a great whirlpool; *taralaiḥ*—by the waves; *tāḍitaḥ*—beaten; *kvacit*—sometimes; *yādobhiḥ*—by the aquatic monsters; *bhakṣyate*—he was threatened with being eaten; *kva api*—sometimes; *svayam*—himself; *anyonya*—each other; *ghātibhiḥ*—attacking; *kvacit*—sometimes; *śokam*—depression; *kvacit*—sometimes; *moham*—bewilderment; *kvacit*—sometimes; *duḥkham*—misery; *sukham*—happiness; *bhayam*—fear; *kvacit*—sometimes; *mṛtyum*—death; *avāpnoti*—he experienced; *vyādhi*—by disease; *ādibhiḥ*—and other pains; *uta*—also; *arditaḥ*—distressed.

TRANSLATION

At times he was engulfed by the great whirlpools, sometimes he was beaten by the mighty waves, and at other times the aquatic monsters threatened to devour him as they attacked one another. Sometimes he felt lamentation, bewilderment, misery, happiness or fear, and at other times he experienced such terrible illness and pain that he felt himself dying.

TEXT 19

अयुतायुतवर्षाणां सहस्राणि शतानि च ।
व्यतीयुर्भ्रमतस्तस्मिन् विष्णुमायावृतात्मनः ॥१९॥

ayutāyuta-varṣāṇāṁ
sahasrāṇi śatāni ca
vyatīyur bhramatas tasmin
viṣṇu-māyāvṛtātmanaḥ

ayuta—tens of thousands; *ayuta*—by tens of thousands; *varṣāṇām*—of years; *sahasrāṇi*—thousands; *śatāni*—hundreds; *ca*—and; *vyatīyuḥ*—passed by; *bhramataḥ*—as he wandered; *tasmin*—in that; *viṣṇu-māyā*—by the illusory energy of Lord Viṣṇu; *āvṛta*—covered; *ātmanaḥ*—his mind.

TRANSLATION

Countless millions of years passed as Mārkaṇḍeya wandered about in that deluge, his mind bewildered by the illusory energy of Lord Viṣṇu, the Supreme Personality of Godhead.

TEXT 20

स कदाचिद् भ्रमंस्तस्मिन् पृथिव्याः ककुदि द्विजः ।
न्याग्रोधपोतं ददृशे फलपल्लवशोभितम् ॥२०॥

sa kadācid bhramaṁs tasmin
pṛthivyāḥ kakudi dvijaḥ
nyāgrodha-potaṁ dadṛśe
phala-pallava-śobhitam

saḥ—he; *kadācit*—on one occasion; *bhraman*—while wandering; *tasmin*—in that water; *pṛthivyāḥ*—of earth; *kakudi*—upon a raised place; *dvijaḥ*—the *brāhmaṇa; nyāgrodha-potam*—a young banyan tree; *dadṛśe*—saw; *phala*—with fruits; *pallava*—and blossoms; *śobhitam*—decorated.

TRANSLATION

Once, while wandering in the water, the *brāhmaṇa* Mārkaṇḍeya discovered a small island, upon which stood a young banyan tree bearing blossoms and fruits.

TEXT 21

प्रागुत्तरस्यां शाखायां तस्यापि ददृशे शिशुम् ।
शयानं पर्णपुटके ग्रसन्तं प्रभया तमः ॥२१॥

prāg-uttarasyāṁ śākhāyāṁ
tasyāpi dadṛśe śiśum
śayānaṁ parṇa-puṭake
grasantaṁ prabhayā tamaḥ

prāk-uttarasyām—toward the northeast; *śākhāyām*—upon a branch; *tasya*—of that tree; *api*—indeed; *dadṛśe*—he saw; *śiśum*—an infant boy; *śayānam*—lying; *parṇa-puṭake*—within the concavity of a leaf; *grasantam*—swallowing; *prabhayā*—with His effulgence; *tamaḥ*—the darkness.

TRANSLATION

Upon a branch of the northeast portion of that tree he saw an infant boy lying within a leaf. The child's effulgence was swallowing up the darkness.

TEXTS 22–25

महामरकतश्यामं श्रीमद्वदनपंकजम् ।
कम्बुग्रीवं महोरस्कं सुनासं सुन्दरभ्रुवम् ॥२२॥
श्वासैजदलकाभातं कम्बुश्रीकर्णदाडिमम् ।
विद्रुमाधरभासेषच्छोणायितसुधास्मितम् ॥२३॥
पद्मगर्भारुणापांगं हृद्यहासावलोकनम् ।
श्वासैजद्वलिसंविग्ननिम्ननाभिदलोदरम् ॥२४॥
चार्वंगुलिभ्यां पाणिभ्यामुन्नीय चरणाम्बुजम् ।
मुखे निधाय विप्रेन्द्रो धयन्तं वीक्ष्य विस्मितः ॥२५॥

mahā-marakata-śyāmaṁ
śrīmad-vadana-paṅkajam
kambu-grīvaṁ mahoraskaṁ
su-nasaṁ sundara-bhruvam

śvāsaijad-alakābhātaṁ
kambu-śrī-karṇa-dāḍimam
vidrumādhara-bhāseṣac-
choṇāyita-sudhā-smitam

padma-garbhāruṇāpāṅgaṁ
hṛdya-hāsāvalokanam
śvāsaijad-vali-saṁvigna-
nimna-nābhi-dalodaram

cārv-aṅgulibhyāṁ pāṇibhyām
unnīya caraṇāmbujam
mukhe nidhāya viprendro
dhayantaṁ vīkṣya vismitaḥ

mahā-marakata—like a great emerald; *śyāmam*—dark blue; *śrīmat*—beautiful; *vadana-paṅkajam*—whose lotus face; *kambu*—like a conchshell; *grīvam*—whose throat; *mahā*—broad; *uraskam*—whose chest; *su-nasam*—having a beautiful nose; *sundara-bhruvam*—having beautiful eyebrows; *śvāsa*—by His breath; *ejat*—trembling; *alaka*—with the hair; *ābhātam*—splendid; *kambu*—like a conchshell; *śrī*—beautiful; *karṇa*—His ears; *dāḍimam*—resembling pomegranate flowers; *vidruma*—like coral; *adhara*—of His lips; *bhāsā*—by the effulgence; *īṣat*—slightly; *śoṇāyita*—reddened; *sudhā*—nectarean; *smitam*—His smile; *padma-garbha*—like the whorl of a lotus; *aruṇa*—reddish; *apāṅgam*—the corners of His eyes; *hṛdya*—charming; *hāsa*—with a smile; *avalokanam*—His countenance; *śvāsa*—by His breath; *ejat*—made to move; *vali*—by the lines; *saṁvigna*—contorted; *nimna*—deep; *nābhi*—with His navel; *dala*—like a leaf; *udaram*—whose abdomen; *cāru*—attractive; *aṅgulibhyām*—having fingers; *pāṇibhyām*—by His two hands; *unnīya*—picking up; *caraṇa-ambujam*—His lotus foot; *mukhe*—in His mouth; *nidhāya*—placing; *vipra-indraḥ*—the best of *brāhmaṇas,* Mārkaṇḍeya; *dhayantam*—drinking; *vīkṣya*—seeing; *vismitaḥ*—was amazed.

TRANSLATION

The infant's dark-blue complexion was the color of a flawless emerald, His lotus face shone with a wealth of beauty, and His throat bore marks like the lines on a conchshell. He had a broad chest, a finely shaped nose, beautiful eyebrows, and lovely ears that resembled pomegranate flowers and that had inner folds like a conchshell's spirals. The corners of His eyes were reddish like the whorl of a lotus, and the effulgence of His corallike lips slightly reddened the nectarean, enchanting smile on His face. As He breathed, His splendid hair trembled and His deep navel became distorted by the moving folds of skin on His abdomen, which resembled a banyan leaf. The exalted *brāhmaṇa* watched with amazement as the infant took hold of one of His lotus feet with His graceful fingers, placed a toe within His mouth and began to suck.

PURPORT

The young child was the Supreme Personality of Godhead. According to Śrīla Viśvanātha Cakravartī Ṭhākura, Lord Kṛṣṇa wondered, "So many devotees are hankering for the nectar of My lotus feet. Therefore let Me personally experience that nectar." Thus the Lord, playing like an ordinary baby, began to suck on His toes.

TEXT 26

तद्दर्शनाद् वीतपरिश्रमो मुदा
प्रोत्फुल्लहृत्पद्मविलोचनाम्बुजः ।
प्रहृष्टरोमाद्भुतभावशंकितः
प्रष्टुं पुरस्तं प्रससार बालकम् ॥२६॥

tad-darśanād vīta-pariśramo mudā
protphulla-hṛt-padma-vilocanāmbujaḥ
prahṛṣṭa-romādbhuta-bhāva-śaṅkitaḥ
praṣṭuṁ puras taṁ prasasāra bālakam

tat-darśanāt—by seeing the child; *vīta*—dispelled; *pariśramaḥ*—his weariness; *mudā*—out of pleasure; *protphulla*—expanded wide; *hṛt-padma*—the lotus of his heart; *vilocana-ambujaḥ*—and his lotus eyes; *prahṛṣṭa*—standing on end; *romā*—the hairs on his body; *adbhuta-bhāva*—about the identity of this wonderful form; *śaṅkitaḥ*—confused; *praṣṭum*—in order to inquire; *puraḥ*—in front; *tam*—of Him; *prasasāra*—he approached; *bālakam*—the child.

TRANSLATION

As Mārkaṇḍeya beheld the child, all his weariness vanished. Indeed, so great was his pleasure that the lotus of his heart, along with his lotus eyes, fully blossomed and the hairs on his body stood on end. Confused as to the identity of the wonderful infant, the sage approached Him.

PURPORT

Mārkaṇḍeya wanted to ask the child about His identity and therefore approached Him.

TEXT 27

तावच्छिशोर्वै श्वसितेन भार्गवः
सोऽन्तः शरीरं मशको यथाविशत् ।
तत्राप्यदो न्यस्तमचष्ट कृत्स्नशो
यथा पुरामुह्यदतीव विस्मितः ॥२७॥

tāvac chiśor vai śvasitena bhārgavaḥ
so 'ntaḥ śarīraṁ maśako yathāviśat
tatrāpy ado nyastam acaṣṭa kṛtsnaśo
yathā purāmuhyad atīva vismitaḥ

tāvat—at that very moment; *śiśoḥ*—of the infant; *vai*—indeed; *śvasitena*—with the breathing; *bhārgavaḥ*—the descendant of Bhṛgu; *saḥ*—he; *antaḥ śarīram*—within the body; *maśakaḥ*—a mosquito; *yathā*—just like; *aviśat*—entered; *tatra*—therein; *api*—indeed; *adaḥ*—this universe; *nyastam*—placed; *acaṣṭa*—he saw; *kṛtsnaśaḥ*—entire; *yathā*—as; *purā*—previously; *amuhyat*—he became bewildered; *atīva*—extremely; *vismitaḥ*—surprised.

TRANSLATION

Just then the child inhaled, drawing Mārkaṇḍeya within His body like a mosquito. There the sage found the entire universe arrayed as it had been before its dissolution. Seeing this, Mārkaṇḍeya was most astonished and perplexed.

TEXTS 28–29

खं रोदसी भागणानद्रिसागरान्
द्वीपान् सवर्षान् ककुभः सुरासुरान् ।
वनानि देशान् सरितः पुराकरान्
खेटान् व्रजानाश्रमवर्णवृत्तयः ॥२८॥
महान्ति भूतान्यथ भौतिकान्यसौ
कालं च नानायुगकल्पकल्पनम् ।
यत् किञ्चिदन्यद् व्यवहारकारणं
ददर्श विश्वं सदिवावभासितम् ॥२९॥

khaṁ rodasī bhā-gaṇān adri-sāgarān
dvīpān sa-varṣān kakubhaḥ surāsurān
vanāni deśān saritaḥ purākarān
kheṭān vrajān āśrama-varṇa-vṛttayaḥ

mahānti bhūtāny atha bhautikāny asau
kālaṁ ca nānā-yuga-kalpa-kalpanam
yat kiñcid anyad vyavahāra-kāraṇaṁ
dadarśa viśvaṁ sad ivāvabhāsitam

kham—the sky; *rodasī*—the heavens and earth; *bhā-gaṇān*—all the stars; *adri*—the mountains; *sāgarān*—and oceans; *dvīpān*—the great islands; *sa-varṣān*—along with the continents; *kakubhaḥ*—the directions; *sura-asurān*—the saintly devotees and the demons; *vanāni*—the forests; *deśān*—the various countries; *saritaḥ*—the rivers; *pura*—the cities; *ākarān*—and the mines; *kheṭān*—the agricultural villages; *vrajān*—the cow pastures; *āśrama-varṇa*—of the various spiritual and occupational divisions of society; *vṛttayaḥ*—the engagements; *mahānti bhūtāni*—the basic elements of nature; *atha*—and; *bhautikāni*—all their gross manifestations; *asau*—he; *kālam*—time; *ca*—also; *nānā-yuga-kalpa*—of the different millennia and the days of Brahmā; *kalpanam*—the regulating agent; *yat kiñcit*—whatever; *anyat*—other; *vyavahāra-kāraṇam*—object intended for use in material life; *dadarśa*—he saw; *viśvam*—the universe; *sat*—real; *iva*—as if; *avabhāsitam*—manifest.

TRANSLATION

The sage saw the entire universe: the sky, heavens and earth, the stars, mountains, oceans, great islands and continents, the expanses in every direction, the saintly and demoniac living beings, the forests, countries, rivers, cities and mines, the agricultural villages and cow pastures, and the occupational and spiritual activities of the various social divisions. He also saw the basic elements of creation along with all their by-products, as well as time itself, which regulates the progression of countless ages within the days of Brahmā. In addition, he saw everything else created for use in material life. All this he saw manifested before him as if it were real.

TEXT 30

हिमालयं पुष्पवहां च तां नदीं
निजाश्रमं यत्र ऋषी अपश्यत ।
विश्वं विपश्यञ्छ्‌वसिताच्छिशोर्वै
बहिर्निरस्तो न्यपतल्लयाब्धौ ॥३०॥

himālayaṁ puṣpavahāṁ ca tāṁ nadīṁ
nijāśramaṁ yatra ṛṣī apaśyata
viśvaṁ vipaśyañ chvasitāc chiśor vai
bahir nirasto nyapatal layābdhau

himālayam—the Himālaya Mountains; *puṣpa-vahām*—Puṣpabhadrā; *ca*—and; *tām*—that; *nadīm*—river; *nija-āśramam*—his own hermitage; *yatra*—where; *ṛṣī*—the two sages, Nara-Nārāyaṇa; *apaśyata*—he saw; *viśvam*—the universe; *vipaśyan*—while observing; *śvasitāt*—by the breath; *śiśoḥ*—of the infant; *vai*—indeed; *bahiḥ*—outside; *nirastaḥ*—expelled; *nyapatat*—he fell; *laya-abdhau*—into the ocean of dissolution.

TRANSLATION

He saw before him the Himālaya Mountains, the Puṣpabhadrā River, and his own hermitage, where he had had the audience of the sages Nara-Nārāyaṇa. Then, as Mārkaṇḍeya beheld the entire universe, the infant exhaled, expelling the sage from His body and casting him back into the ocean of dissolution.

TEXTS 31–32

तस्मिन् पृथिव्याः ककुदि प्ररूढं
वटं च तत्पर्णपुटे शयानम् ।
तोकं च तत्प्रेमसुधास्मितेन
निरीक्षितोऽपांगनिरीक्षणेन ॥३१॥
अथ तं बालकं वीक्ष्य नेत्राभ्यां धिष्ठितं हृदि ।
अभ्ययादतिसङ्क्लिष्टः परिष्वक्तुमधोक्षजम् ॥३२॥

tasmin pṛthivyāḥ kakudi prarūḍhaṁ
vaṭaṁ ca tat-parṇa-puṭe śayānam
tokaṁ ca tat-prema-sudhā-smitena
nirīkṣito 'pāṅga-nirīkṣaṇena

atha taṁ bālakaṁ vīkṣya
netrābhyāṁ dhiṣṭhitaṁ hṛdi
abhyayād ati-saṅkliṣṭaḥ
pariṣvaktum adhokṣajam

tasmin—in that water; *pṛthivyāḥ*—of land; *kakudi*—on the raised place; *prarūḍham*—growing up; *vaṭam*—the banyan tree; *ca*—and; *tat*—of it; *parṇa-puṭe*—within the slight depression of the leaf; *śayānam*—lying; *tokam*—the child; *ca*—and; *tat*—for himself; *prema*—of love; *sudhā*—like nectar; *smitena*—with a smile; *nirīkṣitaḥ*—being looked upon; *apāṅga*—of the corner of His eyes; *nirīkṣaṇena*—by the glance; *atha*—then; *tam*—that; *bālakam*—infant; *vīkṣya*—looking upon; *netrābhyām*—by his eyes; *dhiṣṭhitam*—placed; *hṛdi*—within his heart; *abhyayāt*—ran forward; *ati-saṅkliṣṭaḥ*—greatly agitated; *pariṣvaktum*—to embrace; *adhokṣajam*—the transcendental Supreme Lord.

TRANSLATION

In that vast sea he again saw the banyan tree growing on the tiny island and the infant boy lying within the leaf. The child glanced at him from the corner of His eyes with a smile imbued with the nectar of love, and Mārkaṇḍeya took Him into his heart through his eyes. Greatly agitated, the sage ran to embrace the transcendental Personality of Godhead.

TEXT 33

तावत् स भगवान् साक्षाद् योगाधीशो गुहाशयः ।
अन्तर्दध ऋषेः सद्यो यथेहानीशनिर्मिता ॥३३॥

tāvat sa bhagavān sākṣād
yogādhīśo guhā-śayaḥ
antardadha ṛṣeḥ sadyo
yathehānīśa-nirmitā

tāvat—just then; *saḥ*—He; *bhagavān*—the Personality of Godhead; *sākṣāt*—directly; *yoga-adhīśaḥ*—the supreme master of *yoga; guhā-śayaḥ*—who is hidden within the heart of all living beings; *antardadhe*—disappeared; *ṛṣeḥ*—in front of the sage; *sadyaḥ*—suddenly; *yathā*—in the same way as; *īhā*—the object of endeavor; *anīśa*—by an incompetent person; *nirmitā*—created.

TRANSLATION

At that moment the Supreme Personality of Godhead, who is the original master of all mysticism and who is hidden within everyone's heart, became invisible to the sage, just as the achievements of an incompetent person can suddenly vanish.

TEXT 34

तमन्वथ वटो ब्रह्मन् सलिलं लोकसम्प्लवः ।
तिरोधायि क्षणादस्य स्वाश्रमे पूर्ववत् स्थितः ॥३४॥

tam anv atha vaṭo brahman
salilaṁ loka-samplavaḥ
tirodhāyi kṣaṇād asya
svāśrame pūrva-vat sthitaḥ

tam—Him; *anu*—following; *atha*—then; *vaṭaḥ*—the banyan tree; *brahman*—O *brāhmaṇa*, Śaunaka; *salilam*—the water; *loka-samplavaḥ*—the annihilation of the universe; *tirodhāyi*—they disappeared; *kṣaṇāt*—immediately; *asya*—in front of him; *sva-āśrame*—in his own hermitage; *pūrva-vat*—as previously; *sthitaḥ*—he was present.

TRANSLATION

After the Lord disappeared, O *brāhmaṇa*, the banyan tree, the great water and the dissolution of the universe all vanished as well, and in an instant Mārkaṇḍeya found himself back in his own hermitage, just as before.

Thus end the purports of the humble servant of His Divine Grace A. C. Bhaktivedanta Swami Prabhupāda to the Twelfth Canto, Ninth Chapter, of the Śrīmad-Bhāgavatam, *entitled "Mārkaṇḍeya Ṛṣi Sees the Illusory Potency of the Lord."*

CHAPTER TEN

Lord Śiva and Umā Glorify Mārkaṇḍeya Ṛṣi

In this chapter Śrī Sūta Gosvāmī describes how Mārkaṇḍeya Ṛṣi received benedictions from Lord Śiva.

Once, as Lord Śiva was traveling in the sky with his wife, Pārvatī, he came across Śrī Mārkaṇḍeya merged in meditative trance. At the request of Pārvatī, Lord Śiva presented himself before the sage to grant him the result of his austerities. Coming out of his trance, Śrī Mārkaṇḍeya saw Lord Śiva, the spiritual master of the three worlds, together with Pārvatī, and he worshiped them by offering them obeisances, words of greeting and a sitting place.

Then Lord Śiva praised the saintly devotees of the Personality of Godhead and requested Śrī Mārkaṇḍeya to choose whatever benediction he desired. Mārkaṇḍeya begged for unflinching devotion to the Supreme Lord Śrī Hari, to the devotees of the Supreme Lord and to Lord Śiva himself. Satisfied with Mārkaṇḍeya's devotion, Lord Śiva awarded him the boons of renown, freedom from old age and death until the time of universal dissolution, knowledge of all three phases of time, renunciation, realized knowledge and the position of a teacher of the *Purāṇas.*

Those who chant and hear the story of Mārkaṇḍeya Ṛṣi will attain liberation from material life, which is based on the accumulated desires generated from fruitive work.

TEXT 1

सूत उवाच
स एवमनुभूयेदं नारायणविनिर्मितम् ।
वैभवं योगमायायास्तमेव शरणं ययौ ॥१॥

sūta uvāca
sa evam anubhūyedaṁ
nārāyaṇa-vinirmitam
vaibhavaṁ yoga-māyāyās
tam eva śaraṇaṁ yayau

sūtaḥ uvāca—Sūta Gosvāmī said; *saḥ*—he, Mārkaṇḍeya; *evam*—in this way; *anubhūya*—experiencing; *idam*—this; *nārāyaṇa-vinirmitam*—manufactured by the Supreme Personality of Godhead, Nārāyaṇa; *vaibhavam*—the opulent exhibition; *yoga-māyāyāḥ*—of His internal mystic energy; *tam*—to Him; *eva*—indeed; *śaraṇam*—for shelter; *yayau*—he went.

TRANSLATION

Sūta Gosvāmī said: The Supreme Lord Nārāyaṇa arranged this opulent display of His bewildering potency. Mārkaṇḍeya Ṛṣi, having experienced it, took shelter of the Lord.

TEXT 2

श्रीमार्कण्डेय उवाच
प्रपन्नोऽस्म्यङ्घ्रिमूलं ते प्रपन्नाभयदं हरे ।
यन्माययापि विबुधा मुह्यन्ति ज्ञानकाशया ॥२॥

śrī-mārkaṇḍeya uvāca
prapanno 'smy aṅghri-mūlaṁ te
prapannābhaya-daṁ hare
yan-māyayāpi vibudhā
muhyanti jñāna-kāśayā

śrī-mārkaṇḍeyaḥ uvāca—Śrī Mārkaṇḍeya said; *prapannaḥ*—surrendered; *asmi*—I am; *aṅghri-mūlam*—to the soles of the lotus feet; *te*—Your; *prapanna*—of those who surrender; *abhaya-dam*—the giver of fearlessness; *hare*—O Lord Hari; *yat-māyayā*—by whose illusory potency; *api*—even; *vibudhāḥ*—intelligent demigods; *muhyanti*—become bewildered; *jñāna-kāśayā*—which falsely appears as knowledge.

TRANSLATION

Śrī Mārkaṇḍeya said: O Lord Hari, I take shelter of the soles of Your lotus feet, which bestow fearlessness upon all who surrender to them. Even the great demigods are bewildered by Your illusory energy, which appears to them in the guise of knowledge.

PURPORT

Conditioned souls are attracted to material sense gratification, and thus they meticulously study the workings of nature. Although they appear to be advancing in scientific knowledge, they become increasingly entangled in their false identification with the material body and therefore increasingly merge into ignorance.

TEXT 3

सूत उवाच
तमेवं निभृतात्मानं वृषेण दिवि पर्यटन् ।
रुद्राण्या भगवान् रुद्रो ददर्श स्वगणैर्वृतः ॥३॥

sūta uvāca
tam evaṁ nibhṛtātmānaṁ
vṛṣeṇa divi paryaṭan
rudrāṇyā bhagavān rudro
dadarśa sva-gaṇair vṛtaḥ

sūtaḥ uvāca—Sūta Gosvāmī said; *tam*—him, Mārkaṇḍeya Ṛṣi; *evam*—thus; *nibhṛta-ātmānam*—his mind completely absorbed in trance; *vṛṣeṇa*—on his bull; *divi*—in the sky; *paryaṭan*—traveling; *rudrāṇyā*—accompanied by his consort, Rudrāṇī (Umā); *bhagavān*—the powerful lord; *rudraḥ*—Śiva; *dadarśa*—saw; *sva-gaṇaiḥ*—by his entourage; *vṛtaḥ*—surrounded.

TRANSLATION

Sūta Gosvāmī said: Lord Rudra, traveling in the sky on his bull and accompanied by his consort, Rudrāṇī, as well as his personal associates, observed Mārkaṇḍeya in trance.

TEXT 4

अथोमा तमृषिं वीक्ष्य गिरिशं समभाषत ।
पश्येमं भगवन् विप्रं निभृतात्मेन्द्रियाशयम् ॥४॥

athomā tam ṛṣiṁ vīkṣya
giriśaṁ samabhāṣata
paśyemaṁ bhagavan vipraṁ
nibhṛtātmendriyāśayam

atha—then; *umā*—Umā; *tam*—that; *ṛṣim*—sage; *vīkṣya*—seeing; *giriśam*—to Lord Śiva; *samabhāṣata*—spoke; *paśya*—just see; *imam*—this; *bhagavan*—my lord; *vipram*—learned *brāhmaṇa; nibhṛta*—motionless; *ātma-indriya-āśayam*—his body, senses and mind.

TRANSLATION

Goddess Umā, seeing the sage, addressed Lord Giriśa: My lord, just see this learned *brāhmaṇa*, his body, mind and senses motionless in trance.

TEXT 5

निभृतोदझषव्रातो वातापाये यथार्णवः ।
कुर्वस्य तपसः साक्षात् संसिद्धिं सिद्धिदो भवान् ॥५॥

nibhṛtoda-jhaṣa-vrāto
vātāpāye yathārṇavaḥ
kurv asya tapasaḥ sākṣāt
saṁsiddhiṁ siddhi-do bhavān

nibhṛta—stationary; *uda*—water; *jhaṣa-vrātaḥ*—and schools of fish; *vāta*—of the wind; *apāye*—upon the ceasing; *yathā*—just as; *arṇavaḥ*—the ocean; *kuru*—please make; *asya*—his; *tapasaḥ*—of the austerities; *sākṣāt*—manifest; *saṁsiddhim*—perfection; *siddhi-daḥ*—the bestower of perfection; *bhavān*—you.

TRANSLATION

He is as calm as the waters of the ocean when the wind has ceased and the fish remain still. Therefore, my lord, since you bestow perfection on the performers of austerity, please award this sage the perfection that is obviously due him.

TEXT 6

श्रीभगवानुवाच
नैवेच्छत्याशिषः क्वापि ब्रह्मर्षिर्मोक्षमप्युत ।
भक्तिं परां भगवति लब्धवान् पुरुषेऽव्यये ॥६॥

śrī-bhagavān uvāca
naivecchaty āśiṣaḥ kvāpi
brahmarṣir mokṣam apy uta
bhaktiṁ parāṁ bhagavati
labdhavān puruṣe 'vyaye

śrī-bhagavān uvāca—the powerful lord said; *na*—not; *eva*—indeed; *icchati*—desires; *āśiṣaḥ*—benedictions; *kva api*—in any realm; *brahma-ṛṣiḥ*—the saintly *brāhmaṇa; mokṣam*—liberation; *api uta*—even; *bhaktim*—devotional service; *parām*—transcendental; *bhagavati*—for the Supreme Lord; *labdhavān*—he has achieved; *puruṣe*—for the Personality of Godhead; *avyaye*—who is inexhaustible.

TRANSLATION

Lord Śiva replied: Surely this saintly *brāhmaṇa* does not desire any benediction, not even liberation itself, for he has attained pure devotional service unto the inexhaustible Personality of Godhead.

PURPORT

The words *naivecchaty āśiṣaḥ kvāpi* indicate that Mārkaṇḍeya Ṛṣi was uninterested in any reward available on any planet within the universe. Nor did he want liberation, for he had achieved the Supreme Lord Himself.

TEXT 7

अथापि संवदिष्यामो भवान्येतेन साधुना ।
अयं हि परमो लाभो नृणां साधुसमागमः ॥७॥

athāpi saṁvadiṣyāmo
bhavāny etena sādhunā
ayaṁ hi paramo lābho
nṛṇāṁ sādhu-samāgamaḥ

atha api—nevertheless; *saṁvadiṣyāmaḥ*—we shall converse; *bhavāni*—my dear Bhavānī; *etena*—with this; *sādhunā*—pure devotee; *ayam*—this; *hi*—indeed; *paramaḥ*—the best; *lābhaḥ*—gain; *nṛṇām*—for men; *sādhu-samāgamaḥ*—the association of saintly devotees.

TRANSLATION

Still, my dear Bhavānī, let us talk with this saintly personality. After all, association with saintly devotees is man's highest achievement.

TEXT 8

सूत उवाच
इत्युक्त्वा तमुपेयाय भगवान् स सतां गतिः ।
ईशानः सर्वविद्यानामीश्वरः सर्वदेहिनाम् ॥८॥

sūta uvāca
ity uktvā tam upeyāya
bhagavān sa satāṁ gatiḥ
īśānaḥ sarva-vidyānām
īśvaraḥ sarva-dehinām

sūtaḥ uvāca—Sūta Gosvāmī said; *iti*—thus; *uktvā*—having said; *tam*—to the sage; *upeyāya*—going; *bhagavān*—the exalted demigod; *saḥ*—he; *satām*—of the pure souls; *gatiḥ*—the shelter; *īśānaḥ*—the master; *sarva-vidyānām*—of all branches of knowledge; *īśvaraḥ*—the controller; *sarva-dehinām*—of all embodied living beings.

TRANSLATION

Sūta Gosvāmī said: Having spoken thus, Lord Śaṅkara—the shelter of pure souls, master of all spiritual sciences and controller of all embodied living beings—approached the sage.

TEXT 9

तयोरागमनं साक्षादीशयोर्जगदात्मनोः ।
न वेद रुद्धधीवृत्तिरात्मानं विश्वमेव च ॥९॥

tayor āgamanaṁ sākṣād
īśayor jagad-ātmanoḥ
na veda ruddha-dhī-vṛttir
ātmānaṁ viśvam eva ca

tayoḥ—of the two of them; *āgamanam*—the arrival; *sākṣāt*—in person; *īśayoḥ*—of the powerful personalities; *jagat-ātmanoḥ*—the controllers of the universe; *na veda*—he did not notice; *ruddha*—checked; *dhī-vṛttiḥ*—the functioning of his mind; *ātmānam*—himself; *viśvam*—the external universe; *eva*—indeed; *ca*—also.

TRANSLATION

Because Mārkaṇḍeya's material mind had stopped functioning, the sage failed to notice that Lord Śiva and his wife, the controllers of the universe, had personally come to see him. Mārkaṇḍeya was so absorbed in meditation that he was unaware of either himself or the external world.

TEXT 10

भगवांस्तदभिज्ञाय गिरिशो योगमायया ।
आविशत्तद्गुहाकाशं वायुश्छिद्रमिवेश्वरः ॥१०॥

bhagavāṁs tad abhijñāya
giriśo yoga-māyayā
āviśat tad-guhākāśaṁ
vāyuś chidram iveśvaraḥ

bhagavān—the great personality; *tat*—that; *abhijñāya*—understanding; *giriśaḥ*—Lord Giriśa; *yoga-māyayā*—by his mystic power; *āviśat*—entered; *tat*—of Mārkaṇḍeya; *guhā-ākāśam*—the hidden sky of the heart; *vāyuḥ*—the air; *chidram*—a hole; *iva*—as if; *īśvaraḥ*—the lord.

TRANSLATION

Understanding the situation very well, the powerful Lord Śiva employed his mystic power to enter within the sky of Mārkaṇḍeya's heart, just as the wind passes through an opening.

TEXTS 11–13

आत्मन्यपि शिवं प्राप्तं तडित्पिंगजटाधरम् ।
त्र्यक्षं दशभुजं प्रांशुमुद्यन्तमिव भास्करम् ॥११॥
व्याघ्रचर्माम्बरं शूलधनुरिष्वसिचर्मभिः ।
अक्षमालाडमरुककपालं परशुं सह ॥१२॥
बिभ्राणं सहसा भातं विचक्ष्य हृदि विस्मितः ।
किमिदं कुत एवेति समाधेर्विरतो मुनिः ॥१३॥

ātmany api śivaṁ prāptaṁ
taḍit-piṅga-jaṭā-dharam
try-akṣaṁ daśa-bhujaṁ prāṁśum
udyantam iva bhāskaram

vyāghra-carmāmbaraṁ śūla-
dhanur-iṣv-asi-carmabhiḥ
akṣa-mālā-ḍamaruka-
kapālaṁ paraśuṁ saha

bibhrāṇaṁ sahasā bhātaṁ
vicakṣya hṛdi vismitaḥ
kim idaṁ kuta eveti
samādher virato muniḥ

ātmani—within himself; *api*—also; *śivam*—Lord Śiva; *prāptam*—arrived; *taḍit*—like lightning; *piṅga*—yellowish; *jaṭā*—locks of hair; *dharam*—carrying; *tri-akṣam*—with three eyes; *daśa-bhujam*—and ten arms; *prāṁśum*—very tall; *udyantam*—rising; *iva*—as; *bhāskaram*—the sun; *vyāghra*—of a tiger; *carma*—the fur; *ambaram*—as his garment; *śūla*—with his trident; *dhanuḥ*—bow; *iṣu*—arrows; *asi*—sword; *carma-bhiḥ*—and shield; *akṣa-mālā*—his prayer beads; *ḍamaruka*—small drum;

kapālam—and skull; *paraśum*—ax; *saha*—together with; *bibhrāṇam*—exhibiting; *sahasā*—suddenly; *bhātam*—manifest; *vicakṣya*—seeing; *hṛdi*—in his heart; *vismitaḥ*—surprised; *kim*—what; *idam*—this; *kutaḥ*—from where; *eva*—indeed; *iti*—thus; *samādheḥ*—from his trance; *virataḥ*—desisted; *muniḥ*—the sage.

TRANSLATION

Śrī Mārkaṇḍeya saw Lord Śiva suddenly appear within his heart. Lord Śiva's golden hair resembled lightning, and he had three eyes, ten arms and a tall body that shone like the rising sun. He wore a tiger skin, and he carried a trident, a bow, arrows, a sword and a shield, along with prayer beads, a *ḍamaru* drum, a skull and an ax. Astonished, the sage came out of his trance and thought, "Who is this, and where has he come from?"

TEXT 14

नेत्रे उन्मील्य ददृशे सगणं सोमयागतम् ।
रुद्रं त्रिलोकैकगुरुं ननाम शिरसा मुनिः ॥१४॥

netre unmīlya dadṛśe
sa-gaṇaṁ somayāgatam
rudraṁ tri-lokaika-guruṁ
nanāma śirasā muniḥ

netre—his eyes; *unmīlya*—opening; *dadṛśe*—he saw; *sa-gaṇam*—with his associates; *sa-umayā*—and with Umā; *āgatam*—having arrived; *rudram*—Lord Rudra; *tri-loka*—of the three worlds; *eka-gurum*—the one spiritual master; *nanāma*—he offered his obeisances; *śirasā*—with his head; *muniḥ*—the sage.

TRANSLATION

Opening his eyes, the sage saw Lord Rudra, the spiritual master of the three worlds, together with Umā and Rudra's followers. Mārkaṇḍeya then offered his respectful obeisances by bowing his head.

PURPORT

When Mārkaṇḍeya Ṛṣi saw Lord Śiva and Umā within his heart, he immediately became aware of them and thus also of his own individual self. During his trance, on the other hand, he had simply been absorbed in awareness of the Supreme Lord and had thus forgotten himself as the conscious perceiver.

TEXT 15

तस्मै सपर्यां व्यदधात् सगणाय सहोमया ।
स्वागतासनपाद्यार्घ्यगन्धस्रग्धूपदीपकैः ॥१५॥

tasmai saparyāṁ vyadadhāt
sa-gaṇāya sahomayā
svāgatāsana-pādyārghya-
gandha-srag-dhūpa-dīpakaiḥ

tasmai—to him; *saparyām*—worship; *vyadadhāt*—he offered; *sa-gaṇāya*—together with his associates; *saha umayā*—together with Umā; *su-āgata*—by words of greeting; *āsana*—offering of sitting places; *pādya*—water for bathing the feet; *arghya*—fragrant drinking water; *gandha*—perfumed oil; *srak*—garlands; *dhūpa*—incense; *dīpakaiḥ*—and lamps.

TRANSLATION

Mārkaṇḍeya worshiped Lord Śiva, along with Umā and Śiva's associates, by offering them words of welcome, sitting places, water for washing their feet, scented drinking water, fragrant oils, flower garlands and *ārati* lamps.

TEXT 16

आह त्वात्मानुभावेन पूर्णकामस्य ते विभो ।
करवाम किमीशान येनेदं निर्वृतं जगत् ॥१६॥

āha tv ātmānubhāvena
pūrṇa-kāmasya te vibho
karavāma kim īśāna
yenedaṁ nirvṛtaṁ jagat

āha—Mārkaṇḍeya said; *tu*—indeed; *ātma-anubhāvena*—by your own experience of ecstasy; *pūrṇa-kāmasya*—who is satisfied in all respects; *te*—for you; *vibho*—O mighty one; *karavāma*—I can do; *kim*—what; *īśāna*—O lord; *yena*—by whom; *idam*—this; *nirvṛtam*—is made peaceful; *jagat*—the entire world.

TRANSLATION

Mārkaṇḍeya said: O mighty lord, what can I possibly do for you, who are fully satisfied by your own ecstasy? Indeed, by your mercy you satisfy this entire world.

TEXT 17

नमः शिवाय शान्ताय सत्त्वाय प्रमृडाय च ।
रजोजुषेऽथ घोराय नमस्तुभ्यं तमोजुषे ॥१७॥

namaḥ śivāya śāntāya
sattvāya pramṛḍāya ca
rajo-juṣe 'tha ghorāya
namas tubhyaṁ tamo-juṣe

namaḥ—obeisances; *śivāya*—to the all-auspicious; *śāntāya*—peaceful; *sattvāya*—the personification of material goodness; *pramṛḍāya*—the giver of pleasure; *ca*—and; *rajaḥ-juṣe*—to him who is in contact with the mode of passion; *atha*—also; *ghorāya*—terrible; *namaḥ*—obeisances; *tubhyam*—to you; *tamaḥ-juṣe*—who associates with the mode of ignorance.

TRANSLATION

Again and again I offer my obeisances unto you, O all-auspicious transcendental personality. As the lord of goodness you give

pleasure, in contact with the mode of passion you appear most fearful, and you also associate with the mode of ignorance.

TEXT 18

सूत उवाच
एवं स्तुतः स भगवानादिदेवः सतां गतिः ।
परितुष्टः प्रसन्नात्मा प्रहसंस्तमभाषत ॥१८॥

sūta uvāca
evaṁ stutaḥ sa bhagavān
ādi-devaḥ satāṁ gatiḥ
parituṣṭaḥ prasannātmā
prahasaṁs tam abhāṣata

sūtaḥ uvāca—Sūta Gosvāmī said; *evam*—in these words; *stutaḥ*—praised; *saḥ*—he; *bhagavān*—the powerful Lord Śiva; *ādi-devaḥ*—the foremost of demigods; *satām*—of the saintly devotees; *gatiḥ*—the shelter; *parituṣṭaḥ*—perfectly satisfied; *prasanna-ātmā*—happy in his mind; *prahasan*—smiling; *tam*—to Mārkaṇḍeya; *abhāṣata*—spoke.

TRANSLATION

Sūta Gosvāmī said: Lord Śiva, the foremost demigod and the shelter of the saintly devotees, was satisfied by Mārkaṇḍeya's praise. Pleased, he smiled and addressed the sage.

TEXT 19

श्रीभगवानुवाच
वरं वृणीष्व नः कामं वरदेशा वयं त्रयः ।
अमोघं दर्शनं येषां मर्त्यो यद् विन्दतेऽमृतम् ॥१९॥

śrī-bhagavān uvāca
varaṁ vṛṇīṣva naḥ kāmaṁ
vara-deśā vayaṁ trayaḥ
amoghaṁ darśanaṁ yeṣāṁ
martyo yad vindate 'mṛtam

śrī-bhagavān uvāca—Lord Śiva said; *varam*—a benediction; *vṛṇīṣva*—please choose; *naḥ*—from us; *kāmam*—as desired; *vara-da*—of all givers of benedictions; *īśāḥ*—the controlling lords; *vayam*—we; *trayaḥ*—three (Brahmā, Viṣṇu and Maheśvara); *amogham*—never in vain; *darśanam*—the seeing; *yeṣām*—of whom; *martyaḥ*—a mortal being; *yat*—by which; *vindate*—achieves; *amṛtam*—immortality.

TRANSLATION

Lord Śiva said: Please ask me for some benediction, since among all givers of benedictions, we three—Brahmā, Viṣṇu and I—are the best. Seeing us never goes in vain, because simply by seeing us a mortal achieves immortality.

TEXTS 20–21

ब्राह्मणाः साधवः शान्ता निःसंगा भूतवत्सलाः ।
एकान्तभक्ता अस्मासु निर्वैराः समदर्शिनः ॥२०॥
सलोका लोकपालास्तान् वन्दन्त्यर्चन्त्युपासते ।
अहं च भगवान् ब्रह्मा स्वयं च हरिरीश्वरः ॥२१॥

brāhmaṇāḥ sādhavaḥ śāntā
niḥsaṅgā bhūta-vatsalāḥ
ekānta-bhaktā asmāsu
nirvairāḥ sama-darśinaḥ

sa-lokā loka-pālās tān
vandanty arcanty upāsate
ahaṁ ca bhagavān brahmā
svayaṁ ca harir īśvaraḥ

brāhmaṇāḥ—*brāhmaṇas; sādhavaḥ*—saintly in behavior; *śāntāḥ*—peaceful and free of envy and other bad qualities; *niḥsaṅgāḥ*—free of material association; *bhūta-vatsalāḥ*—compassionate to all living beings; *eka-anta-bhaktāḥ*—unalloyed devotees; *asmāsu*—of ourselves (Brahmā, Lord Śrī Hari and Śiva); *nirvairāḥ*—never hateful; *sama-darśinaḥ*—seeing equally; *sa-lokāḥ*—with the inhabitants of all the worlds; *loka-pālāḥ*—the rulers of the various planets; *tān*—those *brāhmaṇas; vandanti*—glorify;

arcanti—worship; *upāsate*—assist; *aham*—I; *ca*—also; *bhagavān*—the great lord; *brahmā*—Brahmā; *svayam*—Himself; *ca*—also; *hariḥ*—Lord Hari; *īśvaraḥ*—the Supreme Personality of Godhead.

TRANSLATION

The inhabitants and ruling demigods of all planets, along with Lord Brahmā, the Supreme Lord Hari and I, glorify, worship and assist those *brāhmaṇas* who are saintly, always peaceful, free of material attachment, compassionate to all living beings, purely devoted to us, devoid of hatred and endowed with equal vision.

TEXT 22

न ते मय्यच्युतेऽजे च भिदामण्वपि चक्षते ।
नात्मनश्च जनस्यापि तद्युष्मान् वयमीमहि ॥२२॥

na te mayy acyute 'je ca
bhidām aṇv api cakṣate
nātmanaś ca janasyāpi
tad yuṣmān vayam īmahi

na—do not; *te*—they; *mayi*—in me; *acyute*—in Lord Viṣṇu; *aje*—in Lord Brahmā; *ca*—and; *bhidām*—difference; *aṇu*—slight; *api*—even; *cakṣate*—see; *na*—not; *ātmanaḥ*—of themselves; *ca*—and; *janasya*—of other people; *api*—also; *tat*—therefore; *yuṣmān*—yourselves; *vayam*—we; *īmahi*—worship.

TRANSLATION

These devotees do not differentiate between Lord Viṣṇu, Lord Brahmā and me, nor do they differentiate between themselves and other living beings. Therefore, because you are this kind of saintly devotee, we worship you.

PURPORT

Lord Brahmā and Lord Śiva are, respectively, manifestations of the creating and annihilating potencies of the Personality of Godhead, Viṣṇu. Thus unity exists among these three ruling deities of the material world.

One should not, on the basis of the modes of nature, find material duality within the ruling potency of the Supreme Lord, although that potency is manifested in three divisions as Brahmā, Viṣṇu and Śiva.

TEXT 23

न ह्यम्मयानि तीर्थानि न देवाश्चेतनोज्झिताः ।
ते पुनन्त्युरुकालेन यूयं दर्शनमात्रतः ॥२३॥

na hy am-mayāni tīrthāni
na devāś cetanojjhitāḥ
te punanty uru-kālena
yūyaṁ darśana-mātrataḥ

na—not; *hi*—indeed; *ap-mayāni*—consisting of sacred water; *tīrthāni*—holy places; *na*—not; *devāḥ*—deity forms of demigods; *cetana-ujjhitāḥ*—devoid of life; *te*—they; *punanti*—purify; *uru-kālena*—after a long time; *yūyam*—yourselves; *darśana-mātrataḥ*—simply by being seen.

TRANSLATION

Mere bodies of water do not constitute holy places, nor are lifeless statues of the demigods actual worshipable deities. Because external vision fails to appreciate the higher essence of the holy rivers and the demigods, these purify only after a considerable time. But devotees like you purify immediately, just by being seen.

TEXT 24

ब्राह्मणेभ्यो नमस्यामो येऽस्मद्रूपं त्रयीमयम् ।
बिभ्रत्यात्मसमाधानतपःस्वाध्यायसंयमैः ॥२४॥

brāhmaṇebhyo namasyāmo
ye 'smad-rūpaṁ trayī-mayam
bibhraty ātma-samādhāna-
tapaḥ-svādhyāya-saṁyamaiḥ

brāhmaṇebhyaḥ—to the *brāhmaṇas; namasyāmaḥ*—we offer our respects; *ye*—who; *asmat-rūpam*—the form of ourselves (Śiva, Brahmā and Viṣṇu); *trayī-mayam*—represented by the three *Vedas; bibhrati*—carry; *ātma-samādhāna*—by meditative trance focused on the Self; *tapaḥ*—by austerities; *svādhyāya*—by study; *saṁyamaiḥ*—and by following regulative principles.

TRANSLATION

By meditating upon the Supreme Soul, performing austerities, engaging in Vedic study and following regulative principles, the *brāhmaṇas* sustain within themselves the three *Vedas*, which are nondifferent from Lord Viṣṇu, Lord Brahmā and me. Therefore I offer my obeisances unto the *brāhmaṇas*.

PURPORT

A pure devotee of the Supreme Lord is considered the most elevated of *brāhmaṇas*, since all spiritual endeavor culminates in the loving service of God.

TEXT 25

श्रवणाद्दर्शनाद् वापि महापातकिनोऽपि वः ।
शुध्येरन्नन्त्यजाश्चापि किमु सम्भाषणादिभिः ॥२५॥

śravaṇād darśanād vāpi
mahā-pātakino 'pi vaḥ
śudhyerann antya-jāś cāpi
kim u sambhāṣaṇādibhiḥ

śravaṇāt—by hearing about; *darśanāt*—by seeing; *vā*—or; *api*—also; *mahā-pātakinaḥ*—those who commit the worst kinds of sins; *api*—even; *vaḥ*—you; *śudhyeran*—they become purified; *antya-jāḥ*—outcasts; *ca*—and; *api*—even; *kim u*—what to speak of; *sambhāṣaṇa-ādibhiḥ*—by directly speaking with, and so on.

TRANSLATION

Even the worst sinners and social outcasts are purified just by hearing about or seeing personalities like you. Imagine, then, how purified they become by directly speaking with you.

TEXT 26

सूत उवाच
इति चन्द्रललामस्य धर्मगुह्योपबृंहितम् ।
वचोऽमृतायनमृषिर्नातृप्यत् कर्णयोः पिबन् ॥२६॥

sūta uvāca
iti candra-lalāmasya
dharma-guhyopabṛṁhitam
vaco 'mṛtāyanam ṛṣir
nātṛpyat karṇayoḥ piban

sūtaḥ uvāca—Sūta Gosvāmī said; *iti*—thus; *candra-lalāmasya*—of Lord Śiva, who is decorated with the moon; *dharma-guhya*—with the secret essence of religion; *upabṛṁhitam*—filled; *vacaḥ*—the words; *amṛta-ayanam*—the reservoir of nectar; *ṛṣiḥ*—the sage; *na atṛpyat*—did not feel satiated; *karṇayoḥ*—with his ears; *piban*—drinking.

TRANSLATION

Sūta Gosvāmī said: Drinking with his ears Lord Śiva's nectarean words, full of the confidential essence of religion, Mārkaṇḍeya Ṛṣi could not be satiated.

PURPORT

Mārkaṇḍeya Ṛṣi was not eager to hear himself praised by Lord Śiva, but he appreciated Lord Śiva's deep realization of religious principles and therefore desired to hear more.

TEXT 27

स चिरं मायया विष्णोर्भ्रामितः कर्शितो भृशम् ।
शिववागमृतध्वस्तक्लेशपुञ्जस्तमब्रवीत् ॥२७॥

sa ciraṁ māyayā viṣṇor
bhrāmitaḥ karśito bhṛśam
śiva-vāg-amṛta-dhvasta-
kleśa-puñjas tam abravīt

saḥ—he; *ciram*—for a long time; *māyayā*—by the illusory energy; *viṣṇoḥ*—of the Supreme Personality of Godhead, Viṣṇu; *bhrāmitaḥ*—made to wander; *karśitaḥ*—exhausted; *bhṛśam*—extremely; *śiva*—of Lord Śiva; *vāk-amṛta*—by the words of nectar; *dhvasta*—destroyed; *kleśa-puñjaḥ*—his heaps of suffering; *tam*—to him; *abravīt*—spoke.

TRANSLATION

Mārkaṇḍeya, having been forced by Lord Viṣṇu's illusory energy to wander about for a long time in the water of dissolution, had become extremely exhausted. But Lord Śiva's words of nectar vanquished his accumulated suffering. Thus he addressed Lord Śiva.

PURPORT

Mārkaṇḍeya Ṛṣi had desired to see Lord Viṣṇu's illusory energy and had suffered extensive miseries. But now, in the person of Śiva, Lord Viṣṇu again appeared before the sage and relieved all his suffering by imparting blissful spiritual instructions.

TEXT 28

श्रीमार्कण्डेय उवाच
अहो ईश्वरलीलेयं दुर्विभाव्या शरीरिणाम् ।
यन्नमन्तीशितव्यानि स्तुवन्ति जगदीश्वराः ॥२८॥

śrī-mārkaṇḍeya uvāca
aho īśvara-līleyaṁ
durvibhāvyā śarīriṇām
yan namantīśitavyāni
stuvanti jagad-īśvarāḥ

śrī-mārkaṇḍeyaḥ uvāca—Śrī Mārkaṇḍeya said; *aho*—ah; *īśvara*—of the great lords; *līlā*—the pastime; *iyam*—this; *durvibhāvyā*—inconceivable; *śarīriṇām*—for embodied souls; *yat*—since; *namanti*—they offer obeisances; *īśitavyāni*—to those who are controlled by them; *stuvanti*—they praise; *jagat-īśvarāḥ*—the rulers of the universe.

TRANSLATION

Śrī Mārkaṇḍeya said: It is indeed most difficult for embodied souls to understand the pastimes of the universal controllers, for such lords bow down to and offer praise to the very living beings they rule.

PURPORT

In the material world, conditioned souls strive to lord it over one another. Therefore they cannot understand the pastimes of the actual lords of the universe. Such bona fide lords have a wonderfully magnanimous mentality and thus sometimes bow down to the most qualified and saintly among their own subjects.

TEXT 29

धर्मं ग्राहयितुं प्राय: प्रवक्तारश्च देहिनाम् ।
आचरन्त्यनुमोदन्ते क्रियमाणं स्तुवन्ति च ॥२९॥

dharmaṁ grāhayituṁ prāyaḥ
pravaktāraś ca dehinām
ācaranty anumodante
kriyamāṇaṁ stuvanti ca

dharmam—religion; *grāhayitum*—to cause the acceptance of; *prāyaḥ*—for the most part; *pravaktāraḥ*—the authorized speakers; *ca*—and; *dehinām*—for ordinary embodied souls; *ācaranti*—they act; *anumodante*—they encourage; *kriyamāṇam*—one who is executing; *stuvanti*—they praise; *ca*—also.

TRANSLATION

Generally it is to induce embodied souls to accept religious principles that the authorized teachers of religion exhibit ideal behavior while encouraging and praising the proper behavior of others.

TEXT 30

नैतावता भगवतः स्वमायामयवृत्तिभिः ।
न दुष्येतानुभावस्तैर्मायिनः कुहकं यथा ॥३०॥

naitāvatā bhagavataḥ
sva-māyā-maya-vṛttibhiḥ
na duṣyetānubhāvas tair
māyinaḥ kuhakaṁ yathā

na—not; *etāvatā*—by such (a show of humility); *bhagavataḥ*—of the Personality of Godhead; *sva-māyā*—of His own illusory energy; *maya*—consisting of; *vṛttibhiḥ*—by the activities; *na duṣyeta*—is not spoiled; *anubhāvaḥ*—the power; *taiḥ*—by them; *māyinaḥ*—of a magician; *kuhakam*—the tricks; *yathā*—just as.

TRANSLATION

This apparent humility is simply a show of mercy. Such behavior of the Supreme Lord and His personal associates, which the Lord effects by His own bewildering potency, does not spoil His power any more than a magician's powers are diminished by his exhibition of tricks.

TEXTS 31–32

सृष्ट्वेदं मनसा विश्वमात्मनानुप्रविश्य यः ।
गुणैः कुर्वद्भिराभाति कर्तेव स्वप्नदृग् यथा ॥३१॥
तस्मै नमो भगवते त्रिगुणाय गुणात्मने ।
केवलायाद्वितीयाय गुरवे ब्रह्ममूर्तये ॥३२॥

sṛṣṭvedaṁ manasā viśvam
ātmanānupraviśya yaḥ
guṇaiḥ kurvadbhir ābhāti
karteva svapna-dṛg yathā

tasmai namo bhagavate
tri-guṇāya guṇātmane
kevalāyādvitīyāya
gurave brahma-mūrtaye

sṛṣṭvā—creating; *idam*—this; *manasā*—by His mind, simply by His desire; *viśvam*—the universe; *ātmanā*—as the Supersoul; *anupraviśya*—subsequently entering; *yaḥ*—who; *guṇaiḥ*—by the modes of nature; *kurvadbhiḥ*—which are acting; *ābhāti*—appears; *kartā iva*—as if the doer; *svapna-dṛk*—a person who is seeing a dream; *yathā*—as; *tasmai*—unto Him; *namaḥ*—obeisances; *bhagavate*—unto the Supreme Personality of Godhead; *tri-guṇāya*—who possesses the three modes of nature; *guṇa-ātmane*—who is the ultimate controller of the modes of nature; *kevalāya*—to the pure; *advitīyāya*—who has no equal; *gurave*—the supreme spiritual master; *brahma-mūrtaye*—the personal form of the Absolute Truth.

TRANSLATION

I offer my obeisances to that Supreme Personality of Godhead, who has created this entire universe simply by His desire and then entered into it as the Supersoul. By making the modes of nature act, He seems to be the direct creator of this world, just as a dreamer seems to be acting within his dream. He is the owner and

ultimate controller of the three modes of nature, yet He remains alone and pure, without any equal. He is the supreme spiritual master of all, the original personal form of the Absolute Truth.

PURPORT

The Supreme Lord releases His material potencies, and by their interaction creation takes place. The Lord remains aloof, as the supreme transcendental entity. Still, because the entire creation unfolds according to His design and will, His controlling hand is perceived within all things. People thus imagine that God is the direct builder of this world, although He remains aloof, creating through the manipulation of His multifarious potencies.

TEXT 33

कं वृणे नु परं भूमन् वरं त्वद्वरदर्शनात् ।
यद्दर्शनात् पूर्णकामः सत्यकामः पुमान् भवेत् ॥३३॥

kaṁ vṛṇe nu paraṁ bhūman
varaṁ tvad vara-darśanāt
yad-darśanāt pūrṇa-kāmaḥ
satya-kāmaḥ pumān bhavet

kam—what; *vṛṇe*—shall I choose; *nu*—indeed; *param*—other; *bhūman*—O all-pervading lord; *varam*—benediction; *tvat*—from you; *vara-darśanāt*—the sight of whom is itself the highest benediction; *yat*—of whom; *darśanāt*—from the seeing; *pūrṇa-kāmaḥ*—full in all desires; *satya-kāmaḥ*—able to achieve anything desired; *pumān*—a person; *bhavet*—becomes.

TRANSLATION

O all-pervading lord, since I have received the benediction of seeing you, what other benediction can I ask for? Simply by seeing you, a person fulfills all his desires and can achieve anything imaginable.

TEXT 34

वरमेकं वृणेऽथापि पूर्णात् कामाभिवर्षणात् ।
भगवत्यच्युतां भक्तिं तत्परेषु तथा त्वयि ॥३४॥

varam ekaṁ vṛṇe 'thāpi
pūrṇāt kāmābhivarṣaṇāt
bhagavaty acyutāṁ bhaktiṁ
tat-pareṣu tathā tvayi

varam—benediction; *ekam*—one; *vṛṇe*—I request; *atha api*—nevertheless; *pūrṇāt*—from him who is completely full; *kāma-abhivarṣaṇāt*—who showers down the fulfillment of desires; *bhagavati*—for the Supreme Personality of Godhead; *acyutām*—infallible; *bhaktim*—devotional service; *tat-pareṣu*—for those who are dedicated to Him; *tathā*—and also; *tvayi*—for yourself.

TRANSLATION

But I do request one benediction from you, who are full of all perfection and able to shower down the fulfillment of all desires. I ask to have unfailing devotion for the Supreme Personality of Godhead and for His dedicated devotees, especially you.

PURPORT

The words *tat-pareṣu tathā tvayi* clearly indicate that Lord Śiva is a devotee of the Supreme Lord, not the Supreme Lord Himself. Because the representative of God is offered the same protocol as God Himself, Mārkaṇḍeya Ṛṣi addressed Lord Śiva as "lord" in previous verses. But now it is clearly revealed that, as stated throughout Vedic literature, Lord Śiva is an eternal servant of God and not God Himself.

Desire manifests itself within the mind and heart according to the subtle laws governing consciousness. Pure desire to engage in the loving service of the Lord brings one to the most exalted platform of consciousness, and such a perfect understanding of life is available only by the special mercy of the Lord's devotees.

TEXT 35

सूत उवाच
इत्यर्चितोऽभिष्टुतश्च मुनिना सूक्तया गिरा ।
तमाह भगवाञ्छर्वः शर्वया चाभिनन्दितः ॥३५॥

sūta uvāca
ity arcito 'bhiṣṭutaś ca
muninā sūktayā girā
tam āha bhagavāñ charvaḥ
śarvayā cābhinanditaḥ

sūtaḥ uvāca—Sūta Gosvāmī said; *iti*—in these words; *arcitaḥ*—worshiped; *abhiṣṭutaḥ*—glorified; *ca*—and; *muninā*—by the sage; *su-uktayā*—well-spoken; *girā*—with words; *tam*—to him; *āha*—spoke; *bhagavān śarvaḥ*—Lord Śiva; *śarvayā*—by his consort, Śarvā; *ca*—and; *abhinanditaḥ*—encouraged.

TRANSLATION

Sūta Gosvāmī said: Thus worshiped and glorified by the eloquent statements of the sage Mārkaṇḍeya, Lord Śarva [Śiva], encouraged by his consort, replied to him as follows.

TEXT 36

कामो महर्षे सर्वोऽयं भक्तिमांस्त्वमधोक्षजे ।
आकल्पान्ताद्यशः पुण्यमजरामरता तथा ॥३६॥

kāmo maharṣe sarvo 'yaṁ
bhaktimāṁs tvam adhokṣaje
ā-kalpāntād yaśaḥ puṇyam
ajarāmaratā tathā

kāmaḥ—desire; *mahā-ṛṣe*—O great sage; *sarvaḥ*—all; *ayam*—this; *bhakti-mān*—full of devotion; *tvam*—you; *adhokṣaje*—for the transcendental Personality of Godhead; *ā-kalpa-antāt*—up until the end of the day of Brahmā; *yaśaḥ*—fame; *puṇyam*—pious; *ajara-amaratā*—freedom from old age and death; *tathā*—also.

TRANSLATION

O great sage, because you are devoted to Lord Adhokṣaja, all your desires will be fulfilled. Until the very end of this creation cycle, you will enjoy pious fame and freedom from old age and death.

TEXT 37

ज्ञानं त्रैकालिकं ब्रह्मन् विज्ञानं च विरक्तिमत् ।
ब्रह्मवर्चस्विनो भूयात् पुराणाचार्यतास्तु ते ॥३७॥

jñānaṁ trai-kālikaṁ brahman
vijñānaṁ ca viraktimat
brahma-varcasvino bhūyāt
purāṇācāryatāstu te

jñānam—knowledge; *trai-kālikam*—of all three phases of time (past, present and future); *brahman*—O *brāhmaṇa; vijñānam*—transcendental realization; *ca*—also; *virakti-mat*—including renunciation; *brahma-varcasvinaḥ*—of him who is endowed with brahminical potency; *bhūyāt*—let there be; *purāṇa-ācāryatā*—the status of being a teacher of the *Purāṇas; astu*—may there be; *te*—of you.

TRANSLATION

O *brāhmaṇa*, may you have perfect knowledge of past, present and future, along with transcendental realization of the Supreme, enriched by renunciation. You have the brilliance of an ideal *brāhmaṇa*, and thus may you achieve the post of spiritual master of the *Purāṇas*.

TEXT 38

सूत उवाच
एवं वरान् स मुनये दत्त्वागात् त्र्यक्ष ईश्वरः ।
देव्यै तत्कर्म कथयन्ननुभूतं पुरामुना ॥३८॥

sūta uvāca
evaṁ varān sa munaye
dattvāgāt try-akṣa īśvaraḥ
devyai tat-karma kathayann
anubhūtaṁ purāmunā

sūtaḥ uvāca—Sūta Gosvāmī said; *evam*—in this way; *varān*—benedictions; *saḥ*—he; *munaye*—to the sage; *dattvā*—giving; *agāt*—went; *tri-akṣaḥ*—he who has three eyes; *īśvaraḥ*—Lord Śiva; *devyai*—to goddess Pārvatī; *tat-karma*—the activities of Mārkaṇḍeya; *kathayan*—recounting; *anubhūtam*—what was experienced; *purā*—before; *amunā*—by him, Mārkaṇḍeya.

TRANSLATION

Sūta Gosvāmī said: Having thus granted Mārkaṇḍeya Ṛṣi benedictions, Lord Śiva went on his way, continuing to describe to goddess Devī the accomplishments of the sage and the direct exhibition of the Lord's illusory power that he had experienced.

TEXT 39

सोऽप्यवाप्तमहायोगमहिमा भार्गवोत्तमः ।
विचरत्यधुनाप्यद्धा हरावेकान्ततां गतः ॥३९॥

so 'py avāpta-mahā-yoga-
mahimā bhārgavottamaḥ
vicaraty adhunāpy addhā
harāv ekāntatāṁ gataḥ

saḥ—he, Mārkaṇḍeya; *api*—indeed; *avāpta*—having achieved; *mahā-yoga*—of the topmost perfection of *yoga; mahimā*—the glories; *bhārgava-uttamaḥ*—the best descendant of Bhṛgu; *vicarati*—is traveling about; *adhunā api*—even today; *addhā*—directly; *harau*—for Lord Hari; *eka-antatām*—the platform of exclusive devotion; *gataḥ*—having attained.

TRANSLATION

Mārkaṇḍeya Ṛṣi, the best of the descendants of Bhṛgu, is glorious because of his achievement of perfection in mystic *yoga*. Even today he travels about this world, fully absorbed in unalloyed devotion for the Supreme Personality of Godhead.

TEXT 40

अनुवर्णितमेतत्ते मार्कण्डेयस्य धीमतः ।
अनुभूतं भगवतो मायावैभवमद्भुतम् ॥४०॥

anuvarṇitam etat te
mārkaṇḍeyasya dhīmataḥ
anubhūtaṁ bhagavato
māyā-vaibhavam adbhutam

anuvarṇitam—described; *etat*—this; *te*—to you; *mārkaṇḍeyasya*—by Mārkaṇḍeya; *dhī-mataḥ*—the intelligent; *anubhūtam*—experienced; *bhagavataḥ*—of the Personality of Godhead; *māyā-vaibhavam*—the opulence of the illusory energy; *adbhutam*—amazing.

TRANSLATION

I have thus narrated to you the activities of the highly intelligent sage Mārkaṇḍeya, especially how he experienced the amazing power of the Supreme Lord's illusory energy.

TEXT 41

एतत् केचिदविद्वांसो मायासंसृतिरात्मनः ।
अनाद्यावर्तितं नृणां कादाचित्कं प्रचक्षते ॥४१॥

etat kecid avidvāṁso
māyā-saṁsṛtir ātmanaḥ
anādy-āvartitaṁ nṛṇāṁ
kādācitkaṁ pracakṣate

etat—this; *kecit*—some persons; *avidvāṁsaḥ*—who are not learned; *māyā-saṁsṛtiḥ*—the illusory creation; *ātmanaḥ*—of the Supreme Soul; *anādi*—from time immemorial; *āvartitam*—repeating; *nṝṇām*—of conditioned living beings; *kādācitkam*—unprecedented; *pracakṣate*—they say.

TRANSLATION

Although this event was unique and unprecedented, some unintelligent persons compare it to the cycle of illusory material existence the Supreme Lord has created for the conditioned souls—an endless cycle that has been continuing since time immemorial.

PURPORT

Mārkaṇḍeya's being drawn into the Lord's body by His inhalation and expelled again by His exhalation should not be considered a symbolic description of the perennial cycles of material creation and annihilation. This portion of the *Śrīmad-Bhāgavatam* describes a real, historical event experienced by a great devotee of the Lord, and those trying to relegate this story to mere symbolic allegory are here declared to be unintelligent fools.

TEXT 42

य एवमेतद् भृगुवर्य वर्णितं
रथांगपाणेरनुभावभावितम् ।
संश्रावयेत् संशृणुयादु तावुभौ
तयोर्न कर्माशयसंसृतिर्भवेत् ॥४२॥

ya evam etad bhṛgu-varya varṇitaṁ
rathāṅga-pāṇer anubhāva-bhāvitam
saṁśrāvayet saṁśṛṇuyād u tāv ubhau
tayor na karmāśaya-saṁsṛtir bhavet

yaḥ—who; *evam*—thus; *etat*—this; *bhṛgu-varya*—O best of the descendants of Bhṛgu (Śaunaka); *varṇitam*—described; *ratha-aṅga-pāṇeḥ*—of Lord Śrī Hari, who carries a chariot wheel in His hand; *anubhāva*—with the potency; *bhāvitam*—infused; *saṁśrāvayet*—causes anyone to hear; *saṁśṛṇuyāt*—himself hears; *u*—or; *tau*—they; *ubhau*—both; *tayoḥ*—of them; *na*—not; *karma-āśaya*—based on the mentality of fruitive work; *saṁsṛtiḥ*—the cycle of material life; *bhavet*—there is.

TRANSLATION

O best of the Bhṛgus, this account concerning Mārkaṇḍeya Ṛṣi conveys the transcendental potency of the Supreme Lord. Anyone who properly narrates or hears it will never again undergo material existence, which is based on the desire to perform fruitive activities.

Thus end the purports of the humble servant of His Divine Grace A. C. Bhaktivedanta Swami Prabhupāda to the Twelfth Canto, Tenth Chapter, of the Śrīmad-Bhāgavatam, *entitled "Lord Śiva and Umā Glorify Mārkaṇḍeya Ṛṣi."*

His Divine Grace
A. C. Bhaktivedanta Swami Prabhupāda
Founder-Ācārya of the International Society for Krishna Consciousness

PLATE ONE: **Sūta Gosvāmī Addresses the Sages at Naimiṣāraṇya**

Śaunaka, the leader of the sages gathered at the forest of Naimiṣāraṇya, said to Sūta Gosvāmī, the speaker of *Śrīmad-Bhāgavatam*, "O Sūta, may you live a long life! O saintly one, best of speakers, please continue speaking to us. Indeed, only you can show men the path out of the ignorance in which they are wandering." Śaunaka then questioned

Sūta about the history of Mārkaṇḍeya Ṛṣi, a great sage who had survived the previous annihilation of the universe. Sūta Gosvāmī replies, "O great sage Śaunaka, your very question will help remove everyone's illusion, for it leads to the topics of Lord Nārāyāṇa [the Supreme Personality of Godhead], which cleanse away the contamination of this Kali age." (*pp. 22–25*)

PLATE TWO: **Mārkaṇḍeya Ṛṣi Tempted by Cupid and Celestial Maidens**

Mārkaṇḍeya Ṛṣi, a great devotional mystic, resided in a hermitage on the northern side of the Himalaya Mountains. Observing that the sage was becoming very powerful by performing severe penances and austerities, the demigod Indra became fearful of his growing mystic potency. To ruin Mārkaṇḍeya's spiritual practice, Indra sent Cupid along with greed and intoxication personified and beautiful celestial maidens expert in the arts of singing and dancing. Springtime itself appeared at the sage's *āśrama*. But in the midst of all these disturbing influences, Mārkaṇḍeya remained fixed in his meditation, defeating Cupid and his associates by burning them with his mystic potency. (*pp. 30–41*)

PLATE THREE: **Nara and Nārāyaṇa Appear before Mārkaṇḍeya Ṛṣi to Offer Him a Benediction**

"Desiring to bestow His mercy upon the saintly Mārkaṇḍeya, who had perfectly fixed his mind in self-realization through penance, Vedic study and observance of regulative principles, the Supreme Personality of Godhead personally appeared before the sage in the forms of Nara and Nārāyaṇa. One of Them was of a whitish complexion, the other blackish, and They both had four arms. Their eyes resembled the petals of blooming lotuses, and They wore garments of black deerskin and bark, along with the three-stringed sacred thread. In Their hands, which were most purifying, They carried the mendicant's waterpot, straight bamboo staff and lotus-seed prayer beads, as well as the all-purifying *Vedas* in the symbolic form of bundles of *darbha* grass. Their bearing was tall and Their yellow effulgence the color of radiant lightning." *(pp. 40–41)*

PLATE FOUR: **Mārkaṇḍeya Ṛṣi Sees the Illusory Potency of the Lord**

"Satisfied by the prayers Śrī Mārkaṇḍeya had offered, the Supreme Lord told him to ask for a benediction, and the sage said he wanted to see the Lord's illusory energy. The Supreme Lord Śrī Hari, present before Mārkaṇḍeya in the form of Nara-Nārāyaṇa, replied, "So be it," and then left for Badarikāśrama. One day, as Śrī Mārkaṇḍeya was offering his evening prayers, the water of devastation suddenly flooded the three worlds. With great difficulty, Mārkaṇḍeya moved about all alone in this water for a long time, until he came upon a Banyan tree. Lying upon a leaf of that tree was an infant boy glowing with a charming effulgence. As Mārkaṇḍeya moved toward the leaf, he was pulled by the boy's inhalation and, just like a mosquito, drawn within His body.

"Inside the boy's body, Mārkaṇḍeya was amazed to see the entire universe just as it had been before the annihilation. After a moment the sage was carried out by the force of the child's exhalation and hurled back into the ocean of annihilation. Then, seeing that the child on the leaf was actually Śrī Hari, the transcendental Lord situated within his own heart, Śrī Mārkaṇḍeya tried to embrace Him. But at that moment Lord Hari, the master of all mystic power, disappeared. Then the waters of annihilation disappeared as well, and Śrī Mārkaṇḍeya found himself in his own *āśrama* just as before." (*pp. 55–78*)

PLATE FIVE: **Lord Śiva Appears to Mārkaṇḍeya Ṛṣi**

Once while traveling through the sky upon his bull carrier, Lord Śiva came upon the great sage Mārkaṇḍeya Ṛṣi seated in trance. Upon emerging from his meditation upon the Supreme Personality of Godhead, Mārkaṇḍeya offered respectful greetings to Lord Śiva, who asked him to choose any benediction he desired. Mārkaṇḍeya requested only unflinching devotion to the Supreme Lord Hari and His devotees as well as Lord Śiva. Pleased with Mārkaṇḍeya, Lord Śiva told him that all of his desires would be fulfilled and awarded him the benedictions of renown, freedom from old age and death until the time of universal dissolution, knowledge of all three phases of time, renunciation, realized knowledge and the position of a teacher of the Vedic histories called the *Purāṇas*. (*pp. 79–103*)

PLATE SIX: **Lord Kṛṣṇa, the Supreme Personality of Godhead**

Explaining the importance of *Śrīmad-Bhāgavatam,* Sūta Gosvāmī told the sages gathered in the forest of Naimiṣāraṇya, "Those words describing the glories of the all-famous Personality of Godhead are attractive, relishable and ever-fresh. Indeed, such words are a perpetual festival for the mind, and they dry up the ocean of misery. Those words that do not describe the glories of the Lord, who alone can sanctify the atmosphere of the whole universe, are considered to be like unto a place of pilgrimage for crows, and are never resorted to by those situated in transcendental knowledge. The pure and saintly devotees take interest only in topics glorifying the infallible Supreme Lord. On the other hand, that literature which is full of descriptions of the transcendental glories of the name, fame, forms, pastimes and so on of the unlimited Supreme Lord is a different creation, full of transcendental words directed toward bringing about a revolution in the impious lives of this world's misdirected civilization." (*pp. 176–178*)

PLATE SEVEN: **Nārada Muni Instructs Śrīla Vyāsadeva**

Śrīla Vyāsadeva heard the transcendental knowledge of *Śrīmad-Bhāgavatam* from his spiritual master, Nārada Muni, who hear it from his father, Brahmā, the first created being in the universe. Brahmā had personally received this torchlight of knowledge from the Supreme Personality of Godhead Himself. In turn, Śrīla Vyāsadeva communicated the message of *Śrīmad-Bhāgavatam* to his son, Śukadeva Gosvāmī, who

spoke it to King Parīkṣit. Sūta Gosvāmī, a disciple of Śukadeva Gosvāmī, was present when King Parīkṣit heard the *Bhāgavatam* and later explained the same knowledge to the sages at Naimiṣāraṇya. This is the system for receiving transcendental knowledge. Whoever faithfully hears the *Śrīmad-Bhāgavatam* from a bona fide representative of the Supreme Lord attains complete liberation from material existence. (*pp. 206–207*)

CHAPTER ELEVEN

Summary Description of the Mahāpuruṣa

In the context of worship, this chapter describes the Mahāpuruṣa and the various expansions of the sun in each month. Śrī Sūta first tells Śaunaka Ṛṣi about the material objects through which one can understand the major limbs, the secondary limbs, the weapons and the garments of Lord Śrī Hari. Then he outlines the process of practical service by which a mortal soul can attain immortality. When Śaunaka shows further interest in learning about the expansion of Lord Hari in the form of the sun-god, Sūta replies that Lord Śrī Hari—the indwelling controller of the universe and its original creator—manifests Himself in the form of the demigod of the sun. Sages describe this sun-god in many features according to his different material designations. To sustain the world, the Personality of Godhead manifests His potency of time as the sun and travels throughout the twelve months, beginning with Caitra, along with twelve sets of personal associates. One who remembers the opulences of the Personality of Godhead Śrī Hari in His form as the sun will become free of his sinful reactions.

TEXT 1

श्रीशौनक उवाच

अथेममर्थं पृच्छामो भवन्तं बहुवित्तमम् ।
समस्ततन्त्रराद्धान्ते भवान् भागवत तत्त्ववित् ॥१॥

śrī-śaunaka uvāca
athemam arthaṁ pṛcchāmo
bhavantaṁ bahu-vittamam
samasta-tantra-rāddhānte
bhavān bhāgavata tattva-vit

śrī-śaunakaḥ uvāca—Śrī Śaunaka said; *atha*—now; *imam*—this; *artham*—matter; *pṛcchāmaḥ*—we are inquiring about; *bhavantam*—from you; *bahu-vit-tamam*—the possessor of the broadest knowledge; *samasta*—of all; *tantra*—the scriptures prescribing practical methods of worship; *rāddha-ante*—in the definitive conclusions; *bhavān*—you; *bhāgavata*—O great devotee of the Supreme Lord; *tattva-vit*—the knower of the essential facts.

TRANSLATION

Śrī Śaunaka said: O Sūta, you are the best of learned men and a great devotee of the Supreme Lord. Therefore we now inquire from you about the definitive conclusion of all *tantra* scriptures.

TEXTS 2–3

तान्त्रिकाः परिचर्यायां केवलस्य श्रियः पतेः ।
अंगोपांगायुधाकल्पं कल्पयन्ति यथा च यैः ॥२॥
तन्नो वर्णय भद्रं ते क्रियायोगं बुभुत्सताम् ।
येन क्रियानैपुणेन मर्त्यो यायादमर्त्यताम् ॥३॥

tāntrikāḥ paricaryāyāṁ
kevalasya śriyaḥ pateḥ
aṅgopāṅgāyudhākalpaṁ
kalpayanti yathā ca yaiḥ

tan no varṇaya bhadraṁ te
kriyā-yogaṁ bubhutsatām
yena kriyā-naipuṇena
martyo yāyād amartyatām

tāntrikāḥ—the followers of the methods of the tantric literatures; *paricaryāyām*—in regulated worship; *kevalasya*—who is pure spirit; *śriyaḥ*—of the goddess of fortune; *pateḥ*—of the master; *aṅga*—His limbs, such as His feet; *upāṅga*—His secondary limbs, such as associates like Garuḍa; *āyudha*—His weapons, such as the Sudarśana disc;

ākalpam—and His ornaments, such as the Kaustubha gem; *kalpayanti*—they conceive of; *yathā*—how; *ca*—and; *yaiḥ*—by which (material representations); *tat*—that; *naḥ*—to us; *varṇaya*—please describe; *bhadram*—all-auspiciousness; *te*—unto you; *kriyā-yogam*—the practical method of cultivation; *bubhutsatām*—who are eager to learn; *yena*—by which; *kriyā*—in the systematic practice; *naipuṇena*—expertise; *martyaḥ*—a mortal being; *yāyāt*—may attain; *amartyatām*—immortality.

TRANSLATION

All good fortune to you! Please explain to us, who are very eager to learn, the process of *kriyā-yoga* practiced through regulated worship of the transcendental Lord, the husband of the goddess of fortune. Please also explain how the Lord's devotees conceive of His limbs, associates, weapons and ornaments in terms of particular material representations. By expertly worshiping the Supreme Lord, a mortal can attain immortality.

TEXT 4

सूत उवाच
नमस्कृत्य गुरून् वक्ष्ये विभूतीर्वैष्णवीरपि ।
याः प्रोक्ता वेदतन्त्राभ्यामाचार्यैः पद्मजादिभिः ॥४॥

sūta uvāca
namaskṛtya gurūn vakṣye
vibhūtīr vaiṣṇavīr api
yāḥ proktā veda-tantrābhyām
ācāryaiḥ padmajādibhiḥ

sūtaḥ uvāca—Sūta Gosvāmī said; *namaskṛtya*—offering obeisances; *gurūn*—to the spiritual masters; *vakṣye*—I shall speak; *vibhūtīḥ*—the opulences; *vaiṣṇavīḥ*—belonging to Lord Viṣṇu; *api*—indeed; *yāḥ*—which; *proktāḥ*—are described; *veda-tantrābhyām*—by the *Vedas* and the *tantras; ācāryaiḥ*—by standard authorities; *padmaja-ādibhiḥ*—beginning with Lord Brahmā.

TRANSLATION

Sūta Gosvāmī said: Offering obeisances to my spiritual masters, I shall repeat to you the description of the opulences of Lord Viṣṇu given in the *Vedas* and *tantras* by great authorities, beginning from lotus-born Brahmā.

TEXT 5

मायाद्यैर्नवभिस्तत्त्वैः स विकारमयो विराट् ।
निर्मितो दृश्यते यत्र सचित्के भुवनत्रयम् ॥५॥

māyādyair navabhis tattvaiḥ
sa vikāra-mayo virāṭ
nirmito dṛśyate yatra
sa-citke bhuvana-trayam

māyā-ādyaiḥ—beginning with the unmanifest stage of nature; *navabhiḥ*—with the nine; *tattvaiḥ*—elements; *saḥ*—that; *vikāra-mayaḥ*—also comprising the transformations (of the eleven senses and the five gross elements); *virāṭ*—the universal form of the Lord; *nirmitaḥ*—constructed; *dṛśyate*—are seen; *yatra*—in which; *sa-citke*—being conscious; *bhuvana-trayam*—the three planetary systems.

TRANSLATION

The universal form [*virāṭ*] of the Personality of Godhead includes the nine basic elements of creation, starting with the unmanifest nature, and their subsequent transformations. Once this universal form is instilled with consciousness, the three planetary systems become visible within it.

PURPORT

The nine basic elements of creation are *prakṛti, sūtra, mahat-tattva,* false ego, and the five subtle perceptions. The transformations are the eleven senses and the five gross material elements.

TEXTS 6–8

एतद् वै पौरुषं रूपं भूः पादौ द्यौः शिरो नभः ।
नाभिः सूर्योऽक्षिणी नासे वायुः कर्णौ दिशः प्रभोः ॥६॥
प्रजापतिः प्रजननम् अपानो मृत्युरीशितुः ।
तद्बाहवो लोकपाला मनश्चन्द्रो भ्रुवौ यमः ॥७॥
लज्जोत्तरोऽधरो लोभो दन्ता ज्योत्स्ना स्मयो भ्रमः ।
रोमाणि भूरुहा भूम्नो मेघाः पुरुषमूर्धजाः ॥८॥

etad vai pauruṣaṁ rūpaṁ
bhūḥ pādau dyauḥ śiro nabhaḥ
nābhiḥ sūryo 'kṣiṇī nāse
vāyuḥ karṇau diśaḥ prabhoḥ

prajāpatiḥ prajananam
apāno mṛtyur īśituḥ
tad-bāhavo loka-pālā
manaś candro bhruvau yamaḥ

lajjottaro 'dharo lobho
dantā jyotsnā smayo bhramaḥ
romāṇi bhūruhā bhūmno
meghāḥ puruṣa-mūrdhajāḥ

etat—this; *vai*—indeed; *pauruṣam*—of the Virāṭ-puruṣa; *rūpam*—the form; *bhūḥ*—the earth; *pādau*—His feet; *dyauḥ*—heaven; *śiraḥ*—His head; *nabhaḥ*—the sky; *nābhiḥ*—His navel; *sūryaḥ*—the sun; *akṣiṇī*—His eyes; *nāse*—His nostrils; *vāyuḥ*—the air; *karṇau*—His ears; *diśaḥ*—the directions; *prabhoḥ*—of the Supreme Lord; *prajā-patiḥ*—the demigod of procreation; *prajananam*—His genital; *apānaḥ*—His anus; *mṛtyuḥ*—death; *īśituḥ*—of the absolute controller; *tat-bāhavaḥ*—His many arms; *loka-pālāḥ*—the presiding demigods of the various planets; *manaḥ*—His mind; *candraḥ*—the moon; *bhruvau*—His eyebrows; *yamaḥ*—the god of death; *lajjā*—shame; *uttaraḥ*—His upper lip; *adharaḥ*—His lower lip; *lobhaḥ*—greed; *dantāḥ*—His teeth; *jyotsnā*—the light of the moon;

smayaḥ—His smile; *bhramaḥ*—delusion; *romāṇi*—the hairs of the body; *bhū-ruhāḥ*—the trees; *bhūmnaḥ*—of the almighty Lord; *meghāḥ*—the clouds; *puruṣa*—of the Virāṭ-puruṣa; *mūrdha-jāḥ*—the hairs upon the head.

TRANSLATION

This is the representation of the Supreme Lord as the universal person, in which the earth is His feet, the sky His navel, the sun His eyes, the wind His nostrils, the demigod of procreation His genital, death His anus and the moon His mind. The heavenly planets are His head, the directions His ears, and the demigods protecting the various planets His many arms. The god of death is His eyebrows, shame His lower lip, greed His upper lip, delusion His smile, and moonshine His teeth, while the trees are the almighty Puruṣa's bodily hairs, and the clouds the hair on His head.

PURPORT

Various aspects of material creation, such as the earth, the sun and the trees, are sustained by various limbs of the universal body of the Lord. Thus they are considered nondifferent from Him, as described in this verse, which is meant for meditation.

TEXT 9

यावानयं वै पुरुषो यावत्या संस्थया मितः ।
तावानसावपि महापुरुषो लोकसंस्थया ॥९॥

yāvān ayaṁ vai puruṣo
yāvatyā saṁsthayā mitaḥ
tāvān asāv api mahā-
puruṣo loka-saṁsthayā

yāvān—to which extent; *ayam*—this; *vai*—indeed; *puruṣaḥ*—ordinary individual person; *yāvatyā*—extending to which dimensions; *saṁsthayā*—by the position of his limbs; *mitaḥ*—measured; *tāvān*—to that extent; *asau*—He; *api*—also; *mahā-puruṣaḥ*—the transcendental personality; *loka-saṁsthayā*—according to the positions of the planetary systems.

TRANSLATION

Just as one can determine the dimensions of an ordinary person of this world by measuring his various limbs, one can determine the dimensions of the Mahāpuruṣa by measuring the arrangement of the planetary systems within His universal form.

TEXT 10

कौस्तुभव्यपदेशेन स्वात्मज्योतिर्बिभर्त्यजः ।
तत्प्रभा व्यापिनी साक्षात् श्रीवत्समुरसा विभुः ॥१०॥

kaustubha-vyapadeśena
svātma-jyotir bibharty ajaḥ
tat-prabhā vyāpinī sākṣāt
śrīvatsam urasā vibhuḥ

kaustubha-vyapadeśena—represented by the Kaustubha gem; *sva-ātma*—of the pure *jīva* soul; *jyotiḥ*—the spiritual light; *bibharti*—carries; *ajaḥ*—the unborn Lord; *tat-prabhā*—the effulgence of this (Kaustubha); *vyāpinī*—expansive; *sākṣāt*—directly; *śrīvatsam*—of the Śrīvatsa mark; *urasā*—upon His chest; *vibhuḥ*—the almighty.

TRANSLATION

Upon His chest the almighty, unborn Personality of Godhead bears the Kaustubha gem, which represents the pure spirit soul, along with the Śrīvatsa mark, which is the direct manifestation of this gem's expansive effulgence.

TEXTS 11–12

स्वमायां वनमालाख्यां नानागुणमयीं दधत् ।
वासश्छन्दोमयं पीतं ब्रह्मसूत्रं त्रिवृत् स्वरम् ॥११॥

बिभर्ति सांख्यं योगं च देवो मकरकुण्डले ।
मौलिं पदं पारमेष्ठ्यं सर्वलोकाभयंकरम् ॥१२॥

sva-māyāṁ vana-mālākhyāṁ
nānā-guṇa-mayīṁ dadhat
vāsaś chando-mayaṁ pītaṁ
brahma-sūtraṁ tri-vṛt svaram

bibharti sāṅkhyaṁ yogaṁ ca
devo makara-kuṇḍale
mauliṁ padaṁ pārameṣṭhyaṁ
sarva-lokābhayaṅ-karam

sva-māyām—His own material energy; *vana-mālā-ākhyām*—represented as His flower garland; *nānā-guṇa*—various combinations of the modes of nature; *mayīm*—composed of; *dadhat*—wearing; *vāsaḥ*—His garment; *chandaḥ-mayam*—consisting of the Vedic meters; *pītam*—yellow; *brahma-sūtram*—His sacred thread; *tri-vṛt*—threefold; *svaram*—the sacred sound *oṁkāra; bibharti*—He carries; *sāṅkhyam*—the process of Sāṅkhya; *yogam*—the process of *yoga; ca*—and; *devaḥ*—the Lord; *makara-kuṇḍale*—His shark-shaped earrings; *maulim*—His crown; *padam*—the position; *pārameṣṭhyam*—supreme (of Lord Brahmā); *sarva-loka*—to all the worlds; *abhayam*—fearlessness; *karam*—which gives.

TRANSLATION

His flower garland is His material energy, comprising various combinations of the modes of nature. His yellow garment is the Vedic meters, and His sacred thread the syllable *oṁ* composed of three sounds. In the form of His two shark-shaped earrings, the Lord carries the processes of Sāṅkhya and *yoga*, and His crown, bestowing fearlessness on the inhabitants of all the worlds, is the supreme position of Brahmaloka.

TEXT 13

अव्याकृतमनन्ताख्यमासनं यदधिष्ठितः ।
धर्मज्ञानादिभिर्युक्तं सत्त्वं पद्ममिहोच्यते ॥१३॥

avyākṛtam anantākhyam
āsanaṁ yad-adhiṣṭhitaḥ
dharma-jñānādibhir yuktaṁ
sattvaṁ padmam ihocyate

avyākṛtam—the unmanifest phase of material creation; *ananta-ākhyam*—known as Lord Ananta; *āsanam*—His personal seat; *yat-adhiṣṭhitaḥ*—upon which He is sitting; *dharma-jñāna-ādibhiḥ*—together with religion, knowledge and so on; *yuktam*—conjoined; *sattvam*—in the mode of goodness; *padmam*—His lotus; *iha*—thereupon; *ucyate*—is said.

TRANSLATION

Ananta, the Lord's sitting place, is the unmanifest phase of material nature, and the Lord's lotus throne is the mode of goodness, endowed with religion and knowledge.

TEXTS 14–15

ओजःसहोबलयुतं मुख्यतत्त्वं गदां दधत् ।
अपां तत्त्वं दरवरं तेजस्तत्त्वं सुदर्शनम् ॥१४॥
नभोनिभं नभस्तत्त्वमसिं चर्म तमोमयम् ।
कालरूपं धनुः शार्ङ्गं तथा कर्ममयेषुधिम् ॥१५॥

ojaḥ-saho-bala-yutaṁ
mukhya-tattvaṁ gadāṁ dadhat
apāṁ tattvaṁ dara-varaṁ
tejas-tattvaṁ sudarśanam

nabho-nibhaṁ nabhas-tattvam
asiṁ carma tamo-mayam
kāla-rūpaṁ dhanuḥ śārṅgaṁ
tathā karma-mayeṣudhim

ojaḥ-sahaḥ-bala—with the power of the senses, the power of the mind and the power of the body; *yutam*—conjoined; *mukhya-tattvam*—the principle element, air, which is the vital force within the material body;

gadām—His club; *dadhat*—carrying; *apām*—of water; *tattvam*—the element; *dara*—His conchshell; *varam*—excellent; *tejaḥ-tattvam*—the element fire; *sudarśanam*—His Sudarśana disc; *nabhaḥ-nibham*—just like the sky; *nabhaḥ-tattvam*—the element ether; *asim*—His sword; *carma*—His shield; *tamaḥ-mayam*—composed of the mode of ignorance; *kāla-rūpam*—appearing as time; *dhanuḥ*—His bow; *śārṅgam*—named Śārṅga; *tathā*—and; *karma-maya*—representing the active senses; *iṣu-dhim*—the quiver holding His arrows.

TRANSLATION

The club the Lord carries is the chief element, *prāṇa*, incorporating the potencies of sensory, mental and physical strength. His excellent conchshell is the element water, His Sudarśana disc the element fire, and His sword, pure as the sky, the element ether. His shield embodies the mode of ignorance, His bow, named Śārṅga, time, and His arrow-filled quiver the working sensory organs.

TEXT 16

इन्द्रियाणि शरानाहुराकूतीरस्य स्यन्दनम् ।
तन्मात्राण्यस्याभिव्यक्तिं मुद्रयार्थक्रियात्मताम् ॥१६॥

indriyāṇi śarān āhur
ākūtīr asya syandanam
tan-mātrāṇy asyābhivyaktiṁ
mudrayārtha-kriyātmatām

indriyāṇi—the senses; *śarān*—His arrows; *āhuḥ*—they say; *ākūtīḥ*—(the mind with its) active functions; *asya*—of Him; *syandanam*—the chariot; *tat-mātrāṇi*—the objects of perception; *asya*—His; *abhivyaktim*—external appearance; *mudrayā*—by the gestures of His hands (symbolizing the giving of benedictions, the offering of fearlessness, and so on); *artha-kriyā-ātmatām*—the essence of purposeful activity.

TRANSLATION

His arrows are said to be the senses, and His chariot is the active, forceful mind. His external appearance is the subtle objects of

perception, and the gestures of His hands are the essence of all purposeful activity.

PURPORT

All activity is ultimately aimed at the supreme perfection of life, and this perfection is awarded by the merciful hands of the Lord. The gestures of the Lord remove all fear from the heart of a devotee and elevate him to the Lord's own association in the spiritual sky.

TEXT 17

मण्डलं देवयजनं दीक्षा संस्कार आत्मनः ।
परिचर्या भगवत आत्मनो दुरितक्षयः ॥१७॥

maṇḍalaṁ deva-yajanaṁ
dīkṣā saṁskāra ātmanaḥ
paricaryā bhagavata
ātmano durita-kṣayaḥ

maṇḍalam—the sun globe; *deva-yajanam*—the place where the Supreme Lord is worshiped; *dīkṣā*—spiritual initiation; *saṁskāraḥ*—the process of purification; *ātmanaḥ*—for the spirit soul; *paricaryā*—devotional service; *bhagavataḥ*—of the Personality of Godhead; *ātmanaḥ*—for the *jīva* soul; *durita*—of sinful reactions; *kṣayaḥ*—the destruction.

TRANSLATION

The sun globe is the place where the Supreme Lord is worshiped, spiritual initiation is the means of purification for the spirit soul, and rendering devotional service to the Personality of Godhead is the process for eradicating all one's sinful reactions.

PURPORT

One should meditate on the fiery sun globe as a place where God is worshiped. Lord Kṛṣṇa is the reservoir of all effulgence, and thus it is fitting that He be properly worshiped on the glowing sun.

TEXT 18

भगवान् भगशब्दार्थं लीलाकमलमुद्वहन् ।
धर्मं यशश्च भगवांश्चामरव्यजनेऽभजत् ॥१८॥

bhagavān bhaga-śabdārthaṁ
līlā-kamalam udvahan
dharmaṁ yaśaś ca bhagavāṁś
cāmara-vyajane 'bhajat

bhagavān—the Personality of Godhead; *bhaga-śabda*—of the word *bhaga; artham*—the meaning (namely, "opulence"); *līlā-kamalam*—His pastime lotus; *udvahan*—carrying; *dharmam*—religion; *yaśaḥ*—fame; *ca*—and; *bhagavān*—the Personality of Godhead; *cāmara-vyajane*—the pair of yak-tail fans; *abhajat*—has accepted.

TRANSLATION

Playfully carrying a lotus, which represents the various opulences designated by the word *bhaga*, the Supreme Lord accepts service from a pair of *cāmara* fans, which are religion and fame.

TEXT 19

आतपत्रं तु वैकुण्ठं द्विजा धामाकुतोभयम् ।
त्रिवृद् वेदः सुपर्णाख्यो यज्ञं वहति पूरुषम् ॥१९॥

ātapatraṁ tu vaikuṇṭhaṁ
dvijā dhāmākuto-bhayam
tri-vṛd vedaḥ suparṇākhyo
yajñaṁ vahati pūruṣam

ātapatram—His umbrella; *tu*—and; *vaikuṇṭham*—His spiritual abode, Vaikuṇṭha; *dvijāḥ*—O *brāhmaṇas; dhāma*—His personal abode, the spiritual world; *akutaḥ-bhayam*—free from fear; *tri-vṛt*—threefold; *vedaḥ*—the *Veda; suparṇa-ākhyaḥ*—named Suparṇa, or Garuḍa; *yajñam*—sacrifice personified; *vahati*—carried; *pūruṣam*—the Supreme Personality of Godhead.

TRANSLATION

O *brāhmaṇas,* the Lord's umbrella is His spiritual abode, Vaikuṇṭha, where there is no fear, and Garuḍa, who carries the Lord of sacrifice, is the threefold *Veda.*

TEXT 20

अनपायिनी भगवती श्रीः साक्षादात्मनो हरेः ।
विष्वक्सेनस्तन्त्रमूर्तिर्विदितः पार्षदाधिपः ।
नन्दादयोऽष्टौ द्वाःस्थाश्च तेऽणिमाद्या हरेर्गुणाः ॥२०॥

anapāyinī bhagavatī
śrīḥ sākṣād ātmano hareḥ
viṣvaksenas tantra-mūrtir
viditaḥ pārṣadādhipaḥ
nandādayo 'ṣṭau dvāḥ-sthāś ca
te 'ṇimādyā harer guṇāḥ

anapāyinī—inseparable; *bhagavatī*—the goddess of fortune; *śrīḥ*—Śrī; *sākṣāt*—directly; *ātmanaḥ*—of the internal nature; *hareḥ*—of Lord Hari; *viṣvaksenaḥ*—Viṣvaksena; *tantra-mūrtiḥ*—as the personification of the *tantra* scriptures; *viditaḥ*—is known; *pārṣada-adhipaḥ*—the chief of His personal associates; *nanda-ādayaḥ*—Nanda and the others; *aṣṭau*—the eight; *dvāḥ-sthāḥ*—doorkeepers; *ca*—and; *te*—they; *aṇimā-ādyāḥ*—*aṇimā* and the other mystic perfections; *hareḥ*—of the Supreme Lord; *guṇāḥ*—the qualities.

TRANSLATION

The goddess of fortune, Śrī, who never leaves the Lord's side, appears with Him in this world as the representation of His internal potency. Viṣvaksena, the chief among His personal associates, is known to be the personification of the *Pañcarātra* and other *tantras.* And the Lord's eight doorkeepers, headed by Nanda, are His mystic perfections, beginning with *aṇimā.*

PURPORT

According to Śrīla Jīva Gosvāmī, the goddess of fortune is the original source of all material opulence. Material nature is directly controlled by the Lord's inferior energy, Mahā-māyā, whereas the goddess of fortune is His internal, superior energy. Still, the opulence of the Lord's inferior nature has its source in the supreme spiritual opulence of the goddess of fortune. As stated in *Śrī Hayaśīrṣa Pañcarātra:*

paramātmā harir devas
tac-chaktiḥ śrīr ihoditā
śrīr devī prakṛtiḥ proktā
keśavaḥ puruṣaḥ smṛtaḥ
na viṣṇunā vinā devī
na hariḥ padmajāṁ vinā

"The Supreme Soul is Lord Hari, and His potency is known in this world as Śrī. Goddess Śrī is known as *prakṛti,* and the Supreme Lord Keśava is known as the *puruṣa.* The divine goddess is never present without Him, nor does He ever appear without her."

Also, *Śrī Viṣṇu Purāṇa* (1.8.15) states:

nityaiva sā jagan-mātā
viṣṇoḥ śrīr anapāyinī
yathā sarva-gato viṣṇus
tathaiveyaṁ dvijottamāḥ

"She is the eternal mother of the universe, the goddess of fortune of Lord Viṣṇu, and she is never separated from Him. In the same way that Lord Viṣṇu is present everywhere, so is she, O best of *brāhmaṇas.*"

Also in *Viṣṇu Purāṇa* (1.9.140):

evaṁ yathā jagat-svāmī
deva-devo janārdanaḥ
avatāraṁ karoty eva
tathā śrīs tat-sahāyinī

"Thus, in the same way that the Lord of the universe, the God of gods, Janārdana, descends to this world, so His consort, the goddess of fortune, does also."

The pure spiritual status of the goddess of fortune is described in the *Skanda Purāṇa:*

aparaṁ tv akṣaraṁ yā sā
prakṛtir jaḍa-rūpikā
śrīḥ parā prakṛtiḥ proktā
cetanā viṣṇu-saṁśrayā

taṁ akṣaraṁ paraṁ prāhuḥ
parataḥ param akṣaram
harir evākhila-guṇo 'py
akṣara-trayam īritam

"The inferior infallible entity is that nature who manifests as the material world. The goddess of fortune, on the other hand, is known as the superior nature. She is pure consciousness and is under the direct shelter of Lord Viṣṇu. While she is said to be the superior infallible entity, that infallible entity who is greater than the greatest is Lord Hari Himself, the original possessor of all transcendental qualities. In this way, three distinct infallible entities are described."

Thus, although the inferior energy of the Lord is infallible in her function, her power to manifest temporary illusory opulences exists by the grace of the internal energy, the goddess of fortune, who is the personal consort of the Supreme Lord.

The *Padma Purāṇa* (256.9–21) lists eighteen doorkeepers of the Lord: Nanda, Sunanda, Jaya, Vijaya, Caṇḍa, Pracaṇḍa, Bhadra, Subhadra, Dhātā, Vidhātā, Kumuda, Kumudākṣa, Pundarikṣa, Vāmana, Śaṅkukarṇa, Sarvanetra, Sumukha and Supratiṣṭhita.

TEXT 21

वासुदेवः संकर्षणः प्रद्युम्नः पुरुषः स्वयम् ।
अनिरुद्ध इति ब्रह्मन्मूर्तिव्यूहोऽभिधीयते ॥२१॥

vāsudevaḥ saṅkarṣaṇaḥ
pradyumnaḥ puruṣaḥ svayam
aniruddha iti brahman
mūrti-vyūho 'bhidhīyate

vāsudevaḥ saṅkarṣaṇaḥ pradyumnaḥ—Vāsudeva, Saṅkarṣaṇa and Pradyumna; *puruṣaḥ*—the Supreme Personality of Godhead; *svayam*—Himself; *aniruddhaḥ*—Aniruddha; *iti*—thus; *brahman*—O *brāhmaṇa*,

Śaunaka; *mūrti-vyūhaḥ*—the expansion of personal forms; *abhidhīyate*—is designated.

TRANSLATION

Vāsudeva, Saṅkarṣaṇa, Pradyumna and Aniruddha are the names of the direct personal expansions of the Supreme Godhead, O *brāhmaṇa* Śaunaka.

TEXT 22

स विश्वस्तैजसः प्राज्ञस्तुरीय इति वृत्तिभिः ।
अर्थेन्द्रियाशयज्ञानैर्भगवान् परिभाव्यते ॥२२॥

sa viśvas taijasaḥ prājñas
turīya iti vṛttibhiḥ
arthendriyāśaya-jñānair
bhagavān paribhāvyate

saḥ—He; *viśvaḥ taijasaḥ prājñaḥ*—the manifestations of waking consciousness, sleep and deep sleep; *turīyaḥ*—the fourth, transcendental stage; *iti*—thus termed; *vṛttibhiḥ*—by the functions; *artha*—by the external objects of perception; *indriya*—the mind; *āśaya*—covered consciousness; *jñānaiḥ*—and spiritual knowledge; *bhagavān*—the Personality of Godhead; *paribhāvyate*—is conceived of.

TRANSLATION

One can conceive of the Supreme Personality of Godhead in terms of awakened consciousness, sleep and deep sleep—which function respectively through external objects, the mind and material intelligence—and also in terms of the fourth, transcendental level of consciousness, which is characterized by pure knowledge.

TEXT 23

अंगोपांगायुधाकल्पैर्भगवांस्तच्चतुष्टयम् ।
बिभर्ति स्म चतुर्मूर्तिर्भगवान् हरिरीश्वरः ॥२३॥

aṅgopāṅgāyudhākalpair
bhagavāṁs tac catuṣṭayam
bibharti sma catur-mūrtir
bhagavān harir īśvaraḥ

aṅga—with His major limbs; *upāṅga*—minor limbs; *āyudha*—weapons; *ākalpaiḥ*—and ornaments; *bhagavān*—the Personality of Godhead; *tat catuṣṭayam*—these four manifestations (of *viśva, taijasa, prājña* and *turīya*); *bibharti*—maintains; *sma*—indeed; *catuḥ-mūrtiḥ*—in His four personal features (Vāsudeva, Saṅkarṣaṇa, Pradyumna and Aniruddha); *bhagavān*—the Lord; *hariḥ*—Hari; *īśvaraḥ*—the supreme controller.

TRANSLATION

The Supreme Personality of Godhead, Lord Hari, thus appears in four personal expansions, each exhibiting major limbs, minor limbs, weapons and ornaments. Through these distinct features, the Lord maintains the four phases of existence.

PURPORT

The Lord's spiritual body, weapons, ornaments and associates are all pure transcendental existence, identical with Him.

TEXT 24

द्विजऋषभ स एष ब्रह्मयोनिः स्वयंदृक्
स्वमहिमपरिपूर्णो मायया च स्वयैतत् ।
सृजति हरति पातीत्याख्ययानावृताक्षो
विवृत इव निरुक्तस्तत्परैरात्मलभ्यः ॥२४॥

dvija-ṛṣabha sa eṣa brahma-yoniḥ svayaṁ-dṛk
sva-mahima-paripūrṇo māyayā ca svayaitat
sṛjati harati pātīty ākhyayānāvṛtākṣo
vivṛta iva niruktas tat-parair ātma-labhyaḥ

dvija-ṛṣabha—O best of the *brāhmaṇas; saḥ eṣaḥ*—He alone; *brahma-yoniḥ*—the source of the *Vedas; svayam-dṛk*—who is self-illuminating;

sva-mahima—in His own glory; *paripūrṇaḥ*—perfectly complete; *māyayā*—by the material energy; *ca*—and; *svayā*—His own; *etat*—this universe; *sṛjati*—He creates; *harati*—He withdraws; *pāti*—He maintains; *iti ākhyayā*—conceived of as such; *anāvṛta*—uncovered; *akṣaḥ*—His transcendental awareness; *vivṛtaḥ*—materially divided; *iva*—as if; *niruktaḥ*—described; *tat-paraiḥ*—by those who are devoted to Him; *ātma*—as their very Soul; *labhyaḥ*—realizable.

TRANSLATION

O best of *brāhmaṇas*, He alone is the self-luminous, original source of the *Vedas*, perfect and complete in His own glory. By His material energy He creates, destroys and maintains this entire universe. Because He is the performer of various material functions, He is sometimes described as materially divided, yet He always remains transcendentally situated in pure knowledge. Those who are dedicated to Him in devotion can realize Him to be their true Soul.

PURPORT

Śrīla Viśvanātha Cakravartī Ṭhākura recommends that we become humble by practicing the following meditation: "The earth, which is always visible to me, is the expansion of the lotus feet of my Lord, who is always to be meditated upon. All moving and nonmoving living beings have taken shelter of the earth and are thus sheltered at the lotus feet of my Lord. For this reason I should respect every living being and not envy anyone. In fact, all living entities constitute the Kaustubha gem on My Lord's chest. Therefore I should never envy or deride any living entity." By practicing this meditation one can achieve success in life.

TEXT 25

श्रीकृष्ण कृष्णसख वृष्ण्यृषभावनिध्रुग्-
राजन्यवंशदहनानपवर्गवीर्य ।
गोविन्द गोपवनिताव्रजभृत्यगीत-
तीर्थश्रवः श्रवणमंगल पाहि भृत्यान् ॥२५॥

śrī-kṛṣṇa kṛṣṇa-sakha vṛṣṇy-ṛṣabhāvani-dhrug-
rājanya-vaṁśa-dahanānapavarga-vīrya
govinda gopa-vanitā-vraja-bhṛtya-gīta-
tīrtha-śravaḥ śravaṇa-maṅgala pāhi bhṛtyān

śrī-kṛṣṇa—O Śrī Kṛṣṇa; *kṛṣṇa-sakha*—O friend of Arjuna; *vṛṣṇi*—of the descendants of Vṛṣṇi; *ṛṣabha*—O chief; *avani*—on the earth; *dhruk*—rebellious; *rājanya-vaṁśa*—of the dynasties of kings; *dahana*—O annihilator; *anapavarga*—without deterioration; *vīrya*—whose prowess; *govinda*—O proprietor of Goloka-dhāma; *gopa*—of the cowherd men; *vanitā*—and the cowherd women; *vraja*—by the multitude; *bhṛtya*—and by their servants; *gīta*—sung; *tīrtha*—pious, as the most holy place of pilgrimage; *śravaḥ*—whose glories; *śravaṇa*—just to hear about whom; *maṅgala*—auspicious; *pāhi*—please protect; *bhṛtyān*—Your servants.

TRANSLATION

O Kṛṣṇa, O friend of Arjuna, O chief among the descendants of Vṛṣṇi, You are the destroyer of those political parties that are disturbing elements on this earth. Your prowess never deteriorates. You are the proprietor of the transcendental abode, and Your most sacred glories, which are sung by Vṛndāvana's cowherd men and women and their servants, bestow all auspiciousness just by being heard. O Lord, please protect Your devotees.

TEXT 26

य इदं कल्य उत्थाय महापुरुषलक्षणम् ।
तच्चित्तः प्रयतो जप्त्वा ब्रह्म वेद गुहाशयम् ॥२६॥

ya idaṁ kalya utthāya
mahā-puruṣa-lakṣaṇam
tac-cittaḥ prayato japtvā
brahma veda guhāśayam

yaḥ—anyone who; *idam*—this; *kalye*—at dawn; *utthāya*—rising; *mahā-puruṣa-lakṣaṇam*—the characteristics of the Supreme Personality in His universal form; *tat-cittaḥ*—with mind absorbed in Him; *prayataḥ*—purified; *japtvā*—chanting to oneself; *brahma*—the Absolute Truth; *veda*—he comes to know; *guhā-śayam*—situated within the heart.

TRANSLATION

Anyone who rises early in the morning and, with a purified mind fixed upon the Mahāpuruṣa, quietly chants this description of His characteristics will realize Him as the Supreme Absolute Truth residing within the heart.

TEXTS 27–28

श्रीशौनक उवाच
शुको यदाह भगवान् विष्णुराताय शृण्वते ।
सौरो गणो मासि मासि नाना वसति सप्तकः ॥२७॥
तेषां नामानि कर्माणि नियुक्तानामधीश्वरैः ।
ब्रूहि नः श्रद्दधानानां व्यूहं सूर्यात्मनो हरेः ॥२८॥

śrī-śaunaka uvāca
śuko yad āha bhagavān
viṣṇu-rātāya śṛṇvate
sauro gaṇo māsi māsi
nānā vasati saptakaḥ

teṣāṁ nāmāni karmāṇi
niyuktānām adhīśvaraiḥ
brūhi naḥ śraddadhānānāṁ
vyūhaṁ sūryātmano hareḥ

śrī-śaunakaḥ uvāca—Śrī Śaunaka said; *śukaḥ*—Sūkadeva Gosvāmī; *yat*—which; *āha*—described; *bhagavān*—the great sage; *viṣṇu-rātāya*—to King Parīkṣit; *śṛṇvate*—who was listening; *sauraḥ*—of the sun-god; *gaṇaḥ*—the associates; *māsi māsi*—in each month; *nānā*—various; *vasati*—who reside; *saptakaḥ*—the group of seven; *teṣām*—of them; *nāmāni*—the names; *karmāṇi*—the activities; *niyuktānām*—who are engaged; *adhīśvaraiḥ*—by the various features of the sun-god, who are their controllers; *brūhi*—please speak; *naḥ*—to us; *śraddadhānānām*—who are faithful; *vyūham*—the personal expansions; *sūrya-ātmanaḥ*—in His personal expansion as the sun-god; *hareḥ*—of the Supreme Personality of Godhead, Lord Hari.

TRANSLATION

Śrī Śaunaka said: Please describe to us, who have great faith in your words, the different sets of seven personal features and associates the sun-god exhibits during each month, along with their names and activities. The associates of the sun-god, who serve their lord, are personal expansions of the Supreme Personality of Godhead Hari in His feature as the presiding deity of the sun.

PURPORT

After hearing an account of the exalted conversation between Śukadeva Gosvāmī and Mahārāja Parīkṣit, Śaunaka now inquires about the sun as the expansion of the Supreme Lord. Although the sun is the king of all planets, Śrī Śaunaka is specifically interested in this effulgent globe as the expansion of Śrī Hari, the Supreme Personality of Godhead.

The personalities related with the sun are of seven categories. In the course of the sun's orbit there are twelve months, and in each month a different sun-god and a different set of his six associates preside. In each of the twelve months beginning from Vaiśākha there are different names for the sun-god himself, the sage, the Yakṣa, the Gandharva, the Apsarā, the Rākṣasa and the Nāga, making a total of seven categories.

TEXT 29

सूत उवाच
अनाद्यविद्यया विष्णोरात्मनः सर्वदेहिनाम् ।
निर्मितो लोकतन्त्रोऽयं लोकेषु परिवर्तते ॥२९॥

sūta uvāca
anādy-avidyayā viṣṇor
ātmanaḥ sarva-dehinām
nirmito loka-tantro 'yaṁ
lokeṣu parivartate

sūtaḥ uvāca—Sūta Gosvāmī said; *anādi*—beginningless; *avidyayā*—by the illusory energy; *viṣṇoḥ*—of Lord Viṣṇu; *ātmanaḥ*—who is the Supreme Soul; *sarva-dehinām*—of all embodied living beings; *nirmitaḥ*—produced; *loka-tantraḥ*—the regulator of the planets; *ayam*—this; *lokeṣu*—among the planets; *parivartate*—travels.

TRANSLATION

Sūta Gosvāmī said: The sun travels among all the planets and thus regulates their movements. It has been created by Lord Viṣṇu, the Supreme Soul of all embodied beings, through His beginningless material energy.

TEXT 30

एक एव हि लोकानां सूर्य आत्मादिकृद्धरिः ।
सर्ववेदक्रियामूलमृषिभिर्बहुधोदितः ॥३०॥

eka eva hi lokānāṁ
sūrya ātmādi-kṛd dhariḥ
sarva-veda-kriyā-mūlam
ṛṣibhir bahudhoditaḥ

ekaḥ—one; *eva*—only; *hi*—indeed; *lokānām*—of the worlds; *sūryaḥ*—the sun; *ātmā*—their soul; *ādi-kṛt*—the original creator; *hariḥ*—the Personality of Godhead, Hari; *sarva-veda*—in all the *Vedas; kriyā*—of the ritualistic activities; *mūlam*—the basis; *ṛṣibhiḥ*—by the sages; *bahudhā*—variously; *uditaḥ*—designated.

TRANSLATION

The sun-god, being nondifferent from Lord Hari, is the one soul of all the worlds and their original creator. He is the source of all the ritualistic activities prescribed in the *Vedas* and has been given many names by the Vedic sages.

TEXT 31

कालो देशः क्रिया कर्ता करणं कार्यमागमः ।
द्रव्यं फलमिति ब्रह्मन्नवधोक्तोऽजया हरिः ॥३१॥

kālo deśaḥ kriyā kartā
karaṇaṁ kāryam āgamaḥ
dravyaṁ phalam iti brahman
navadhokto 'jayā hariḥ

kālaḥ—time; *deśaḥ*—place; *kriyā*—endeavor; *kartā*—performer; *karaṇam*—instrument; *kāryam*—specific ritual; *āgamaḥ*—scripture; *dravyam*—paraphernalia; *phalam*—result; *iti*—thus; *brahman*—O *brāhmaṇa*, Śaunaka; *navadhā*—in nine phases; *uktaḥ*—described; *ajayā*—in terms of the material energy; *hariḥ*—Lord Hari.

TRANSLATION

Being the source of the material energy, the Personality of Godhead Lord Hari in His expansion as the sun-god is described in nine aspects, O Śaunaka: the time, the place, the endeavor, the performer, the instrument, the specific ritual, the scripture, the paraphernalia of worship and the result to be achieved.

TEXT 32

मध्वादिषु द्वादशसु भगवान् कालरूपधृक् ।
लोकतन्त्राय चरति पृथग् द्वादशभिर्गणैः ॥३२॥

madhv-ādiṣu dvādaśasu
bhagavān kāla-rūpa-dhṛk
loka-tantrāya carati
pṛthag dvādaśabhir gaṇaiḥ

madhu-ādiṣu—beginning with Madhu; *dvādaśasu*—in the twelve (months); *bhagavān*—the Supreme Lord; *kāla-rūpa*—the form of time;

dhṛk—assuming; *loka-tantrāya*—to regulate planetary motion; *carati*—travels; *pṛthak*—separately; *dvādaśabhiḥ*—with twelve; *gaṇaiḥ*—sets of associates.

TRANSLATION

The Supreme Personality of Godhead, manifesting His potency of time as the sun-god, travels about in each of the twelve months, beginning with Madhu, to regulate planetary motion within the universe. Traveling with the sun-god in each of the twelve months is a different set of six associates.

TEXT 33

धाता कृतस्थली हेतिर्वासुकी रथकृन्मुने ।
पुलस्त्यस्तुम्बुरुरिति मधुमासं नयन्त्यमी ॥३३॥

dhātā kṛtasthalī hetir
vāsukī rathakṛn mune
pulastyas tumburur iti
madhu-māsaṁ nayanty amī

dhātā kṛtasthalī hetiḥ—Dhātā, Kṛtasthalī and Heti; *vāsukiḥ rathakṛt*—Vāsuki and Rathakṛt; *mune*—O sage; *pulastyaḥ tumburuḥ*—Pulastya and Tumburu; *iti*—thus; *madhu-māsam*—the month of Madhu (Caitra, at the time of the spring equinox); *nayanti*—lead forth; *amī*—these.

TRANSLATION

My dear sage, Dhātā as the sun-god, Kṛtasthalī as the Apsarā, Heti as the Rākṣasa, Vāsuki as the Nāga, Rathakṛt as the Yakṣa, Pulastya as the sage and Tumburu as the Gandharva rule the month of Madhu.

TEXT 34

अर्यमा पुलहोऽथौजाः प्रहेतिः पुञ्जिकस्थली ।
नारदः कच्छनीरश्च नयन्त्येते स्म माधवम् ॥३४॥

aryamā pulaho 'thaujāḥ
prahetiḥ puñjikasthalī
nāradaḥ kacchanīraś ca
nayanty ete sma mādhavam

aryamā pulahaḥ athaujāḥ—Aryamā, Pulaha and Athaujā; *prahetiḥ puñjikasthalī*—Praheti and Puñjikasthalī; *nāradaḥ kacchanīraḥ*—Nārada and Kacchanīra; *ca*—also; *nayanti*—rule; *ete*—these; *sma*—indeed; *mādhavam*—the month of Mādhava (Vaiśākha).

TRANSLATION

Aryamā as the sun-god, Pulaha as the sage, Athaujā as the Yakṣa, Praheti as the Rākṣasa, Puñjikasthalī as the Apsarā, Nārada as the Gandharva and Kacchanīra as the Nāga rule the month of Mādhava.

TEXT 35

मित्रोऽत्रिः पौरुषेयोऽथ तक्षको मेनका हहाः ।
रथस्वन इति ह्येते शुक्रमासं नयन्त्यमी ॥३५॥

mitro 'triḥ pauruṣeyo 'tha
takṣako menakā hahāḥ
rathasvana iti hy ete
śukra-māsaṁ nayanty amī

mitraḥ atriḥ pauruṣeyaḥ—Mitra, Atri and Pauruṣeya; *atha*—as well; *takṣakaḥ menakā hahāḥ*—Takṣaka, Menakā and Hāhā; *rathasvanaḥ*—Rathasvana; *iti*—thus; *hi*—indeed; *ete*—these; *śukra-māsam*—the month of Śukra (Jyaiṣṭha); *nayanti*—rule; *amī*—these.

TRANSLATION

Mitra as the sun-god, Atri as the sage, Pauruṣeya as the Rākṣasa, Takṣaka as the Nāga, Menakā as the Apsarā, Hāhā as the Gandharva and Rathasvana as the Yakṣa rule the month of Śukra.

TEXT 36

वसिष्ठो वरुणो रम्भा सहजन्यस्तथा हुहूः ।
शुक्रश्चित्रस्वनश्चैव शुचिमासं नयन्त्यमी ॥३६॥

vasiṣṭho varuṇo rambhā
sahajanyas tathā huhūḥ
śukraś citrasvanaś caiva
śuci-māsaṁ nayanty amī

vasiṣṭhaḥ varuṇaḥ rambhā—Vasiṣṭha, Varuṇa and Rambhā; *sahajanyaḥ*—Sahajanya; *tathā*—also; *huhūḥ*—Hūhū; *śukraḥ citrasvanaḥ*—Śukra and Citrasvana; *ca eva*—as well; *śuci-māsam*—the month of Śuci (Āṣāḍha); *nayanti*—rule; *amī*—these.

TRANSLATION

Vasiṣṭha as the sage, Varuṇa as the sun-god, Rambhā as the Apsarā, Sahajanya as the Rākṣasa, Hūhū as the Gandharva, Śukra as the Nāga and Citrasvana as the Yakṣa rule the month of Śuci.

TEXT 37

इन्द्रो विश्वावसुः श्रोता एलापत्रस्तथाङ्गिराः ।
प्रम्लोचा राक्षसो वर्यो नभोमासं नयन्त्यमी ॥३७॥

indro viśvāvasuḥ śrotā
elāpatras tathāṅgirāḥ
pramlocā rākṣaso varyo
nabho-māsaṁ nayanty amī

indraḥ viśvāvasuḥ śrotāḥ—Indra, Viśvāvasu and Śrotā; *elāpatraḥ*—Elāpatra; *tathā*—and; *aṅgirāḥ*—Aṅgirā; *pramlocā*—Pramlocā; *rākṣasaḥ varyaḥ*—the Rākṣasa named Varya; *nabhaḥ-māsam*—the month of Nabhas (Śrāvaṇa); *nayanti*—rule; *amī*—these.

TRANSLATION

Indra as the sun-god, Viśvāvasu as the Gandharva, Śrotā as the Yakṣa, Elāpatra as the Nāga, Aṅgirā as the sage, Pramlocā as the Apsarā and Varya as the Rākṣasa rule the month of Nabhas.

TEXT 38

विवस्वानुग्रसेनश्च व्याघ्र आसारणो भृगुः ।
अनुम्लोचा शंखपालो नभस्याख्यं नयन्त्यमी ॥३८॥

vivasvān ugrasenaś ca
vyāghra āsāraṇo bhṛguḥ
anumlocā śaṅkhapālo
nabhasyākhyaṁ nayanty amī

vivasvān ugrasenaḥ—Vivasvān and Ugrasena; *ca*—also; *vyāghraḥ āsāraṇaḥ bhṛguḥ*—Vyāghra, Āsāraṇa and Bhṛgu; *anumlocā śaṅkha-pālaḥ*—Anumlocā and Śaṅkhapāla; *nabhasya-ākhyam*—the month named Nabhasya (Bhādra); *nayanti*—rule; *amī*—these.

TRANSLATION

Vivasvān as the sun-god, Ugrasena as the Gandharva, Vyāghra as the Rākṣasa, Āsāraṇa as the Yakṣa, Bhṛgu as the sage, Anumlocā as the Apsarā and Śaṅkhapāla as the Nāga rule the month of Nabhasya.

TEXT 39

पूषा धनञ्जयो वातः सुषेणः सुरुचिस्तथा ।
घृताची गौतमश्चेति तपोमासं नयन्त्यमी ॥३९॥

pūṣā dhanañjayo vātaḥ
suṣeṇaḥ surucis tathā
ghṛtācī gautamaś ceti
tapo-māsaṁ nayanty amī

pūṣā dhanañjayaḥ vātaḥ—Pūṣā, Dhanañjaya and Vāta; *suṣeṇaḥ suruciḥ*—Suṣeṇa and Suruci; *tathā*—also; *ghṛtācī gautamaḥ*—Ghṛtācī and Gautama; *ca*—as well; *iti*—thus; *tapaḥ-māsam*—the month of Tapas (Māgha); *nayanti*—rule; *amī*—these.

TRANSLATION

Pūṣā as the sun-god, Dhanañjaya as the Nāga, Vāta as the Rākṣasa, Suṣeṇa as the Gandharva, Suruci as the Yakṣa, Ghṛtācī as the Apsarā and Gautama as the sage rule the month of Tapas.

TEXT 40

ऋतुर्वर्चा भरद्वाजः पर्जन्यः सेनजित्तथा ।
विश्व ऐरावतश्चैव तपस्याख्यं नयन्त्यमी ॥४०॥

ṛtur varcā bharadvājaḥ
parjanyaḥ senajit tathā
viśva airāvataś caiva
tapasyākhyaṁ nayanty amī

ṛtuḥ varcā bharadvājaḥ—Ṛtu, Varcā and Bharadvāja; *parjanyaḥ senajit*—Parjanya and Senajit; *tathā*—also; *viśvaḥ airāvataḥ*—Viśva and Airāvata; *ca eva*—also; *tapasya-ākhyam*—the month known as Tapasya (Phālguna); *nayanti*—rule; *amī*—these.

TRANSLATION

Ṛtu as the Yakṣa, Varcā as the Rākṣasa, Bharadvāja as the sage, Parjanya as the sun-god, Senajit as the Apsarā, Viśva as the Gandharva and Airāvata as the Nāga rule the month known as Tapasya.

TEXT 41

अथांशुः कश्यपस्तार्क्ष्य ऋतसेनस्तथोर्वशी ।
विद्युच्छत्रुर्महाशंखः सहोमासं नयन्त्यमी ॥४१॥

athāṁśuḥ kaśyapas tārkṣya
ṛtasenas tathorvaśī
vidyucchatrur mahāśaṅkhaḥ
saho-māsaṁ nayanty amī

atha—then; *aṁśuḥ kaśyapaḥ tārkṣyaḥ*—Aṁśu, Kaśyapa and Tārkṣya; *ṛtasenaḥ*—Ṛtasena; *tathā*—and; *urvaśī*—Urvaśī; *vidyucchatruḥ mahāśaṅkhaḥ*—Vidyucchatru and Mahāśaṅkha; *sahaḥ-māsam*—the month of Sahas (Mārgaśīrṣa); *nayanti*—rule; *amī*—these.

TRANSLATION

Aṁśu as the sun-god, Kaśyapa as the sage, Tārkṣya as the Yakṣa, Ṛtasena as the Gandharva, Urvaśī as the Apsarā, Vidyucchatru as the Rākṣasa and Mahāśaṅkha as the Nāga rule the month of Sahas.

TEXT 42

भगः स्फूर्जोऽरिष्टनेमिरूर्ण आयुश्च पञ्चमः ।
कर्कोटकः पूर्वचित्तिः पुष्यमासं नयन्त्यमी ॥४२॥

bhagaḥ sphūrjo 'riṣṭanemir
ūrṇa āyuś ca pañcamaḥ
karkoṭakaḥ pūrvacittiḥ
puṣya-māsaṁ nayanty amī

bhagaḥ sphūrjaḥ ariṣṭanemiḥ—Bhaga, Sphūrja and Ariṣṭanemi; *ūrṇaḥ*—Ūrṇa; *āyuḥ*—Āyur; *ca*—and; *pañcamaḥ*—the fifth associate; *karkoṭakaḥ pūrvacittiḥ*—Karkoṭaka and Pūrvacitti; *puṣya-māsam*—the month of Puṣya; *nayanti*—rule; *amī*—these.

TRANSLATION

Bhaga as the sun-god, Sphūrja as the Rākṣasa, Ariṣṭanemi as the Gandharva, Ūrṇa as the Yakṣa, Āyur as the sage, Karkoṭaka as the Nāga and Pūrvacitti as the Apsarā rule the month of Puṣya.

TEXT 43

त्वष्टा ऋचीकतनयः कम्बलश्च तिलोत्तमा ।
ब्रह्मापेतोऽथ शतजिद्धृतराष्ट्र इषम्भराः ॥४३॥

tvaṣṭā ṛcīka-tanayaḥ
kambalaś ca tilottamā
brahmāpeto 'tha śatajid
dhṛtarāṣṭra iṣam-bharāḥ

tvaṣṭā—Tvaṣṭā; *ṛcīka-tanayaḥ*—the son of Ṛcīka (Jamadagni); *kambalaḥ*—Kambala; *ca*—and; *tilottamā*—Tilottamā; *brahmāpetaḥ*—Brahmāpeta; *atha*—and; *śatajit*—Śatajit; *dhṛtarāṣṭraḥ*—Dhṛtarāṣṭra; *iṣam-bharāḥ*—the maintainers of the month Iṣa (Āśvina).

TRANSLATION

Tvaṣṭā as the sun-god; Jamadagni, the son of Ṛcīka, as the sage; Kambalāśva as the Nāga; Tilottamā as the Apsarā; Brahmāpeta as the Rākṣasa; Śatajit as the Yakṣa; and Dhṛtarāṣṭra as the Gandharva maintain the month of Iṣa.

TEXT 44

विष्णुरश्वतरो रम्भा सूर्यवर्चाश्च सत्यजित् ।
विश्वामित्रो मखापेत ऊर्जमासं नयन्त्यमी ॥४४॥

viṣṇur aśvataro rambhā
sūryavarcāś ca satyajit
viśvāmitro makhāpeta
ūrja-māsaṁ nayanty amī

viṣṇuḥ aśvataraḥ rambhā—Viṣṇu, Aśvatara and Rambhā; *sūrya-varcāḥ*—Sūryavarcā; *ca*—and; *satyajit*—Satyajit; *viśvāmitraḥ makhāpetaḥ*—Viśvāmitra and Makhāpeta; *ūrja-māsam*—the month of Ūrja (Kārttika); *nayanti*—rule; *amī*—these.

TRANSLATION

Viṣṇu as the sun-god, Aśvatara as the Nāga, Rambhā as the Apsarā, Sūryavarcā as the Gandharva, Satyajit as the Yakṣa, Viśvāmitra as the sage and Makhāpeta as the Rākṣasa rule the month of Ūrja.

PURPORT

All these sun-gods and their associates are mentioned in divisions in the *Kūrma Purāṇa*, as follows:

dhātāryamā ca mitraś ca
varuṇaś cendra eva ca
vivasvān atha pūṣā ca
parjanyaś cāṁśur eva ca

bhagas tvaṣṭā ca viṣṇuś ca
ādityā dvādaśa smṛtāḥ
pulastyaḥ pulahaś cātrir
vasiṣṭo 'thāṅgirā bhṛguḥ

gautamo 'tha bharadvājaḥ
kaśyapaḥ kratur eva ca
jamadagniḥ kauśikaś ca
munayo brahma-vādināḥ

rathakṛc cāpy athojāś ca
grāmaṇīḥ surucis tathā
ratha-citrasvanaḥ śrotā
aruṇaḥ senajit tathā
tārkṣya ariṣṭanemiś ca
ṛtajit satyajit tathā

atha hetiḥ prahetiś ca
pauruṣeyo vadhas tathā
varyo vyāghras tathāpaś ca
vāyur vidyud divākaraḥ

brahmāpetaś ca vipendrā
yajñāpetaś ca rākṣakāḥ
vāsukiḥ kacchanīraś ca
takṣakaḥ śukra eva ca

elāpatraḥ śaṅkhapālas
tathairāvata-saṁjñitaḥ
dhanañjayo mahāpadmas
tathā karkoṭako dvijāḥ

kambalo 'śvataraś caiva
vahanty enaṁ yathā-kramam
tumburur nārado hāhā
hūhūr viśvāvasus tathā

ugraseno vasurucir
viśvavasur athāparaḥ
citrasenas tathorṇāyur
dhṛtarāṣṭro dvijottamāḥ

sūryavarcā dvādaśaite
gandharvā gāyatāṁ varāḥ
kṛtasthaly apsaro-varyā
tathānyā puñjikasthalī

menakā sahajanyā ca
pramlocā ca dvijottamāḥ
anumlocā ghṛtācī ca
viśvācī corvaśī tathā

anyā ca pūrvacittiḥ syād
anyā caiva tilottamā
rambhā ceti dvija-śreṣṭhās
tathaivāpsarasaḥ smṛtāḥ

TEXT 45

एता भगवतो विष्णोरादित्यस्य विभूतयः ।
स्मरतां सन्ध्ययोर्नृणां हरन्त्यंहो दिने दिने ॥४५॥

etā bhagavato viṣṇor
ādityasya vibhūtayaḥ
smaratāṁ sandhyayor nṛṇāṁ
haranty aṁho dine dine

etāḥ—these; *bhagavataḥ*—of the Personality of Godhead; *viṣṇoḥ*—Lord Viṣṇu; *ādityasya*—of the sun-god; *vibhūtayaḥ*—the opulences; *smaratām*—for those who remember; *sandhyayoḥ*—at the junctures of the day; *nṛṇām*—for such men; *haranti*—they take away; *aṁhaḥ*—sinful reactions; *dine dine*—day after day.

TRANSLATION

All these personalities are the opulent expansions of the Supreme Personality of Godhead, Viṣṇu, in the form of the sun-god. These deities take away all the sinful reactions of those who remember them each day at dawn and sunset.

TEXT 46

द्वादशस्वपि मासेषु देवोऽसौ षड्भिरस्य वै ।
चरन् समन्तात्तनुते परत्रेह च सन्मतिम् ॥४६॥

dvādaśasv api māseṣu
devo 'sau ṣaḍbhir asya vai
caran samantāt tanute
paratreha ca san-matim

dvādaśasu—in each of the twelve; *api*—indeed; *māseṣu*—months; *devaḥ*—the lord; *asau*—this; *ṣaḍbhiḥ*—with his six types of associates; *asya*—for the population of this universe; *vai*—certainly; *caran*—traveling; *samantāt*—in all directions; *tanute*—spreads; *paratra*—in the next life; *iha*—in this life; *ca*—and; *sat-matim*—pure consciousness.

TRANSLATION

Thus, throughout the twelve months, the lord of the sun travels in all directions with his six types of associates, disseminating among the inhabitants of this universe purity of consciousness for both this life and the next.

TEXTS 47–48

सामर्ग्यजुर्भिस्तल्लिंगैरृषयः संस्तुवन्त्यमुम् ।
गन्धर्वास्तं प्रगायन्ति नृत्यन्त्यप्सरसोऽग्रतः ॥४७॥
उन्नह्यन्ति रथं नागा ग्रामण्यो रथयोजकाः ।
चोदयन्ति रथं पृष्ठे नैरृता बलशालिनः ॥४८॥

sāmarg-yajurbhis tal-liṅgair
ṛṣayaḥ saṁstuvanty amum
gandharvās taṁ pragāyanti
nṛtyanty apsaraso 'grataḥ

unnahyanti rathaṁ nāgā
grāmaṇyo ratha-yojakāḥ
codayanti rathaṁ pṛṣṭhe
nairṛtā bala-śālinaḥ

sāma-ṛk-yajurbhiḥ—with the hymns of the *Sāma*, *Ṛg* and *Yajur Vedas; tat-liṅgaiḥ*—which reveal the sun; *ṛṣayaḥ*—the sages; *saṁstuvanti*—glorify; *amum*—him; *gandharvāḥ*—the Gandharvas; *tam*—about him; *pragāyanti*—sing loudly; *nṛtyanti*—dance; *apsarasaḥ*—the Apsarās; *agrataḥ*—in front; *unnahyanti*—bind up; *ratham*—the chariot; *nāgāḥ*—the Nāgas; *grāmaṇyaḥ*—the Yakṣas; *ratha-yojakāḥ*—those who harness the horses to the chariot; *codayanti*—drive; *ratham*—the chariot; *pṛṣṭhe*—from the rear; *nairṛtāḥ*—the Rākṣasas; *bala-śālinaḥ*—strong.

TRANSLATION

While the sages glorify the sun-god with the hymns of the *Sāma*, *Ṛg* and *Yajur Vedas*, which reveal his identity, the Gandharvas also sing his praises and the Apsarās dance before his chariot. The Nāgas arrange the chariot ropes and the Yakṣas harness the horses to the chariot, while the powerful Rākṣasas push from behind.

TEXT 49

वालखिल्याः सहस्राणि षष्टिर्ब्रह्मर्षयोऽमलाः ।
पुरतोऽभिमुखं यान्ति स्तुवन्ति स्तुतिभिर्विभुम् ॥४९॥

vālakhilyāḥ sahasrāṇi
ṣaṣṭir brahmarṣayo 'malāḥ
purato 'bhimukhaṁ yānti
stuvanti stutibhir vibhum

vālakhilyāḥ—the Vālakhilyas; *sahasrāṇi*—thousands; *ṣaṣṭiḥ*—sixty; *brahma-ṛṣayaḥ*—great sages among the *brāhmaṇas; amalāḥ*—pure; *purataḥ*—in front; *abhimukham*—facing the chariot; *yānti*—they go; *stuvanti*—they offer praise; *stutibhiḥ*—with Vedic prayers; *vibhum*—to the almighty lord.

TRANSLATION

Facing the chariot, the sixty thousand *brāhmaṇa* sages known as Vālakhilyas travel in front and offer prayers to the almighty sun-god with Vedic *mantras.*

TEXT 50

एवं ह्यनादिनिधनो भगवान् हरिरीश्वरः ।
कल्पे कल्पे स्वमात्मानं व्यूह्य लोकानवत्यजः ॥५०॥

evaṁ hy anādi-nidhano
bhagavān harir īśvaraḥ
kalpe kalpe svam ātmānaṁ
vyūhya lokān avaty ajaḥ

evam—thus; *hi*—indeed; *anādi*—without beginning; *nidhanaḥ*—or end; *bhagavān*—the Personality of Godhead; *hariḥ*—Lord Hari; *īśvaraḥ*—the supreme controller; *kalpe kalpe*—in each day of Brahmā;

svam ātmānam—Himself; *vyūhya*—expanding into various forms; *lokān*—the worlds; *avati*—protects; *ajaḥ*—the unborn Lord.

TRANSLATION

For the protection of all the worlds, the Supreme Personality of Godhead Hari, who is unborn and without beginning or end, thus expands Himself during each day of Brahmā into these specific categories of His personal representations.

Thus end the purports of the humble servant of His Divine Grace A. C. Bhaktivedanta Swami Prabhupāda to the Twelfth Canto, Eleventh Chapter, of the Śrīmad-Bhāgavatam, *entitled "Summary Description of the Mahāpuruṣa."*

CHAPTER TWELVE

The Topics of Śrīmad-Bhāgavatam Summarized

In this chapter, Śrī Sūta Gosvāmī summarizes the subjects discussed in *Śrīmad-Bhāgavatam.*

The Supreme Lord, Śrī Hari, personally removes all the distress of a person who hears about His glories. Whatever words glorify the innumerable transcendental qualities of the Personality of Godhead are truthful, auspicious and conducive to piety, whereas all other words are impure. Discussions of topics concerning the Supreme Lord bestow ecstasy, which remains constantly new, but persons who are like crows become absorbed in unessential topics, those unrelated to the Personality of Godhead.

By chanting and hearing the countless names of Lord Śrī Hari, which describe His glorious qualities, all human beings can be relieved of their sins. Neither knowledge devoid of devotion for Lord Viṣṇu nor fruitive work not offered to Him have any real beauty. By constant remembrance of Lord Kṛṣṇa, on the other hand, all one's inauspicious desires are destroyed, one's mind is purified, and one attains devotion for Lord Śrī Hari along with knowledge filled with realization and detachment.

Sūta Gosvāmī then states that previously, in the assembly of Mahārāja Parīkṣit, he heard from the mouth of Śrī Śukadeva the glories of Śrī Kṛṣṇa, which annihilate all sinful reactions, and that now he has related these glories to the sages at Naimiṣāraṇya. By hearing *Śrīmad-Bhāgavatam*, the spirit soul is purified and obtains salvation from all sins and all kinds of fear. Through the study of this scripture, one achieves the same result as that achieved by one who studies all the *Vedas*, and one also achieves the fulfillment of all desires. By studying with a controlled mind this essential compilation of all the *Purāṇas*, one will reach the supreme abode of the Personality of Godhead. Every verse of this scripture, *Śrīmad-Bhāgavatam*, contains the narrations of Lord Śrī Hari, who has innumerable personal forms.

Finally, Śrī Sūta offers obeisances to the unborn and unlimited Supreme Soul, Śrī Kṛṣṇa, as well as to Śrī Śukadeva, the son of Vyāsa, who is capable of destroying the sins of all living beings.

TEXT 1

सूत उवाच
नमो धर्माय महते नमः कृष्णाय वेधसे ।
ब्रह्मणेभ्यो नमस्कृत्य धर्मान् वक्ष्ये सनातनान् ॥१॥

sūta uvāca
namo dharmāya mahate
namaḥ kṛṣṇāya vedhase
brahmaṇebhyo namaskṛtya
dharmān vakṣye sanātanān

sūtaḥ uvāca—Sūta Gosvāmī said; *namaḥ*—obeisances; *dharmāya*—to the principle of religion; *mahate*—greatest; *namaḥ*—obeisances; *kṛṣṇāya*—to Lord Kṛṣṇa; *vedhase*—the creator; *brahmaṇebhyaḥ*—to the *brāhmaṇas; namaskṛtya*—offering my obeisances; *dharmān*—the principles of religion; *vakṣye*—I shall speak; *sanātanān*—eternal.

TRANSLATION

Sūta Gosvāmī said: Offering my obeisances to the supreme religious principle, devotional service; to Lord Kṛṣṇa, the supreme creator; and to all the *brāhmaṇas*, I shall now describe the eternal principles of religion.

PURPORT

In this Twelfth Chapter of the Twelfth Canto, Sūta Gosvāmī will summarize all the topics of *Śrīmad-Bhāgavatam*, beginning from the First Canto.

TEXT 2

एतद्वः कथितं विप्रा विष्णोश्चरितमद्भुतम् ।
भवद्भिर्यदहं पृष्टो नराणां पुरुषोचितम् ॥२॥

etad vaḥ kathitaṁ viprā
viṣṇoś caritam adbhutam
bhavadbhir yad ahaṁ pṛṣṭo
narāṇāṁ puruṣocitam

etat—these; *vaḥ*—to you; *kathitam*—narrated; *viprāḥ*—O sages; *viṣṇoḥ*—of Lord Viṣṇu; *caritam*—the pastimes; *adbhutam*—wonderful; *bhavadbhiḥ*—by your good selves; *yat*—which; *aham*—I; *pṛṣṭaḥ*—was asked about; *narāṇām*—among men; *puruṣa*—for an actual human being; *ucitam*—suitable.

TRANSLATION

O great sages, I have narrated to you the wonderful pastimes of Lord Viṣṇu, as you inquired about them from me. Hearing such narrations is the suitable engagement for a person who is actually a human being.

PURPORT

The words *narāṇāṁ puruṣocitam* indicate that men and women who actually come to the standard of human life hear and chant the glories of the Supreme Lord, whereas uncivilized persons may not be interested in the science of God.

TEXT 3

अत्र संकीर्तितः साक्षात्सर्वपापहरो हरिः ।
नारायणो हृषीकेशो भगवान् सात्वतां पतिः ॥३॥

atra saṅkīrtitaḥ sākṣāt
sarva-pāpa-haro hariḥ
nārāyaṇo hṛṣīkeśo
bhagavān sātvatāṁ patiḥ

atra—here, in the *Śrīmad-Bhāgavatam; saṅkīrtitaḥ*—is fully glorified; *sākṣāt*—directly; *sarva-pāpa*—of all sins; *haraḥ*—the remover; *hariḥ*—the Personality of Godhead, Lord Hari; *nārāyaṇaḥ*—Nārāyaṇa;

hṛṣīkeśaḥ—Hṛṣīkeśa, the Lord of the senses; *bhagavān*—the Supreme Personality; *sātvatām*—of the Yadus; *patiḥ*—the master.

TRANSLATION

This literature fully glorifies the Supreme Personality of Godhead Hari, who removes all His devotees' sinful reactions. The Lord is glorified as Nārāyaṇa, Hṛṣīkeśa and the Lord of the Sātvatas.

PURPORT

Lord Kṛṣṇa's many holy names indicate His extraordinary transcendental qualities. The name *Hari* indicates that the Lord removes all sins from the heart of His devotee. *Nārāyaṇa* indicates that the Lord sustains the existence of all other beings. *Hṛṣīkeśa* indicates that Lord Kṛṣṇa is the ultimate controller of the senses of all living beings. The word *bhagavān* indicates that Lord Kṛṣṇa is the all-attractive Supreme Being. And the words *sātvatāṁ patiḥ* indicate that the Lord is naturally the master of saintly and religious people, especially the members of the exalted Yadu family.

TEXT 4

अत्र ब्रह्म परं गुह्यं जगतः प्रभवाप्ययम् ।
ज्ञानं च तदुपाख्यानं प्रोक्तं विज्ञानसंयुतम् ॥४॥

atra brahma paraṁ guhyaṁ
jagataḥ prabhavāpyayam
jñānaṁ ca tad-upākhyānaṁ
proktaṁ vijñāna-saṁyutam

atra—here; *brahma*—the Absolute Truth; *param*—supreme; *guhyam*—confidential; *jagataḥ*—of this universe; *prabhava*—the creation; *apyayam*—and annihilation; *jñānam*—knowledge; *ca*—and; *tat-upākhyānam*—the means of cultivating it; *proktam*—are spoken; *vijñāna*—transcendental realization; *saṁyutam*—including.

TRANSLATION

This literature describes the mystery of the Supreme Absolute Truth, the source of the creation and annihilation of this universe. Also presented are divine knowledge of Him together with the process of its cultivation, and the transcendental realization one achieves.

TEXT 5

भक्तियोगः समाख्यातो वैराग्यं च तदाश्रयम् ।
पारीक्षितमुपाख्यानं नारदाख्यानमेव च ॥५॥

bhakti-yogaḥ samākhyāto
vairāgyaṁ ca tad-āśrayam
pārīkṣitam upākhyānaṁ
nāradākhyānam eva ca

bhakti-yogaḥ—the process of devotional service; *samākhyātaḥ*—is thoroughly enunciated; *vairāgyam*—renunciation; *ca*—and; *tat-āśrayam*—which is subsidiary to it; *pārīkṣitam*—of Mahārāja Parīkṣit; *upākhyānam*—the history; *nārada*—of Nārada; *ākhyānam*—the history; *eva*—indeed; *ca*—also.

TRANSLATION

The following topics are also narrated: the process of devotional service together with its subsidiary feature of renunciation, and the histories of Mahārāja Parīkṣit and the sage Nārada.

TEXT 6

प्रायोपवेशो राजर्षेर्विप्रशापात् परीक्षितः ।
शुकस्य ब्रह्मर्षभस्य संवादश्च परीक्षितः ॥६॥

prāyopaveśo rājarṣer
vipra-śāpāt parīkṣitaḥ
śukasya brahmarṣabhasya
saṁvādaś ca parīkṣitaḥ

prāya-upaveśaḥ—the fast until death; *rāja-ṛṣeḥ*—of the sage among kings; *vipra-śāpāt*—because of the curse of the *brāhmaṇa's* son; *parīkṣitaḥ*—of King Parīkṣit; *śukasya*—of Śukadeva; *brahma-ṛṣabhasya*—the best of *brāhmaṇas; saṁvādaḥ*—the conversation; *ca*—and; *parīkṣitaḥ*—with Parīkṣit.

TRANSLATION

Also described are saintly King Parīkṣit's sitting down to fast until death in response to the curse of a *brāhmaṇa's* son, and the conversations between Parīkṣit and Śukadeva Gosvāmī, who is the best of all *brāhmaṇas.*

TEXT 7

योगधारणयोत्क्रान्तिः संवादो नारदाजयोः ।
अवतारानुगीतं च सर्गः प्राधानिकोऽग्रतः ॥७॥

yoga-dhāraṇayotkrāntiḥ
saṁvādo nāradājayoḥ
avatārānugītaṁ ca
sargaḥ prādhāniko 'grataḥ

yoga-dhāraṇayā—by fixed meditation in *yoga; utkrāntiḥ*—the attainment of liberation at the time of passing away; *saṁvādaḥ*—the conversation; *nārada-ajayoḥ*—between Nārada and Brahmā; *avatāra-anugītam*—the listing of the incarnations of the Supreme Lord; *ca*—and; *sargaḥ*—the process of creation; *prādhānikaḥ*—from the unmanifest material nature; *agrataḥ*—in progressive order.

TRANSLATION

The *Bhāgavatam* explains how one can attain liberation at the time of death by practicing fixed meditation in *yoga.* It also contains a discussion between Nārada and Brahmā, an enumeration of the incarnations of the Supreme Personality of Godhead, and a description of how the universe was created in progressive sequence, beginning from the unmanifest stage of material nature.

PURPORT

Śrīla Viśvanātha Cakravartī Ṭhākura explains that it would be difficult to give a complete list of the numerous accounts and topics contained in the *Śrīmad-Bhāgavatam*. Therefore it is understood that Sūta Gosvāmī is merely summarizing the topics. We should not consider the topics he fails to mention here less important or superfluous, since every letter and word of *Śrīmad-Bhāgavatam* is absolute, Kṛṣṇa conscious sound vibration.

TEXT 8

विदुरोद्धवसंवादः क्षत्तृमैत्रेययोस्ततः ।
पुराणसंहिताप्रश्नो महापुरुषसंस्थितिः ॥८॥

viduroddhava-saṁvādaḥ
kṣattṛ-maitreyayos tataḥ
purāṇa-saṁhitā-praśno
mahā-puruṣa-saṁsthitiḥ

vidura-uddhava—between Vidura and Uddhava; *saṁvādaḥ*—the discussion; *kṣattṛ-maitreyayoḥ*—between Vidura and Maitreya; *tataḥ*—then; *purāṇa-saṁhitā*—concerning this Purāṇic compilation; *praśnaḥ*—inquiries; *mahā-puruṣa*—within the Supreme Personality of Godhead; *saṁsthitiḥ*—the winding up of creation.

TRANSLATION

This scripture also relates the discussions Vidura had with Uddhava and with Maitreya, inquiries about the subject matter of this *Purāṇa*, and the winding up of creation within the body of the Supreme Lord at the time of annihilation.

TEXT 9

ततः प्राकृतिकः सर्गः सप्त वैकृतिकाश्च ये ।
ततो ब्रह्माण्डसम्भूतिर्वैराजः पुरुषो यतः ॥९॥

tataḥ prākṛtikaḥ sargaḥ
sapta vaikṛtikāś ca ye
tato brahmāṇḍa-sambhūtir
vairājaḥ puruṣo yataḥ

tataḥ—then; *prākṛtikaḥ*—from material nature; *sargaḥ*—the creation; *sapta*—the seven; *vaikṛtikāḥ*—stages of creation derived by transformation; *ca*—and; *ye*—which; *tataḥ*—then; *brahma-aṇḍa*—of the universal egg; *sambhūtiḥ*—the construction; *vairājaḥ puruṣaḥ*—the universal form of the Lord; *yataḥ*—from which.

TRANSLATION

The creation effected by the agitation of the modes of material nature, the seven stages of evolution by elemental transformation, and the construction of the universal egg, from which arises the universal form of the Supreme Lord—all these are thoroughly described.

TEXT 10

कालस्य स्थूलसूक्ष्मस्य गतिः पद्मसमुद्भवः ।
भुव उद्धरणेऽम्भोधेर्हिरण्याक्षवधो यथा ॥१०॥

kālasya sthūla-sūkṣmasya
gatiḥ padma-samudbhavaḥ
bhuva uddharaṇe 'mbhodher
hiraṇyākṣa-vadho yathā

kālasya—of time; *sthūla-sūkṣmasya*—gross and subtle; *gatiḥ*—the movement; *padma*—of the lotus; *samudbhavaḥ*—the generation; *bhuvaḥ*—of the earth; *uddharaṇe*—in connection with the deliverance; *ambhodheḥ*—from the ocean; *hiraṇyākṣa-vadhaḥ*—the killing of the demon Hiraṇyākṣa; *yathā*—as it occurred.

TRANSLATION

Other topics include the subtle and gross movements of time, the generation of the lotus from the navel of Garbhodakaśāyī

Viṣṇu, and the killing of the demon Hiraṇyākṣa when the earth was delivered from the Garbhodaka Ocean.

TEXT 11

ऊर्ध्वतिर्यगवाक्सर्गो रुद्रसर्गस्तथैव च ।
अर्धनारीश्वरस्याथ यतः स्वायम्भुवो मनुः ॥११॥

ūrdhva-tiryag-avāk-sargo
rudra-sargas tathaiva ca
ardha-nārīśvarasyātha
yataḥ svāyambhuvo manuḥ

ūrdhva—of the higher species, the demigods; *tiryak*—of the animals; *avāk*—and of lower species; *sargaḥ*—the creation; *rudra*—of Lord Śiva; *sargaḥ*—the creation; *tathā*—and; *eva*—indeed; *ca*—also; *ardha-nārī*—as a half man, half woman; *īśvarasya*—of the lord; *atha*—then; *yataḥ*—from whom; *svāyambhuvaḥ manuḥ*—Svāyambhuva Manu.

TRANSLATION

The *Bhāgavatam* also describes the creation of demigods, animals and demoniac species of life; the birth of Lord Rudra; and the appearance of Svāyambhuva Manu from the half-man, half-woman Īśvara.

TEXT 12

शतरूपा च या स्त्रीणामाद्या प्रकृतिरुत्तमा ।
सन्तानो धर्मपत्नीनां कर्दमस्य प्रजापतेः ॥१२॥

śatarūpā ca yā strīṇām
ādyā prakṛtir uttamā
santāno dharma-patnīnāṁ
kardamasya prajāpateḥ

śatarūpā—Śatarūpā; *ca*—and; *yā*—who; *strīṇām*—of women; *ādyā*—the first; *prakṛtiḥ*—the consort; *uttamā*—best; *santānaḥ*—the progeny;

dharma-patnīnām—of the pious wives; *kardamasya*—of the sage Kardama; *prajāpateḥ*—the progenitor.

TRANSLATION

Also related are the appearance of the first woman, Śatarūpā, who was the excellent consort of Manu, and the offspring of the pious wives of Prajāpati Kardama.

TEXT 13

अवतारो भगवतः कपिलस्य महात्मनः ।
देवहूत्याश्च संवादः कपिलेन च धीमता ॥१३॥

avatāro bhagavataḥ
kapilasya mahātmanaḥ
devahūtyāś ca saṁvādaḥ
kapilena ca dhīmatā

avatāraḥ—the descent; *bhagavataḥ*—of the Supreme Personality of Godhead; *kapilasya*—Lord Kapila; *mahā-ātmanaḥ*—the Supreme Soul; *devahūtyāḥ*—of Devahūti; *ca*—and; *saṁvādaḥ*—the conversation; *kapilena*—with Lord Kapila; *ca*—and; *dhī-matā*—the intelligent.

TRANSLATION

The *Bhāgavatam* describes the incarnation of the Supreme Personality of Godhead as the exalted sage Kapila and records the conversation between that greatly learned soul and His mother, Devahūti.

TEXTS 14–15

नवब्रह्मसमुत्पत्तिर्दक्षयज्ञविनाशनम् ।
ध्रुवस्य चरितं पश्चात्पृथोः प्राचीनबर्हिषः ॥१४॥
नारदस्य च संवादस्ततः प्रैयव्रतं द्विजाः ।
नाभेस्ततोऽनुचरितमृषभस्य भरतस्य च ॥१५॥

nava-brahma-samutpattir
dakṣa-yajña-vināśanam
dhruvasya caritaṁ paścāt
pṛthoḥ prācīnabarhiṣaḥ

nāradasya ca saṁvādas
tataḥ praiyavrataṁ dvijāḥ
nābhes tato 'nucaritam
ṛṣabhasya bharatasya ca

nava-brahma—of the nine *brāhmaṇas* (the sons of Lord Brahmā, headed by Marīci); *samutpattiḥ*—the descendants; *dakṣa-yajña*—of the sacrifice performed by Dakṣa; *vināśanam*—the destruction; *dhruvasya*—of Dhruva Mahārāja; *caritam*—the history; *paścāt*—then; *pṛthoḥ*—of King Pṛthu; *prācīnabarhiṣaḥ*—of Prācīnabarhi; *nāradasya*—with Nārada Muni; *ca*—and; *saṁvādaḥ*—his conversation; *tataḥ*—then; *praiyavratam*—the story of Mahārāja Priyavrata; *dvijāḥ*—O *brāhmaṇas; nābheḥ*—of Nābhi; *tataḥ*—then; *anucaritam*—the life story; *ṛṣabhasya*—of Lord Ṛṣabha; *bharatasya*—of Bharata Mahārāja; *ca*—and.

TRANSLATION

Also described are the progeny of the nine great *brāhmaṇas*, the destruction of Dakṣa's sacrifice, and the history of Dhruva Mahārāja, followed by the histories of King Pṛthu and King Prācīnabarhi, the discussion between Prācīnabarhi and Nārada, and the life of Mahārāja Priyavrata. Then, O *brāhmaṇas*, the *Bhāgavatam* tells of the character and activities of King Nābhi, Lord Ṛṣabha and King Bharata.

TEXT 16

द्वीपवर्षसमुद्राणां गिरिनद्युपवर्णनम् ।
ज्योतिश्चक्रस्य संस्थानं पातालनरकस्थितिः ॥१६॥

dvīpa-varṣa-samudrāṇāṁ
giri-nady-upavarṇanam
jyotiś-cakrasya saṁsthānaṁ
pātāla-naraka-sthitiḥ

dvīpa-varṣa-samudrāṇām—of the continents, great islands and oceans; *giri-nadī*—of the mountains and rivers; *upavarṇanam*—the detailed description; *jyotiḥ-cakrasya*—of the celestial sphere; *saṁsthānam*—the arrangement; *pātāla*—of the subterranean regions; *naraka*—and of hell; *sthitiḥ*—the situation.

TRANSLATION

The *Bhāgavatam* gives an elaborate description of the earth's continents, regions, oceans, mountains and rivers. Also described are the arrangement of the celestial sphere and the conditions found in the subterranean regions and in hell.

TEXT 17

दक्षजन्म प्रचेतोभ्यस्तत्पुत्रीणां च सन्ततिः ।
यतो देवासुरनरास्तिर्यङ्नगखगादयः ॥१७॥

dakṣa-janma pracetobhyas
tat-putrīṇāṁ ca santatiḥ
yato devāsura-narās
tiryaṅ-naga-khagādayaḥ

dakṣa-janma—the birth of Dakṣa; *pracetobhyaḥ*—from the Pracetās; *tat-putrīṇām*—of his daughters; *ca*—and; *santatiḥ*—the progeny; *yataḥ*—from which; *deva-asura-narāḥ*—the demigods, demons and human beings; *tiryak-naga-khaga-ādayaḥ*—the animals, serpents, birds and other species.

TRANSLATION

The rebirth of Prajāpati Dakṣa as the son of the Pracetās, and the progeny of Dakṣa's daughters, who initiated the races of demigods, demons, human beings, animals, serpents, birds and so on—all this is described.

TEXT 18

त्वाष्ट्रस्य जन्मनिधनं पुत्रयोश्च दितेर्द्विजाः ।
दैत्येश्वरस्य चरितं प्रह्रादस्य महात्मनः ॥१८॥

tvāṣṭrasya janma-nidhanaṁ
putrayoś ca diter dvijāḥ
daityeśvarasya caritaṁ
prahrādasya mahātmanaḥ

tvāṣṭrasya—of the son of Tvaṣṭā (Vṛtra); *janma-nidhanam*—the birth and death; *putrayoḥ*—of the two sons, Hiraṇyākṣa and Hiraṇyakaśipu; *ca*—and; *diteḥ*—of Diti; *dvijāḥ*—O *brāhmaṇas; daitya-īśvarasya*—of the greatest of the Daityas; *caritam*—the history; *prahrādasya*—of Prahlāda; *mahā-ātmanaḥ*—the great soul.

TRANSLATION

O *brāhmaṇas*, also recounted are the births and deaths of Vṛtrāsura and of Diti's sons Hiraṇyākṣa and Hiraṇyakaśipu, as well as the history of the greatest of Diti's descendants, the exalted soul Prahlāda.

TEXT 19

मन्वन्तरानुकथनं गजेन्द्रस्य विमोक्षणम् ।
मन्वन्तरावताराश्च विष्णोर्हयशिरादयः ॥१९॥

manv-antarānukathanaṁ
gajendrasya vimokṣaṇam
manv-antarāvatārāś ca
viṣṇor hayaśirādayaḥ

manu-antara—of reigns of the various Manus; *anukathanam*—the detailed description; *gaja-indrasya*—of the king of the elephants; *vimokṣaṇam*—the liberation; *manu-antara-avatārāḥ*—the particular incarnations of the Supreme Personality of Godhead in each *manv-antara; ca*—and; *viṣṇoḥ*—of Lord Viṣṇu; *hayaśirā-ādayaḥ*—such as Lord Hayaśīrṣā.

TRANSLATION

The reign of each Manu, the liberation of Gajendra, and the special incarnations of Lord Viṣṇu in each *manv-antara*, such as Lord Hayaśīrṣā, are described as well.

TEXT 20

कौर्मं मात्स्यं नारसिंहं वामनं च जगत्पतेः ।
क्षीरोदमथनं तद्वदमृतार्थे दिवौकसाम् ॥२०॥

kaurmaṁ mātsyaṁ nārasiṁhaṁ
vāmanaṁ ca jagat-pateḥ
kṣīroda-mathanaṁ tadvad
amṛtārthe divaukasām

kaurmam—the incarnation as a tortoise; *mātsyam*—as a fish; *nāra-siṁham*—as a man-lion; *vāmanam*—as a dwarf; *ca*—and; *jagat-pateḥ*—of the Lord of the universe; *kṣīra-uda*—of the ocean of milk; *mathanam*—the churning; *tadvat*—thus; *amṛta-arthe*—for the sake of nectar; *diva-okasām*—on the part of the inhabitants of heaven.

TRANSLATION

The *Bhāgavatam* also tells of the appearances of the Lord of the universe as Kūrma, Matsya, Narasiṁha and Vāmana, and of the demigods' churning of the milk ocean to obtain nectar.

TEXT 21

देवासुरमहायुद्धं राजवंशानुकीर्तनम् ।
इक्ष्वाकुजन्म तद्वंशः सुद्युम्नस्य महात्मनः ॥२१॥

devāsura-mahā-yuddhaṁ
rāja-vaṁśānukīrtanam
ikṣvāku-janma tad-vaṁśaḥ
sudyumnasya mahātmanaḥ

deva-asura—of the demigods and demons; *mahā-yuddham*—the great war; *rāja-vaṁśa*—of the dynasties of kings; *anukīrtanam*—the reciting in sequence; *ikṣvāku-janma*—the birth of Ikṣvāku; *tat-vaṁśaḥ*—his dynasty; *sudyumnasya*—(and the dynasty) of Sudyumna; *mahā-ātmanaḥ*—the great soul.

TRANSLATION

An account of the great battle fought between the demigods and the demons, a systematic description of the dynasties of various kings, and narrations concerning Ikṣvāku's birth, his dynasty and the dynasty of the pious Sudyumna—all are presented within this literature.

TEXT 22

इलोपाख्यानमत्रोक्तं तारोपाख्यानमेव च ।
सूर्यवंशानुकथनं शशादाद्या नृगादयः ॥२२॥

ilopākhyānam atroktaṁ
tāropākhyānam eva ca
sūrya-vaṁśānukathanaṁ
śaśādādyā nṛgādayaḥ

ilā-upākhyānam—the history of Ilā; *atra*—herein; *uktam*—is spoken; *tārā-upākhyānam*—the history of Tārā; *eva*—indeed; *ca*—also; *sūrya-vaṁśa*—of the dynasty of the sun-god; *anukathanam*—the narration; *śaśāda-ādyāḥ*—Śaśāda and others; *nṛga-ādayaḥ*—Nṛga and others.

TRANSLATION

Also related are the histories of Ilā and Tārā, and the description of the descendants of the sun-god, including such kings as Śaśāda and Nṛga.

TEXT 23

सौकन्यं चाथ शर्यातेः ककुत्स्थस्य च धीमतः ।
खट्वांगस्य च मान्धातुः सौभरेः सगरस्य च ॥२३॥

saukanyaṁ cātha śaryāteḥ
kakutsthasya ca dhīmataḥ
khaṭvāṅgasya ca māndhātuḥ
saubhareḥ sagarasya ca

saukanyam—the story of Sukanyā; *ca*—and; *atha*—then; *śaryāteḥ*—that of Śaryāti; *kakutsthasya*—of Kakutstha; *ca*—and; *dhī-mataḥ*—who was an intelligent king; *khaṭvāṅgasya*—of Khaṭvāṅga; *ca*—and; *māndhātuḥ*—of Māndhātā; *saubhareḥ*—of Saubhari; *sagarasya*—of Sagara; *ca*—and.

TRANSLATION

The histories of Sukanyā, Śaryāti, the intelligent Kakutstha, Khaṭvāṅga, Māndhātā, Saubhari and Sagara are narrated.

TEXT 24

रामस्य कोशलेन्द्रस्य चरितं किल्बिषापहम् ।
निमेरंगपरित्यागो जनकानां च सम्भवः ॥२४॥

rāmasya kośalendrasya
caritaṁ kilbiṣāpaham
nimer aṅga-parityāgo
janakānāṁ ca sambhavaḥ

rāmasya—of Lord Rāmacandra; *kośala-indrasya*—the King of Kośala; *caritam*—the pastimes; *kilbiṣa-apaham*—which drive away all sins; *nimeḥ*—of King Nimi; *aṅga-parityāgaḥ*—the giving up of his body; *janakānām*—of the descendants of Janaka; *ca*—and; *sambhavaḥ*—the appearance.

TRANSLATION

The *Bhāgavatam* narrates the sanctifying pastimes of Lord Rāmacandra, the King of Kośala, and also explains how King Nimi abandoned his material body. The appearance of the descendants of King Janaka is also mentioned.

TEXTS 25–26

रामस्य भार्गवेन्द्रस्य निःक्षत्रीकरणं भुवः ।
ऐलस्य सोमवंशस्य ययातेर्नहुषस्य च ॥२५॥
दौष्मन्तेर्भरतस्यापि शान्तनोस्तत्सुतस्य च ।
ययातेर्ज्येष्ठपुत्रस्य यदोर्वंशोऽनुकीर्तितः ॥२६॥

rāmasya bhārgavendrasya
niḥkṣatrī-karaṇaṁ bhuvaḥ
ailasya soma-vaṁśasya
yayāter nahuṣasya ca

dauṣmanter bharatasyāpi
śāntanos tat-sutasya ca
yayāter jyeṣṭha-putrasya
yador vaṁśo 'nukīrtitaḥ

rāmasya—by Lord Paraśurāma; *bhārgava-indrasya*—the greatest of the descendants of Bhṛgu Muni; *niḥkṣatrī-karaṇam*—the elimination of all the *kṣatriyas; bhuvaḥ*—of the earth; *ailasya*—of Mahārāja Aila; *soma-vaṁśasya*—of the dynasty of the moon-god; *yayāteḥ*—of Yayāti; *nahuṣasya*—of Nahuṣa; *ca*—and; *dauṣmanteḥ*—of the son of Duṣmanta; *bharatasya*—Bharata; *api*—also; *śāntanoḥ*—of King Śāntanu; *tat*—his; *sutasya*—of the son, Bhīṣma; *ca*—and; *yayāteḥ*—of Yayāti; *jyeṣṭha-putrasya*—of the eldest son; *yadoḥ*—Yadu; *vaṁśaḥ*—the dynasty; *anukīrtitaḥ*—is glorified.

TRANSLATION

The *Śrīmad-Bhāgavatam* describes how Lord Paraśurāma, the greatest descendant of Bhṛgu, annihilated all the *kṣatriyas* on the face of the earth. It further recounts the lives of glorious kings who appeared in the dynasty of the moon-god—kings such as Aila, Yayāti, Nahuṣa, Duṣmanta's son Bharata, Śāntanu and Śāntanu's son Bhīṣma. Also described is the great dynasty founded by King Yadu, the eldest son of Yayāti.

TEXT 27

यत्रावतीर्णो भगवान् कृष्णाख्यो जगदीश्वरः ।
वसुदेवगृहे जन्म ततो वृद्धिश्च गोकुले ॥२७॥

yatrāvatīrṇo bhagavān
kṛṣṇākhyo jagad-īśvaraḥ
vasudeva-gṛhe janma
tato vṛddhiś ca gokule

yatra—in which dynasty; *avatīrṇaḥ*—descended; *bhagavān*—the Supreme Personality of Godhead; *kṛṣṇa-ākhyaḥ*—known as Kṛṣṇa; *jagat-īśvaraḥ*—the Lord of the universe; *vasudeva-gṛhe*—in the home of Vasudeva; *janma*—His birth; *tataḥ*—subsequently; *vṛddhiḥ*—His growing up; *ca*—and; *gokule*—in Gokula.

TRANSLATION

How Śrī Kṛṣṇa, the Supreme Personality of Godhead and Lord of the universe, descended into this Yadu dynasty, how He took birth in the home of Vasudeva and how He then grew up in Gokula—all this is described in detail.

TEXTS 28–29

तस्य कर्माण्यपाराणि कीर्तितान्यसुरद्विषः ।
पूतनासुपयःपानं शकटोच्चाटनं शिशोः ॥२८॥
तृणावर्तस्य निष्पेषस्तथैव बकवत्सयोः ।
अघासुरवधो धात्रा वत्सपालावगूहनम् ॥२९॥

tasya karmāṇy apārāṇi
kīrtitāny asura-dviṣaḥ
pūtanāsu-payaḥ-pānaṁ
śakaṭoccāṭanaṁ śiśoḥ

tṛṇāvartasya niṣpeṣas
tathaiva baka-vatsayoḥ
aghāsura-vadho dhātrā
vatsa-pālāvagūhanam

tasya—His; *karmāṇi*—activities; *apārāṇi*—innumerable; *kīrtitāni*—are glorified; *asura-dviṣaḥ*—of the enemy of the demons; *pūtanā*—of the witch Pūtanā; *asu*—along with her life air; *payaḥ*—of the milk; *pānam*—the drinking; *śakaṭa*—of the cart; *uccāṭanam*—the breaking; *śiśoḥ*—by the child; *tṛṇāvartasya*—of Tṛṇāvarta; *niṣpeṣaḥ*—the trampling; *tathā*—and; *eva*—indeed; *baka-vatsayoḥ*—of the demons named Baka and Vatsa; *agha-asura*—of the demon Agha; *vadhaḥ*—the killing; *dhātrā*—by Lord Brahmā; *vatsa-pāla*—of the calves and cowherd boys; *avagūhanam*—the hiding away.

TRANSLATION

Also glorified are the innumerable pastimes of Śrī Kṛṣṇa, the enemy of the demons, including His childhood pastimes of sucking the breast-milk of Pūtanā along with her life air, breaking the cart, trampling down Tṛṇāvarta, killing Bakāsura, Vatsāsura and Aghāsura, and the pastimes He enacted when Lord Brahmā hid His calves and cowherd boyfriends in a cave.

TEXT 30

धेनुकस्य सहभ्रातुः प्रलम्बस्य च सङ्क्षयः ।
गोपानां च परित्राणं दावाग्नेः परिसर्पतः ॥३०॥

dhenukasya saha-bhrātuḥ
pralambasya ca saṅkṣayaḥ
gopānāṁ ca paritrāṇaṁ
dāvāgneḥ parisarpataḥ

dhenukasya—of Dhenuka; *saha-bhrātuḥ*—along with his companions; *pralambasya*—of Pralamba; *ca*—and; *saṅkṣayaḥ*—the destruction; *gopānām*—of the cowherd boys; *ca*—and; *paritrāṇam*—the saving; *dāva-agneḥ*—from the forest fire; *parisarpataḥ*—which was encircling.

TRANSLATION

The *Śrīmad-Bhāgavatam* tells how Lord Kṛṣṇa and Lord Balarāma killed the demon Dhenukāsura and his companions, how Lord Balarāma destroyed Pralambāsura, and also how Kṛṣṇa saved the cowherd boys from a raging forest fire that had encircled them.

TEXTS 31–33

दमनं कालियस्याहेर्महाहेर्नन्दमोक्षणम् ।
व्रतचर्या तु कन्यानां यत्र तुष्टोऽच्युतो व्रतैः ॥३१॥
प्रसादो यज्ञपत्नीभ्यो विप्राणां चानुतापनम् ।
गोवर्धनोद्धारणं च शक्रस्य सुरभेरथ ॥३२॥
यज्ञाभिषेकः कृष्णस्य स्त्रीभिः क्रीडा च रात्रिषु ।
शंखचूडस्य दुर्बुद्धेर्वधोऽरिष्टस्य केशिनः ॥३३॥

damanaṁ kāliyasyāher
mahāher nanda-mokṣaṇam
vrata-caryā tu kanyānāṁ
yatra tuṣṭo 'cyuto vrataiḥ

prasādo yajña-patnībhyo
viprāṇāṁ cānutāpanam
govardhanoddhāraṇaṁ ca
śakrasya surabher atha

yajñābhiṣekaḥ kṛṣṇasya
strībhiḥ krīḍā ca rātriṣu
śaṅkhacūḍasya durbuddher
vadho 'riṣṭasya keśinaḥ

damanam—the subduing; *kāliyasya*—of Kāliya; *aheḥ*—the snake; *mahā-aheḥ*—from the great serpent; *nanda-mokṣaṇam*—the rescue of Mahārāja Nanda; *vrata-caryā*—the execution of austere vows; *tu*—and; *kanyānām*—of the *gopīs; yatra*—by which; *tuṣṭaḥ*—became satisfied; *acyutaḥ*—Lord Kṛṣṇa; *vrataiḥ*—with their vows; *prasādaḥ*—the mercy;

yajña-patnībhyaḥ—to the wives of the *brāhmaṇas* performing Vedic sacrifices; *viprāṇām*—of the *brāhmaṇa* husbands; *ca*—and; *anutāpanam*—the experience of remorse; *govardhana-uddhāraṇam*—the lifting of Govardhana Hill; *ca*—and; *śakrasya*—by Indra; *surabheḥ*—along with the Surabhi cow; *atha*—then; *yajña-abhiṣekaḥ*—the worship and ritual bathing; *kṛṣṇasya*—of Lord Kṛṣṇa; *strībhiḥ*—together with the women; *krīḍā*—the sporting; *ca*—and; *rātriṣu*—in the nights; *śaṅkhacūḍasya*—of the demon Śaṅkhacūḍa; *durbuddheḥ*—who was foolish; *vadhaḥ*—the killing; *ariṣṭasya*—of Ariṣṭa; *keśinaḥ*—of Keśī.

TRANSLATION

The chastisement of the serpent Kāliya; the rescue of Nanda Mahārāja from a great snake; the severe vows performed by the young *gopīs*, who thus satisfied Lord Kṛṣṇa; the mercy He showed the wives of the Vedic *brāhmaṇas*, who felt remorse; the lifting of Govardhana Hill followed by the worship and bathing ceremony performed by Indra and the Surabhi cow; Lord Kṛṣṇa's nocturnal pastimes with the cowherd girls; and the killing of the foolish demons Śaṅkhacūḍa, Ariṣṭa and Keśī—all these pastimes are elaborately recounted.

TEXT 34

अक्रूरागमनं पश्चात्प्रस्थानं रामकृष्णयोः ।
व्रजस्त्रीणां विलापश्च मथुरालोकनं ततः ॥३४॥

akrūrāgamanaṁ paścāt
prasthānaṁ rāma-kṛṣṇayoḥ
vraja-strīṇāṁ vilāpaś ca
mathurālokanaṁ tataḥ

akrūra—of Akrūra; *āgamanam*—the coming; *paścāt*—after that; *prasthānam*—the departure; *rāma-kṛṣṇayoḥ*—of Lord Balarāma and Lord Kṛṣṇa; *vraja-strīṇām*—of the women of Vṛndāvana; *vilāpaḥ*—the lamentation; *ca*—and; *mathurā-ālokanam*—the seeing of Mathurā; *tataḥ*—then.

TRANSLATION

The *Bhāgavatam* describes the arrival of Akrūra, the subsequent departure of Kṛṣṇa and Balarāma, the lamentation of the *gopīs* and the touring of Mathurā.

TEXT 35

गजमुष्टिकचाणूरकंसादीनां तथा वधः ।
मृतस्यानयनं सूनोः पुनः सान्दीपनेर्गुरोः ॥३५॥

gaja-muṣṭika-cāṇūra-
kaṁsādīnāṁ tathā vadhaḥ
mṛtasyānayanaṁ sūnoḥ
punaḥ sāndīpaner guroḥ

gaja—of the elephant Kuvalayāpīḍa; *muṣṭika-cāṇūra*—of the wrestlers Muṣṭika and Cāṇūra; *kaṁsa*—of Kaṁsa; *ādīnām*—and of others; *tathā*—also; *vadhaḥ*—the killing; *mṛtasya*—who had died; *ānayanam*—the bringing back; *sūnoḥ*—of the son; *punaḥ*—again; *sāndīpaneḥ*—of Sāndīpani; *guroḥ*—their spiritual master.

TRANSLATION

Also narrated are how Kṛṣṇa and Balarāma killed the elephant Kuvalayāpīḍa, the wrestlers Muṣṭika and Cāṇūra, and Kaṁsa and other demons, as well as how Kṛṣṇa brought back the dead son of His spiritual master, Sāndīpani Muni.

TEXT 36

मथुरायां निवसता यदुचक्रस्य यत्प्रियम् ।
कृतमुद्धवरामाभ्यां युतेन हरिणा द्विजाः ॥३६॥

mathurāyāṁ nivasatā
yadu-cakrasya yat priyam
kṛtam uddhava-rāmābhyāṁ
yutena hariṇā dvijāḥ

mathurāyām—in Mathurā; *nivasatā*—by Him who was residing; *yadu-cakrasya*—for the circle of Yadus; *yat*—which; *priyam*—gratifying; *kṛtam*—was done; *uddhava-rāmābhyām*—with Uddhava and Balarāma; *yutena*—joined; *hariṇā*—by Lord Hari; *dvijāḥ*—O *brāhmaṇas.*

TRANSLATION

Then, O *brāhmaṇas*, this scripture recounts how Lord Hari, while residing in Mathurā in the company of Uddhava and Balarāma, performed pastimes for the satisfaction of the Yadu dynasty.

TEXT 37

जरासन्धसमानीतसैन्यस्य बहुशो वधः ।
घातनं यवनेन्द्रस्य कुशस्थल्या निवेशनम् ॥३७॥

jarāsandha-samānīta-
sainyasya bahuśo vadhaḥ
ghātanaṁ yavanendrasya
kuśasthalyā niveśanam

jarāsandha—by King Jarāsandha; *samānīta*—assembled; *sainyasya*—of the army; *bahuśaḥ*—many times; *vadhaḥ*—the annihilation; *ghātanam*—the killing; *yavana-indrasya*—of the king of the barbarians; *kuśasthalyāḥ*—of Dvārakā; *niveśanam*—the founding.

TRANSLATION

Also described are the annihilation of each of the many armies brought by Jarāsandha, the killing of the barbarian king Kālayavana and the establishment of Dvārakā City.

TEXT 38

आदानं पारिजातस्य सुधर्मायाः सुरालयात् ।
रुक्मिण्या हरणं युद्धे प्रमथ्य द्विषतो हरेः ॥३८॥

ādānaṁ pārijātasya
sudharmāyāḥ surālayāt
rukmiṇyā haraṇaṁ yuddhe
pramathya dviṣato hareḥ

ādānam—the receiving; *pārijātasya*—of the *pārijāta* tree; *sudharmāyāḥ*—of the Sudharmā assembly hall; *sura-ālayāt*—from the abode of the demigods; *rukmiṇyāḥ*—of Rukmiṇī; *haraṇam*—the kidnapping; *yuddhe*—in battle; *pramathya*—defeating; *dviṣataḥ*—His rivals; *hareḥ*—by Lord Hari.

TRANSLATION

This work also describes how Lord Kṛṣṇa brought from heaven the *pārijāta* tree and the Sudharmā assembly hall, and how He kidnapped Rukmiṇī by defeating all His rivals in battle.

TEXT 39

हरस्य जृम्भणं युद्धे बाणस्य भुजकृन्तनम् ।
प्राग्ज्योतिषपतिं हत्वा कन्यानां हरणं च यत् ॥३९॥

harasya jṛmbhaṇaṁ yuddhe
bāṇasya bhuja-kṛntanam
prāgjyotiṣa-patiṁ hatvā
kanyānāṁ haraṇaṁ ca yat

harasya—of Lord Śiva; *jṛmbhaṇam*—the forced yawning; *yuddhe*—in battle; *bāṇasya*—of Bāṇa; *bhuja*—of the arms; *kṛntanam*—the cutting; *prāgjyotiṣa-patim*—the master of the city Prāgjyotiṣa; *hatvā*—killing; *kanyānām*—of the unmarried virgins; *haraṇam*—the removal; *ca*—and; *yat*—which.

TRANSLATION

Also narrated are how Lord Kṛṣṇa, in the battle with Bāṇāsura, defeated Lord Śiva by making him yawn, how the Lord cut off

Bāṇāsura's arms and how He killed the master of Prāgjyotiṣapura and then rescued the young princesses held captive in that city.

TEXTS 40–41

चैद्यपौण्ड्रकशाल्वानां दन्तवक्रस्य दुर्मतेः ।
शम्बरो द्विविदः पीठो मुरः पञ्चजनादयः ॥४०॥
माहात्म्यं च वधस्तेषां वाराणस्याश्च दाहनम् ।
भारावतरणं भूमेर्निमित्तीकृत्य पाण्डवान् ॥४१॥

caidya-pauṇḍraka-śālvānāṁ
dantavakrasya durmateḥ
śambaro dvividaḥ pīṭho
muraḥ pañcajanādayaḥ

māhātmyaṁ ca vadhas teṣāṁ
vārāṇasyāś ca dāhanam
bhārāvataraṇaṁ bhūmer
nimittī-kṛtya pāṇḍavān

caidya—of the King of Cedi, Śiśupāla; *pauṇḍraka*—of Pauṇḍraka; *śālvānām*—and of Śālva; *dantavakrasya*—of Dantavakra; *durmateḥ*—the foolish; *śambaraḥ dvividaḥ pīṭhaḥ*—the demons Śambara, Dvivida and Pīṭha; *muraḥ pañcajana-ādayaḥ*—Mura, Pañcajana and others; *māhātmyam*—the prowess; *ca*—and; *vadhaḥ*—the death; *teṣām*—of these; *vārāṇasyāḥ*—of the holy city of Benares; *ca*—and; *dāhanam*—the burning; *bhāra*—of the burden; *avataraṇam*—the reduction; *bhūmeḥ*—of the earth; *nimittī-kṛtya*—making the apparent cause; *pāṇḍavān*—the sons of Pāṇḍu.

TRANSLATION

There are descriptions of the powers and the deaths of the King of Cedi, Pauṇḍraka, Śālva, the foolish Dantavakra, Śambara, Dvivida, Pīṭha, Mura, Pañcajana and other demons, along with a description of how Vārāṇasī was burned to the ground. The *Bhāgavatam* also recounts how Lord Kṛṣṇa relieved the earth's burden by engaging the Pāṇḍavas in the Battle of Kurukṣetra.

TEXTS 42–43

विप्रशापापदेशेन संहारः स्वकुलस्य च ।
उद्धवस्य च संवादो वसुदेवस्य चाद्भुतः ॥४२॥
यत्रात्मविद्या ह्यखिला प्रोक्ता धर्मविनिर्णयः ।
ततो मर्त्यपरित्याग आत्मयोगानुभावतः ॥४३॥

vipra-śāpāpadeśena
saṁhāraḥ sva-kulasya ca
uddhavasya ca saṁvādo
vasudevasya cādbhutaḥ

yatrātma-vidyā hy akhilā
proktā dharma-vinirṇayaḥ
tato martya-parityāga
ātma-yogānubhāvataḥ

vipra-śāpa—of the curse by the *brāhmaṇas; apadeśena*—on the pretext; *saṁhāraḥ*—the withdrawal; *sva-kulasya*—of His own family; *ca*—and; *uddhavasya*—with Uddhava; *ca*—and; *saṁvādaḥ*—the discussion; *vasudevasya*—of Vasudeva (with Nārada); *ca*—and; *adbhutaḥ*—wonderful; *yatra*—in which; *ātma-vidyā*—the science of the self; *hi*—indeed; *akhilā*—completely; *proktā*—was spoken; *dharma-vinirṇayaḥ*—the ascertainment of the principles of religion; *tataḥ*—then; *martya*—of the mortal world; *parityāgaḥ*—the giving up; *ātma-yoga*—of His personal mystic power; *anubhāvataḥ*—on the strength.

TRANSLATION

How the Lord withdrew His own dynasty on the pretext of the *brāhmaṇas'* curse; Vasudeva's conversation with Nārada; the extraordinary conversation between Uddhava and Kṛṣṇa, which reveals the science of the self in complete detail and elucidates the religious principles of human society; and then how Lord Kṛṣṇa gave up this mortal world by His own mystic power—the *Bhāgavatam* narrates all these events.

TEXT 44

युगलक्षणवृत्तिश्च कलौ नृणामुपप्लवः ।
चतुर्विधश्च प्रलय उत्पत्तिस्त्रिविधा तथा ॥४४॥

yuga-lakṣaṇa-vṛttiś ca
kalau nṝṇām upaplavaḥ
catur-vidhaś ca pralaya
utpattis tri-vidhā tathā

yuga—of the different ages; *lakṣaṇa*—the characteristics; *vṛttiḥ*—and the corresponding activities; *ca*—also; *kalau*—in the present age of Kali; *nṝṇām*—of men; *upaplavaḥ*—the total disturbance; *catuḥ-vidhaḥ*—fourfold; *ca*—and; *pralayaḥ*—the process of annihilation; *utpattiḥ*—creation; *tri-vidhā*—of three kinds; *tathā*—and.

TRANSLATION

This work also describes people's characteristics and behavior in the different ages, the chaos men experience in the age of Kali, the four kinds of annihilation and the three kinds of creation.

TEXT 45

देहत्यागश्च राजर्षेर्विष्णुरातस्य धीमतः ।
शाखाप्रणयनमृषेर्मार्कण्डेयस्य सत्कथा ।
महापुरुषविन्यासः सूर्यस्य जगदात्मनः ॥४५॥

deha-tyāgaś ca rājarṣer
viṣṇu-rātasya dhīmataḥ
śākhā-praṇayanam ṛṣer
mārkaṇḍeyasya sat-kathā
mahā-puruṣa-vinyāsaḥ
sūryasya jagad-ātmanaḥ

deha-tyāgaḥ—the relinquishing of his body; *ca*—and; *rāja-ṛṣeḥ*—by the saintly king; *viṣṇu-rātasya*—Parīkṣit; *dhī-mataḥ*—the intelligent; *śākhā*—of the branches of the *Vedas; praṇayanam*—the dissemination; *ṛṣeḥ*—from the great sage Vyāsadeva; *mārkaṇḍeyasya*—of Mārkaṇḍeya Ṛṣi; *sat-kathā*—the pious narration; *mahā-puruṣa*—of the universal form of the Lord; *vinyāsaḥ*—the detailed arrangement; *sūryasya*—of the sun; *jagat-ātmanaḥ*—who is the soul of the universe.

TRANSLATION

There are also an account of the passing away of the wise and saintly King Viṣṇurāta [Parīkṣit], an explanation of how Śrīla Vyāsadeva disseminated the branches of the *Vedas*, a pious narration concerning Mārkaṇḍeya Ṛṣi, and a description of the detailed arrangement of the Lord's universal form and His form as the sun, the soul of the universe.

TEXT 46

इति चोक्तं द्विजश्रेष्ठा यत्पृष्टोऽहमिहास्मि वः ।
लीलावतारकर्माणि कीर्तितानीह सर्वशः ॥४६॥

iti coktaṁ dvija-śreṣṭhā
yat pṛṣṭo 'ham ihāsmi vaḥ
līlāvatāra-karmāṇi
kīrtitānīha sarvaśaḥ

iti—thus; *ca*—and; *uktam*—spoken; *dvija-śreṣṭhāḥ*—O best of the *brāhmaṇas; yat*—what; *pṛṣṭaḥ*—inquired; *aham*—I; *iha*—here; *asmi*—have been; *vaḥ*—by you; *līlā-avatāra*—of the divine descents of the Supreme Lord for His own enjoyment; *karmāṇi*—the activities; *kīrtitāni*—have been glorified; *iha*—in this scripture; *sarvaśaḥ*—completely.

TRANSLATION

Thus, O best of the *brāhmaṇas*, I have explained herein what you have inquired from me. This literature has glorified in full detail the activities of the Lord's pastime incarnations.

TEXT 47

पतितः स्खलितश्चार्तः क्षुत्त्वा वा विवशो गृणन् ।
हरये नम इत्युच्चैर्मुच्यते सर्वपातकात् ॥४७॥

patitaḥ skhalitaś cārtaḥ
kṣuttvā vā vivaśo gṛṇan
haraye nama ity uccair
mucyate sarva-pātakāt

patitaḥ—falling; *skhalitaḥ*—tripping; *ca*—and; *ārtaḥ*—feeling pain; *kṣuttvā*—sneezing; *vā*—or; *vivaśaḥ*—involuntarily; *gṛṇan*—chanting; *haraye namaḥ*—"obeisances to Lord Hari"; *iti*—thus; *uccaiḥ*—loudly; *mucyate*—one is freed; *sarva-pātakāt*—from all sinful reactions.

TRANSLATION

If when falling, slipping, feeling pain or sneezing one involuntarily cries out in a loud voice, "Obeisances to Lord Hari!" one will be automatically freed from all his sinful reactions.

PURPORT

Śrīla Bhaktisiddhānta Sarasvatī Ṭhākura explains that Lord Śrī Caitanya is always loudly chanting the song *haraye namaḥ kṛṣṇa* in the courtyard of Śrīvāsa Ṭhākura and that this same Lord Caitanya will free us from our materialistic enjoying propensity if we also loudly chant the glories of the Supreme Lord Hari.

TEXT 48

संकीर्त्यमानो भगवाननन्तः
श्रुतानुभावो व्यसनं हि पुंसाम् ।
प्रविश्य चित्तं विधुनोत्यशेषं
यथा तमोऽर्कोऽभ्रमिवातिवातः ॥४८॥

saṅkīrtyamāno bhagavān anantaḥ
śrutānubhāvo vyasanaṁ hi puṁsām
praviśya cittaṁ vidhunoty aśeṣaṁ
yathā tamo 'rko 'bhram ivāti-vātaḥ

saṅkīrtyamānaḥ—being properly chanted about; *bhagavān*—the Supreme Personality of Godhead; *anantaḥ*—the unlimited; *śruta*—being heard about; *anubhāvaḥ*—His potency; *vyasanam*—the misery; *hi*—indeed; *puṁsām*—of persons; *praviśya*—enter; *cittam*—the heart; *vidhunoti*—cleans away; *aśeṣam*—entirely; *yathā*—just as; *tamaḥ*—darkness; *arkaḥ*—the sun; *abhram*—clouds; *iva*—as; *ati-vātaḥ*—a strong wind.

TRANSLATION

When people properly glorify the Supreme Personality of Godhead or simply hear about His power, the Lord personally enters their hearts and cleanses away every trace of misfortune, just as the sun removes the darkness or as a powerful wind drives away the clouds.

PURPORT

One may not be satisfied by the example of the sun removing the darkness, since sometimes the darkness in a cave is not removed by the sun. Therefore the example is given of a strong wind that drives away a cover of clouds. It is thus emphatically stated here that the Supreme Lord will remove from the heart of His devotee the darkness of material illusion.

TEXT 49

मृषा गिरस्ता ह्यसतीरसत्कथा
न कथ्यते यद् भगवानधोक्षजः ।
तदेव सत्यं तदु हैव मंगलं
तदेव पुण्यं भगवद्गुणोदयम् ॥४९॥

mṛṣā giras tā hy asatīr asat-kathā
na kathyate yad bhagavān adhokṣajaḥ
tad eva satyaṁ tad u haiva maṅgalaṁ
tad eva puṇyaṁ bhagavad-guṇodayam

mṛṣāḥ—false; *giraḥ*—words; *tāḥ*—they; *hi*—indeed; *asatīḥ*—untrue; *asat-kathāḥ*—useless discussions of that which is not eternal; *na kathyate*—is not discussed; *yat*—wherein; *bhagavān*—the Personality of Godhead; *adhokṣajaḥ*—the transcendental Lord; *tat*—that; *eva*—alone; *satyam*—true; *tat*—that; *u ha*—indeed; *eva*—alone; *maṅgalam*—auspicious; *tat*—that; *eva*—alone; *puṇyam*—pious; *bhagavat-guṇa*—the qualities of the Supreme Personality; *udayam*—which manifests.

TRANSLATION

Words that do not describe the transcendental Personality of Godhead but instead deal with temporary matters are simply false and useless. Only those words that manifest the transcendental qualities of the Supreme Lord are actually truthful, auspicious and pious.

PURPORT

Sooner or later, all material literature and discussion must fail the test of time. On the other hand, the transcendental descriptions of the Supreme Lord can free us from the bondage of illusion and restore us to our eternal status as loving servants of the Lord. Although men who are like animals may criticize the glorification of the Absolute Truth, those who are civilized should go on vigorously propagating the transcendental glories of the Lord.

TEXT 50

तदेव रम्यं रुचिरं नवं नवं
तदेव शश्वन्मनसो महोत्सवम् ।
तदेव शोकार्णवशोषणं नृणां
यदुत्तमःश्लोकयशोऽनुगीयते ॥५०॥

tad eva ramyaṁ ruciraṁ navaṁ navaṁ
tad eva śaśvan manaso mahotsavam
tad eva śokārṇava-śoṣaṇaṁ nṛṇāṁ
yad uttamaḥśloka-yaśo 'nugīyate

tat—that; *eva*—indeed; *ramyam*—attractive; *ruciram*—palatable; *navam navam*—newer and newer; *tat*—that; *eva*—indeed; *śaśvat*—constantly; *manasaḥ*—for the mind; *mahā-utsavam*—a great festival; *tat*—that; *eva*—indeed; *śoka-arṇava*—the ocean of misery; *śoṣaṇam*—that which dries; *nṛṇām*—for all persons; *yat*—in which; *uttamaḥ-śloka*—of the all-famous Supreme Personality of Godhead; *yaśaḥ*—the glories; *anugīyate*—are sung.

TRANSLATION

Those words describing the glories of the all-famous Personality of Godhead are attractive, relishable and ever fresh. Indeed, such words are a perpetual festival for the mind, and they dry up the ocean of misery.

TEXT 51

न यद्वचश्चित्रपदं हरेर्यशो
जगत्पवित्रं प्रगृणीत कर्हिचित् ।
तद् ध्वाङ्क्षतीर्थं न तु हंससेवितं
यत्राच्युतस्तत्र हि साधवोऽमलाः ॥५१॥

na yad vacaś citra-padaṁ harer yaśo
jagat-pavitraṁ pragṛṇīta karhicit
tad dhvāṅkṣa-tīrthaṁ na tu haṁsa-sevitaṁ
yatrācyutas tatra hi sādhavo 'malāḥ

na—not; *yat*—which; *vacaḥ*—vocabulary; *citra-padam*—decorative words; *hareḥ*—of the Lord; *yaśaḥ*—the glories; *jagat*—the universe; *pavitram*—sanctifying; *pragṛṇīta*—describe; *karhicit*—ever; *tat*—that; *dhvāṅkṣa*—of the crows; *tīrtham*—a place of pilgrimage; *na*—not; *tu*—on the other hand; *haṁsa*—by saintly persons situated in knowledge;

sevitam—served; *yatra*—in which; *acyutaḥ*—Lord Acyuta (is described); *tatra*—there; *hi*—alone; *sādhavaḥ*—the saints; *amalāḥ*—who are pure.

TRANSLATION

Those words that do not describe the glories of the Lord, who alone can sanctify the atmosphere of the whole universe, are considered to be like unto a place of pilgrimage for crows, and are never resorted to by those situated in transcendental knowledge. The pure and saintly devotees take interest only in topics glorifying the infallible Supreme Lord.

TEXT 52

तद्वाग्विसर्गो जनताघसम्प्लवो
यस्मिन् प्रतिश्लोकमबद्धवत्यपि ।
नामान्यनन्तस्य यशोऽङ्कितानि यत्
शृण्वन्ति गायन्ति गृणन्ति साधवः ॥५२॥

tad vāg-visargo janatāgha-samplavo
yasmin prati-ślokam abaddhavaty api
nāmāny anantasya yaśo 'ṅkitāni yat
śṛṇvanti gāyanti gṛṇanti sādhavaḥ

tat—that; *vāk*—vocabulary; *visargaḥ*—creation; *janatā*—of the people in general; *agha*—of the sins; *samplavaḥ*—a revolution; *yasmin*—in which; *prati-ślokam*—each and every stanza; *abaddhavati*—is irregularly composed; *api*—although; *nāmāni*—the transcendental names, etc; *anantasya*—of the unlimited Lord; *yaśaḥ*—the glories; *aṅkitāni*—depicted; *yat*—which; *śṛṇvanti*—do hear; *gāyanti*—do sing; *gṛṇanti*—do accept; *sādhavaḥ*—the purified men who are honest.

TRANSLATION

On the other hand, that literature which is full of descriptions of the transcendental glories of the name, fame, forms, pastimes and so on of the unlimited Supreme Lord is a different creation,

full of transcendental words directed toward bringing about a revolution in the impious lives of this world's misdirected civilization. Such transcendental literatures, even though imperfectly composed, are heard, sung and accepted by purified men who are thoroughly honest.

TEXT 53

नैष्कर्म्यमप्यच्युतभाववर्जितं
न शोभते ज्ञानमलं निरञ्जनम् ।
कुतः पुनः शश्वदभद्रमीश्वरे
न ह्यर्पितं कर्म यदप्यनुत्तमम् ॥५३॥

naiṣkarmyam apy acyuta-bhāva-varjitaṁ
na śobhate jñānam alaṁ nirañjanam
kutaḥ punaḥ śaśvad abhadram īśvare
na hy arpitaṁ karma yad apy anuttamam

naiṣkarmyam—self-realization, being freed from the reactions of fruitive work; *api*—although; *acyuta*—of the infallible Lord; *bhāva*—conception; *varjitam*—devoid of; *na*—does not; *śobhate*—look well; *jñānam*—transcendental knowledge; *alam*—actually; *nirañjanam*—free from designations; *kutaḥ*—where is; *punaḥ*—again; *śaśvat*—always; *abhadram*—uncongenial; *īśvare*—unto the Lord; *na*—not; *hi*—indeed; *arpitam*—offered; *karma*—fruitive work; *yat*—which is; *api*—even; *anuttamam*—unsurpassed.

TRANSLATION

Knowledge of self-realization, even though free from all material affinity, does not look well if devoid of a conception of the Infallible [God]. What, then, is the use of even the most properly performed fruitive activities, which are naturally painful from the very beginning and transient by nature, if they are not utilized for the devotional service of the Lord?

PURPORT

This and the previous two verses are found in a slightly different form in the First Canto of *Śrīmad-Bhāgavatam* (1.5.10-12).

TEXT 54

यशःश्रियामेव परिश्रमः परो
वर्णाश्रमाचारतपःश्रुतादिषु ।
अविस्मृतिः श्रीधरपादपद्मयोर्
गुणानुवादश्रवणादरादिभिः ॥५४॥

yaśaḥ-śriyām eva pariśramaḥ paro
varṇāśramācāra-tapaḥ-śrutādiṣu
avismṛtiḥ śrīdhara-pāda-padmayor
guṇānuvāda-śravaṇādarādibhiḥ

yaśaḥ—in fame; *śriyām*—and opulence; *eva*—only; *pariśramaḥ*—the labor; *paraḥ*—great; *varṇa-āśrama-ācāra*—by one's execution of duties in the *varṇāśrama* system; *tapaḥ*—austerities; *śruta*—hearing of sacred scripture; *ādiṣu*—and so on; *avismṛtiḥ*—remembrance; *śrīdhara*—of the maintainer of the goddess of fortune; *pāda-padmayoḥ*—of the lotus feet; *guṇa-anuvāda*—of the chanting of the qualities; *śravaṇa*—by hearing; *ādara*—respecting; *ādibhiḥ*—and so on.

TRANSLATION

The great endeavor one undergoes in executing the ordinary social and religious duties of the *varṇāśrama* system, in performing austerities, and in hearing from the *Vedas* culminates only in the achievement of mundane fame and opulence. But by respecting and attentively hearing the recitation of the transcendental qualities of the Supreme Lord, the husband of the goddess of fortune, one can remember His lotus feet.

TEXT 55

अविस्मृतिः कृष्णपदारविन्दयोः
क्षिणोत्यभद्राणि च शं तनोति ।
सत्त्वस्य शुद्धिं परमात्मभक्तिं
ज्ञानं च विज्ञानविरागयुक्तम् ॥५५॥

avismṛtiḥ kṛṣṇa-padāravindayoḥ
kṣiṇoty abhadrāṇi ca śaṁ tanoti
sattvasya śuddhiṁ paramātma-bhaktiṁ
jñānaṁ ca vijñāna-virāga-yuktam

avismṛtiḥ—remembrance; *kṛṣṇa-pada-aravindayoḥ*—of Lord Kṛṣṇa's lotus feet; *kṣiṇoti*—destroys; *abhadrāṇi*—everything inauspicious; *ca*—and; *śam*—good fortune; *tanoti*—expands; *sattvasya*—of the heart; *śuddhim*—the purification; *parama-ātma*—for the Supreme Soul; *bhaktim*—devotion; *jñānam*—knowledge; *ca*—and; *vijñāna*—with direct realization; *virāga*—and detachment; *yuktam*—endowed.

TRANSLATION

Remembrance of Lord Kṛṣṇa's lotus feet destroys everything inauspicious and awards the greatest good fortune. It purifies the heart and bestows devotion for the Supreme Soul, along with knowledge enriched with realization and renunciation.

TEXT 56

यूयं द्विजाग्र्या बत भूरिभागा
यच्छश्वदात्मन्यखिलात्मभूतम् ।
नारायणं देवमदेवमीशम्
अजस्रभावा भजताविवेश्य ॥५६॥

yūyaṁ dvijāgryā bata bhūri-bhāgā
yac chaśvad ātmany akhilātma-bhūtam

nārāyaṇaṁ devam adevam īśam
ajasra-bhāvā bhajatāviveśya

yūyam—all of you; *dvija-agryāḥ*—O most eminent of *brāhmaṇas; bata*—indeed; *bhūri-bhāgāḥ*—extremely fortunate; *yat*—because; *śaśvat*—constantly; *ātmani*—in your hearts; *akhila*—of all; *ātma-bhūtam*—who is the ultimate Soul; *nārāyaṇam*—Lord Nārāyaṇa; *devam*—the Personality of Godhead; *adevam*—beyond whom there is no other god; *īśam*—the supreme controller; *ajasra*—without interruption; *bhāvāḥ*—having love; *bhajata*—you should worship; *āviveśya*—placing Him.

TRANSLATION

O most eminent of *brāhmaṇas,* you are all indeed extremely fortunate, since you have already placed within your hearts Lord Śrī Nārāyaṇa—the Personality of Godhead, the supreme controller and the ultimate Soul of all existence—beyond whom there is no other god. You have undeviating love for Him, and thus I request you to worship Him.

TEXT 57

अहं च संस्मारित आत्मतत्त्वं
श्रुतं पुरा मे परमर्षिवक्त्रात् ।
प्रायोपवेशे नृपतेः परीक्षितः
सदस्यृषीणां महतां च शृण्वताम् ॥५७॥

ahaṁ ca saṁsmārita ātma-tattvaṁ
śrutaṁ purā me paramarṣi-vaktrāt
prāyopaveśe nṛpateḥ parīkṣitaḥ
sadasy ṛṣīṇāṁ mahatāṁ ca śṛṇvatām

aham—I; *ca*—also; *saṁsmāritaḥ*—have been made to remember; *ātma-tattvam*—the science of the Supersoul; *śrutam*—heard; *purā*—previously; *me*—by me; *parama-ṛṣi*—of the greatest of sages, Śukadeva; *vaktrāt*—from the mouth; *prāya-upaveśe*—during the fast to death; *nṛpateḥ*—of the king; *parīkṣitaḥ*—Parīkṣit; *sadasi*—in the assembly; *ṛṣīṇām*—of sages; *mahatām*—great; *ca*—and; *śṛṇvatām*—while they were listening.

TRANSLATION

I also have now been fully reminded of the science of God, which I previously heard from the mouth of the great sage Śukadeva Gosvāmī. I was present in the assembly of great sages who heard him speak to King Parīkṣit as the monarch sat fasting until death.

TEXT 58

एतद्वः कथितं विप्राः कथनीयोरुकर्मणः ।
माहात्म्यं वासुदेवस्य सर्वाशुभविनाशनम् ॥५८॥

etad vaḥ kathitaṁ viprāḥ
kathanīyoru-karmaṇaḥ
māhātmyaṁ vāsudevasya
sarvāśubha-vināśanam

etat—this; *vaḥ*—to you; *kathitam*—narrated; *viprāḥ*—O *brāhmaṇas; kathanīya*—of Him who is most worthy of being described; *uru-karmaṇaḥ*—and whose activities are very great; *māhātmyam*—the glories; *vāsudevasya*—of Lord Vāsudeva; *sarva-aśubha*—all inauspiciousness; *vināśanam*—which completely destroys.

TRANSLATION

O *brāhmaṇas,* I have thus described to you the glories of the Supreme Lord Vāsudeva, whose extraordinary activities are most worthy of glorification. This narration destroys all that is inauspicious.

TEXT 59

य एतत् श्रावयेन्नित्यं यामक्षणमनन्यधीः ।
श्लोकमेकं तदर्धं वा पादं पादार्धमेव वा ।
श्रद्धावान् योऽनुशृणुयात् पुनात्यात्मानमेव सः ॥५९॥

ya etat śrāvayen nityaṁ
yāma-kṣaṇam ananya-dhīḥ

ślokam ekaṁ tad-ardhaṁ vā
pādaṁ pādārdham eva vā
śraddhāvān yo 'nuśṛṇuyāt
punāty ātmānam eva saḥ

yaḥ—who; *etat*—this; *śrāvayet*—makes others hear; *nityam*—always; *yāma-kṣaṇam*—every hour and every minute; *ananya-dhīḥ*—with undeviated attention; *ślokam*—verse; *ekam*—one; *tat-ardham*—half of that; *vā*—or; *pādam*—a single line; *pāda-ardham*—half a line; *eva*—indeed; *vā*—or; *śraddhā-vān*—with faith; *yaḥ*—who; *anuśṛṇuyāt*—hears from the proper source; *punāti*—purifies; *ātmānam*—his very self; *eva*—indeed; *saḥ*—he.

TRANSLATION

One who with undeviating attention constantly recites this literature at every moment of every hour, as well as one who faithfully hears even one verse or half a verse or a single line or even half a line, certainly purifies his very self.

TEXT 60

द्वादश्यामेकादश्यां वा शृण्वन्नायुष्यवान् भवेत् ।
पठत्यनश्नन् प्रयतस्पूतो भवति पातकात् ॥६०॥

dvādaśyām ekādaśyāṁ vā
śṛṇvann āyuṣyavān bhavet
paṭhaty anaśnan prayataḥ
pūto bhavati pātakāt

dvādaśyām—on the twelfth day of either fortnight of the month; *ekādaśyām*—on the auspicious eleventh day; *vā*—or; *śṛṇvan*—hearing; *āyuṣya-vān*—possessed of long life; *bhavet*—one becomes; *paṭhati*—if one recites; *anaśnan*—while refraining from eating; *prayataḥ*—with careful attention; *pūtaḥ*—purified; *bhavati*—one becomes; *pātakāt*—from sinful reactions.

TRANSLATION

One who hears this *Bhāgavatam* on the Ekādaśī or Dvādaśī day is assured of long life, and one who recites it with careful attention while fasting is purified of all sinful reactions.

TEXT 61

पुष्करे मथुरायां च द्वारवत्यां यतात्मवान् ।
उपोष्य संहितामेतां पठित्वा मुच्यते भयात् ॥६१॥

puṣkare mathurāyāṁ ca
dvāravatyāṁ yatātmavān
upoṣya saṁhitām etāṁ
paṭhitvā mucyate bhayāt

puṣkare—at the holy place Puṣkara; *mathurāyām*—at Mathurā; *ca*—and; *dvāravatyām*—at Dvārakā; *yata-ātma-vān*—self-controlled; *upoṣya*—fasting; *saṁhitām*—literature; *etām*—this; *paṭhitvā*—reciting; *mucyate*—one becomes freed; *bhayāt*—from fear.

TRANSLATION

One who controls his mind, fasts at the holy places Puṣkara, Mathurā or Dvārakā, and studies this scripture will be freed from all fear.

TEXT 62

देवता मुनयः सिद्धाः पितरो मनवो नृपाः ।
यच्छन्ति कामान् गृणतः शृण्वतो यस्य कीर्तनात् ॥६२॥

devatā munayaḥ siddhāḥ
pitaro manavo nṛpāḥ
yacchanti kāmān gṛṇataḥ
śṛṇvato yasya kīrtanāt

devatāḥ—the demigods; *munayaḥ*—the sages; *siddhāḥ*—the perfected *yogīs; pitaraḥ*—the forefathers; *manavaḥ*—the progenitors of mankind;

nṛpāḥ—the kings of the earth; *yacchanti*—bestow; *kāmān*—desires; *gṛṇataḥ*—to one who is chanting; *śṛṇvataḥ*—or who is hearing; *yasya*—of which; *kīrtanāt*—because of the glorification.

TRANSLATION

Upon the person who glorifies this *Purāṇa* by chanting or hearing it, the demigods, sages, Siddhas, Pitās, Manus and kings of the earth bestow all desirable things.

TEXT 63

ऋचो यजूंषि सामानि द्विजोऽधीत्यानुविन्दते ।
मधुकुल्या घृतकुल्याः पयःकुल्याश्च तत्फलम् ॥६३॥

ṛco yajūṁṣi sāmāni
dvijo 'dhītyānuvindate
madhu-kulyā ghṛta-kulyāḥ
payaḥ-kulyāś ca tat phalam

ṛcaḥ—the *mantras* of the *Ṛg Veda; yajūṁṣi*—those of the *Yajur Veda; sāmāni*—and those of the *Sāma Veda; dvijaḥ*—a *brāhmaṇa; adhītya*—studying; *anuvindate*—obtains; *madhu-kulyāḥ*—rivers of honey; *ghṛta-kulyāḥ*—rivers of ghee; *payaḥ-kulyāḥ*—rivers of milk; *ca*—and; *tat*—that; *phalam*—fruit.

TRANSLATION

By studying this *Bhāgavatam*, a *brāhmaṇa* can enjoy the same rivers of honey, ghee and milk he enjoys by studying the hymns of the *Ṛg*, *Yajur* and *Sāma Vedas*.

TEXT 64

पुराणसंहितामेतामधीत्य प्रयतो द्विजः ।
प्रोक्तं भगवता यत्तु तत्पदं परमं व्रजेत् ॥६४॥

purāṇa-saṁhitām etām
adhītya prayato dvijaḥ
proktaṁ bhagavatā yat tu
tat padaṁ paramaṁ vrajet

purāṇa-saṁhitām—essential compilation of all the *Purāṇas; etām*—this; *adhītya*—studying; *prayataḥ*—carefully; *dvijaḥ*—a *brāhmaṇa; proktam*—described; *bhagavatā*—by the Personality of Godhead; *yat*—which; *tu*—indeed; *tat*—that; *padam*—position; *paramam*—supreme; *vrajet*—he attains.

TRANSLATION

A *brāhmaṇa* who diligently reads this essential compilation of all the *Purāṇas* will go to the supreme destination, which the Supreme Lord Himself has herein described.

TEXT 65

विप्रोऽधीत्याप्नुयात्प्रज्ञां राजन्योदधिमेखलाम् ।
वैश्यो निधिपतित्वं च शूद्रः शुध्येत पातकात् ॥६५॥

vipro 'dhītyāpnuyāt prajñāṁ
rājanyodadhi-mekhalām
vaiśyo nidhi-patitvaṁ ca
śūdraḥ śudhyeta pātakāt

vipraḥ—a *brāhmaṇa; adhītya*—studying; *āpnuyāt*—achieves; *prajñām*—intelligence in devotional service; *rājanya*—a king; *udadhi-mekhalām*—(the earth) bounded by the seas; *vaiśyaḥ*—a businessman; *nidhi*—of treasures; *patitvam*—lordship; *ca*—and; *śūdraḥ*—a worker; *śudhyeta*—becomes purified; *pātakāt*—from sinful reactions.

TRANSLATION

A *brāhmaṇa* who studies the *Śrīmad-Bhāgavatam* achieves firm intelligence in devotional service, a king who studies it gains sovereignty over the earth, a *vaiśya* acquires great treasure and a *śūdra* is freed from sinful reactions.

TEXT 66

कलिमलसंहतिकालनोऽखिलेशो
हरिरितरत्र न गीयते ह्यभीक्ष्णम् ।
इह तु पुनर्भगवानशेषमूर्तिः
परिपठितोऽनुपदं कथाप्रसंगैः ॥६६॥

kali-mala-saṁhati-kālano 'khileśo
harir itaratra na gīyate hy abhīkṣṇam
iha tu punar bhagavān aśeṣa-mūrtiḥ
paripaṭhito 'nu-padaṁ kathā-prasaṅgaiḥ

kali—of the age of quarrel; *mala-saṁhati*—of all the contamination; *kālanaḥ*—the annihilator; *akhila-īśaḥ*—the supreme controller of all beings; *hariḥ*—Lord Hari; *itaratra*—elsewhere; *na gīyate*—is not described; *hi*—indeed; *abhīkṣṇam*—constantly; *iha*—here; *tu*—however; *punaḥ*—on the other hand; *bhagavān*—the Personality of Godhead; *aśeṣa-mūrtiḥ*—who expands in unlimited personal forms; *paripaṭhitaḥ*—is openly described in narration; *anu-padam*—in each and every verse; *kathā-prasaṅgaiḥ*—on the pretext of stories.

TRANSLATION

Lord Hari, the supreme controller of all beings, annihilates the accumulated sins of the Kali age, yet other literatures do not constantly glorify Him. But that Supreme Personality of Godhead, appearing in His innumerable personal expansions, is abundantly and constantly described throughout the various narrations of this *Śrīmad-Bhāgavatam.*

TEXT 67

तमहमजमनन्तमात्मतत्त्वं
जगदुदयस्थितिसंयमात्मशक्तिम् ।
द्युपतिभिरजशक्रशंकराद्यैर्
दुरवसितस्तवमच्युतं नतोऽस्मि ॥६७॥

tam aham ajam anantam ātma-tattvaṁ
jagad-udaya-sthiti-saṁyamātma-śaktim
dyu-patibhir aja-śakra-śaṅkarādyair
duravasita-stavam acyutaṁ nato 'smi

tam—to Him; *aham*—I; *ajam*—to the unborn; *anantam*—the unlimited; *ātma-tattvam*—the original Supersoul; *jagat*—of the material universe; *udaya*—the creation; *sthiti*—maintenance; *saṁyama*—and destruction; *ātma-śaktim*—by whose personal energies; *dyu-patibhiḥ*—by the masters of heaven; *aja-śakra-śaṅkara-ādyaiḥ*—headed by Brahmā, Indra and Śiva; *duravasita*—incomprehensible; *stavam*—whose praises; *acyutam*—to the infallible Supreme Lord; *nataḥ*—bowed down; *asmi*—I am.

TRANSLATION

I bow down to that unborn and infinite Supreme Soul, whose personal energies effect the creation, maintenance and destruction of the material universe. Even Brahmā, Indra, Śaṅkara and the other lords of the heavenly planets cannot fathom the glories of that infallible Personality of Godhead.

TEXT 68

उपचितनवशक्तिभिः स्व आत्मन्य्
उपरचितस्थिरजंगमालयाय ।
भगवत उपलब्धिमात्रधाम्ने
सुरऋषभाय नमः सनातनाय ॥६८॥

upacita-nava-śaktibhiḥ sva ātmany
uparacita-sthira-jaṅgamālayāya
bhagavata upalabdhi-mātra-dhāmne
sura-ṛṣabhāya namaḥ sanātanāya

upacita—fully developed; *nava-śaktibhiḥ*—by His nine energies (*prakṛti, puruṣa, mahat,* false ego and the five subtle forms of perception); *sve ātmani*—within Himself; *uparacita*—arranged in proximity; *sthira-*

jaṅgama—of both the nonmoving and the moving living beings; *ālayāya*—the abode; *bhagavate*—to the Supreme Personality of Godhead; *upalabhdhi-mātra*—pure consciousness; *dhāmne*—whose manifestation; *sura*—of deities; *ṛṣabhāya*—the chief; *namaḥ*—my obeisances; *sanātanāya*—to the eternal Lord.

TRANSLATION

I offer my obeisances to the Supreme Personality of Godhead, who is the eternal Lord and the leader of all other deities, who by evolving His nine material energies has arranged within Himself the abode of all moving and nonmoving creatures, and who is always situated in pure, transcendental consciousness.

TEXT 69

स्वसुखनिभृतचेतास्तद्व्युदस्तान्यभावो
ऽप्यजितरुचिरलीलाकृष्टसारस्तदीयम् ।
व्यतनुत कृपया यस्तत्त्वदीपं पुराणं
तमखिलवृजिनघ्नं व्याससूनुं नतोऽस्मि ॥६९॥

sva-sukha-nibhṛta-cetās tad-vyudastānya-bhāvo
'py ajita-rucira-līlākṛṣṭa-sāras tadīyam
vyatanuta kṛpayā yas tattva-dīpaṁ purāṇaṁ
tam akhila-vṛjina-ghnaṁ vyāsa-sūnuṁ nato 'smi

sva-sukha—in the happiness of the self; *nibhṛta*—solitary; *cetāḥ*—whose consciousness; *tat*—because of that; *vyudasta*—given up; *anya-bhāvaḥ*—any other type of consciousness; *api*—although; *ajita*—of Śrī Kṛṣṇa, the unconquerable Lord; *rucira*—pleasing; *līlā*—by the pastimes; *ākṛṣṭa*—attracted; *sāraḥ*—whose heart; *tadīyam*—consisting of the activities of the Lord; *vyatanuta*—spread, manifested; *kṛpayā*—mercifully; *yaḥ*—who; *tattva-dīpam*—the bright light of the Absolute Truth; *purāṇam*—the *Purāṇa* (*Śrīmad-Bhāgavatam*); *tam*—unto Him; *akhila-vṛjina-ghnam*—defeating everything inauspicious; *vyāsa-sūnum*—son of Vyāsadeva; *nataḥ asmi*—I offer my obeisances.

TRANSLATION

Let me offer my respectful obeisances unto my spiritual master, the son of Vyāsadeva, Śukadeva Gosvāmī. It is he who defeats all inauspicious things within this universe. Although in the beginning he was absorbed in the happiness of Brahman realization and was living in a secluded place, giving up all other types of consciousness, he became attracted by the pleasing, most melodious pastimes of Lord Śrī Kṛṣṇa. He therefore mercifully spoke this supreme *Purāṇa, Śrīmad-Bhāgavatam,* which is the bright light of the Absolute Truth and which describes the activities of the Lord.

PURPORT

Without offering respectful obeisances to Śukadeva Gosvāmī and other great *ācāryas* in his line, one cannot possibly gain the privilege of entering into the deep transcendental meaning of *Śrīmad-Bhāgavatam.*

Thus end the purports of the humble servant of His Divine Grace A. C. Bhaktivedanta Swami Prabhupāda to the Twelfth Canto, Twelfth Chapter, of the Śrīmad-Bhāgavatam, *entitled "The Topics of* Śrīmad-Bhāgavatam *Summarized."*

CHAPTER THIRTEEN

The Glories of Śrīmad-Bhāgavatam

In this final chapter Śrī Sūta Gosvāmī describes the length of each of the *Purāṇas,* along with the subject matter of *Śrīmad-Bhāgavatam,* its purpose, how to give it as a gift, the glories of such gift-giving and the glories of chanting and hearing it.

The total corpus of the *Purāṇas* includes four hundred thousand verses, eighteen thousand of which constitute *Śrīmad-Bhāgavatam.* The Supreme Personality of Godhead, Nārāyaṇa, instructed Brahmā in this *Śrīmad-Bhāgavatam,* whose narrations produce detachment from matter and which contains the essence of all the *Vedānta.* One who gives the *Śrīmad-Bhāgavata Purāṇa* as a gift will attain the highest destination. Among all the *Purāṇas, Śrīmad-Bhāgavatam* is the best, and it is the most dear thing to the Vaiṣṇavas. It reveals that spotless, supreme knowledge accessible to the *paramahaṁsas,* and it also reveals the process by which one can become free from the reactions of material work—a process enriched with knowledge, renunciation and devotion.

Having thus glorified the *Bhāgavatam,* Sūta Gosvāmī meditates upon Lord Śrī Nārāyaṇa as the original Absolute Truth, who is perfectly pure, free from all contamination, devoid of sorrow and immortal. Then he offers obeisances to the greatest *yogī,* Śrī Śukadeva, who is nondifferent from the Absolute Truth. Finally, praying with true devotion, Sūta Gosvāmī offers respects to the Supreme Personality of Godhead, Lord Śrī Hari, who takes away all misery.

TEXT 1

सूत उवाच
यं ब्रह्मा वरुणेन्द्ररुद्रमरुतः स्तुन्वन्ति दिव्यैः स्तवैर्
वेदैः सांगपदक्रमोपनिषदैर्गायन्ति यं सामगाः ।
ध्यानावस्थिततद्गतेन मनसा पश्यन्ति यं योगिनो
यस्यान्तं न विदुः सुरासुरगणा देवाय तस्मै नमः ॥१॥

sūta uvāca
yaṁ brahmā varuṇendra-rudra-marutaḥ stunvanti divyaiḥ stavair
vedaiḥ sāṅga-pada-kramopaniṣadair gāyanti yaṁ sāma-gāḥ
dhyānāvasthita-tad-gatena manasā paśyanti yaṁ yogino
yasyāntaṁ na viduḥ surāsura-gaṇā devāya tasmai namaḥ

sūtaḥ uvāca—Sūta Gosvāmī said; *yam*—whom; *brahmā*—Lord Brahmā; *varuṇa-indra-rudra-marutaḥ*—as well as Varuṇa, Indra, Rudra and the Maruts; *stunvanti*—praise; *divyaiḥ*—with transcendental; *stavaiḥ*—prayers; *vedaiḥ*—with the *Vedas; sa*—along with; *aṅga*—the corollary branches; *pada-krama*—the special sequential arrangement of *mantras; upaniṣadaiḥ*—and the *Upaniṣads; gāyanti*—they sing about; *yam*—whom; *sāma-gāḥ*—the singers of the *Sāma Veda; dhyāna*—in meditative trance; *avasthita*—situated; *tat-gatena*—which is fixed upon Him; *manasā*—within the mind; *paśyanti*—they see; *yam*—whom; *yoginaḥ*—the mystic *yogīs; yasya*—whose; *antam*—end; *na viduḥ*—they do not know; *sura-asura-gaṇāḥ*—all the demigods and demons; *devāya*—to the Supreme Personality of Godhead; *tasmai*—to Him; *namaḥ*—obeisances.

TRANSLATION

Sūta Gosvāmī said: Unto that personality whom Brahmā, Varuṇa, Indra, Rudra and the Maruts praise by chanting transcendental hymns and reciting the *Vedas* with all their corollaries, *pada-kramas* and Upaniṣads, to whom the chanters of the *Sāma Veda* always sing, whom the perfected *yogīs* see within their minds after fixing themselves in trance and absorbing themselves within Him, and whose limit can never be found by any demigod or demon—unto that Supreme Personality of Godhead I offer my humble obeisances.

TEXT 2

पृष्ठे भ्राम्यदमन्दमन्दरगिरिग्रावाग्रकण्डूयनान्
निद्रालोः कमठाकृतेर्भगवतः श्वासानिलाः पान्तु वः ।
यत्संस्कारकलानुवर्तनवशाद् वेलानिभेनाम्भसां
यातायातमतन्द्रितं जलनिधेर्नाद्यापि विश्राम्यति ॥२॥

pṛṣṭhe bhrāmyad amanda-mandara-giri-grāvāgra-kaṇḍūyanān
nidrāloḥ kamaṭhākṛter bhagavataḥ śvāsānilāḥ pāntu vaḥ
yat-saṁskāra-kalānuvartana-vaśād velā-nibhenāmbhasāṁ
yātāyātam atandritaṁ jala-nidher nādyāpi viśrāmyati

pṛṣṭhe—upon His back; *bhrāmyat*—rotating; *amanda*—most heavy; *mandara-giri*—of Mandara Mountain; *grāva-agra*—by the edges of the stones; *kaṇḍūyanāt*—by the scratching; *nidrāloḥ*—who became sleepy; *kamaṭha-ākṛteḥ*—in the form of a tortoise; *bhagavataḥ*—of the Supreme Personality of Godhead; *śvāsa*—coming from the breathing; *anilāḥ*—the winds; *pāntu*—may they protect; *vaḥ*—all of you; *yat*—of which; *saṁskāra*—of the remnants; *kalā*—the traces; *anuvartana-vaśāt*—as the effect of following; *velā-nibhena*—by that which resembles the flow; *ambhasām*—of the water; *yāta-āyātam*—the coming and going; *atandritam*—ceaseless; *jala-nidheḥ*—of the ocean; *na*—does not; *adya api*—even today; *viśrāmyati*—stop.

TRANSLATION

When the Supreme Personality of Godhead appeared as Lord Kūrma, a tortoise, His back was scratched by the sharp-edged stones lying on massive, whirling Mount Mandara, and this scratching made the Lord sleepy. May you all be protected by the winds caused by the Lord's breathing in this sleepy condition. Ever since that time, even up to the present day, the ocean tides have imitated the Lord's inhalation and exhalation by piously coming in and going out.

PURPORT

At times we alleviate an itching sensation by blowing upon it. Similarly, Śrīla Bhaktisiddhānta Sarasvatī Ṭhākura explains, the breathing of the Supreme Personality of Godhead can alleviate the itching sensation within the minds of mental speculators, as well as the itching of the material senses of conditioned souls engaged in sense gratification. Thus by meditating on the windy breath of Lord Kūrma—the tortoise incarnation—all categories of conditioned souls can be relieved of the deficiencies of material existence and come to the liberated, spiritual platform. One must simply allow the pastimes of Lord Kūrma to blow within one's heart like a favorable breeze; then one will surely find spiritual peace.

TEXT 3

पुराणसंख्यासम्भूतिमस्य वाच्यप्रयोजने ।
दानं दानस्य माहात्म्यं पाठादेश्च निबोधत ॥३॥

purāṇa-saṅkhyā-sambhūtim
asya vācya-prayojane
dānaṁ dānasya māhātmyaṁ
pāṭhādeś ca nibodhata

purāṇa—of the *Purāṇas; saṅkhyā*—of the counting (of verses); *sambhūtim*—the summation; *asya*—of this *Bhāgavatam; vācya*—the subject matter; *prayojane*—and the purpose; *dānam*—the method of giving as a gift; *dānasya*—of such gift-giving; *māhātmyam*—the glories; *pāṭha-ādeḥ*—of teaching and so on; *ca*—and; *nibodhata*—please hear.

TRANSLATION

Now please hear a summation of the verse length of each of the *Purāṇas.* Then hear of the prime subject and purpose of this *Bhāgavata Purāṇa,* the proper method of giving it as a gift, the glories of such gift-giving, and finally the glories of hearing and chanting this literature.

PURPORT

Śrīmad-Bhāgavatam is the best of all *Purāṇas.* Śrīla Viśvanātha Cakravartī Ṭhākura explains that the other *Purāṇas* will now be mentioned just as the assistants of a king are mentioned in connection with his glorification.

TEXTS 4–9

ब्राह्मं दश सहस्राणि पाद्मं पञ्चोनषष्टि च ।
श्रीवैष्णवं त्रयोविंशच्चतुर्विंशति शैवकम् ॥४॥
दशाष्टौ श्रीभागवतं नारदं पञ्चविंशति ।
मार्कण्डं नव वाह्नं च दशपञ्च चतुःशतम् ॥५॥

चतुर्दश भविष्यं स्यात्तथा पञ्चशतानि च ।
दशाष्टौ ब्रह्मवैवर्तं लैंगमेकादशैव तु ॥६॥
चतुर्विंशति वाराहमेकाशीतिसहस्रकम् ।
स्कान्दं शतं तथा चैकं वामनं दश कीर्तितम् ॥७॥
कौर्मं सप्तदशाख्यातं मात्स्यं तत्तु चतुर्दश ।
एकोनविंशत्सौपर्णं ब्रह्माण्डं द्वादशैव तु ॥८॥
एवं पुराणसन्दोहश्चतुर्लक्ष उदाहृतः ।
तत्राष्टदशसाहस्रं श्रीभागवतमिष्यते ॥९॥

brāhmaṁ daśa sahasrāṇi
pādmaṁ pañcona-ṣaṣṭi ca
śrī-vaiṣṇavaṁ trayo-viṁśac
catur-viṁśati śaivakam

daśāṣṭau śrī-bhāgavataṁ
nāradaṁ pañca-viṁśati
mārkaṇḍaṁ nava vāhnaṁ ca
daśa-pañca catuḥ-śatam

catur-daśa bhaviṣyaṁ syāt
tathā pañca-śatāni ca
daśāṣṭau brahma-vaivartaṁ
laiṅgam ekādaśaiva tu

catur-viṁśati vārāham
ekāśīti-sahasrakam
skāndaṁ śataṁ tathā caikaṁ
vāmanaṁ daśa kīrtitam

kaurmaṁ sapta-daśākhyātaṁ
mātsyaṁ tat tu catur-daśa
ekona-viṁśat sauparṇaṁ
brahmāṇḍaṁ dvādaśaiva tu

evaṁ purāṇa-sandohaś
catur-lakṣa udāhṛtaḥ
tatrāṣṭadaśa-sāhasraṁ
śrī-bhāgavatam iṣyate

brāhmam—the *Brahmā Purāṇa; daśa*—ten; *sahasrāṇi*—thousands; *pādmam*—the *Padma Purāṇa; pañca-ūna-ṣaṣṭi*—five less than sixty; *ca*—and; *śrī-vaiṣṇavam*—the *Viṣṇu Purāṇa; trayaḥ-viṁśat*—twenty-three; *catuḥ-viṁśati*—twenty-four; *śaivakam*—the *Śiva Purāṇa; daśa-aṣṭau*—eighteen; *śrī-bhāgavatam*—*Śrīmad-Bhāgavatam; nāradam*—the *Nārada Purāṇa; pañca-viṁśati*—twenty-five; *mārkaṇḍam*—the *Mārkaṇḍeya Purāṇa; nava*—nine; *vāhnam*—the *Agni Purāṇa; ca*—and; *daśa-pañca-catuḥ-śatam*—fifteen thousand four hundred; *catuḥ-daśa*—fourteen; *bhaviṣyam*—the *Bhaviṣya Purāṇa; syāt*—consists of; *tathā*—plus; *pañca-śatāni*—five hundred (verses); *ca*—and; *daśa-aṣṭau*—eighteen; *brahma-vaivartam*—the *Brahma-vaivarta Purāṇa; laiṅgam*—the *Liṅga Purāṇa; ekādaśa*—eleven; *eva*—indeed; *tu*—and; *catuḥ-viṁśati*—twenty-four; *vārāham*—the *Varāha Purāṇa; ekāśīti-sahasrakam*—eighty-one thousand; *skāndam*—the *Skanda Purāṇa; śatam*—hundred; *tathā*—plus; *ca*—and; *ekam*—one; *vāmanam*—the *Vāmana Purāṇa; daśa*—ten; *kīrtitam*—is described; *kaurmam*—the *Kūrma Purāṇa; sapta-daśa*—seventeen; *ākhyātam*—is said; *mātsyam*—the *Matsya Purāṇa; tat*—that; *tu*—and; *catuḥ-daśa*—fourteen; *eka-ūna-viṁśat*—nineteen; *sauparṇam*—the *Garuḍa Purāṇa; brahmāṇḍam*—the *Brahmāṇḍa Purāṇa; dvādaśa*—twelve; *eva*—indeed; *tu*—and; *evam*—in this way; *purāṇa*—of the *Purāṇas; sandohaḥ*—the sum; *catuḥ-lakṣaḥ*—four hundred thousand; *udāhṛtaḥ*—is described; *tatra*—therein; *aṣṭa-daśa-sāhasram*—eighteen thousand; *śrī-bhāgavatam*—*Śrīmad-Bhāgavatam; iṣyate*—is said.

TRANSLATION

The *Brahmā Purāṇa* consists of ten thousand verses, the *Padma Purāṇa* of fifty-five thousand, *Śrī Viṣṇu Purāṇa* of twenty-three thousand, the *Śiva Purāṇa* of twenty-four thousand and *Śrīmad-Bhāgavatam* of eighteen thousand. The *Nārada Purāṇa* has twenty-five thousand verses, the *Mārkaṇḍeya Purāṇa* nine thousand, the *Agni Purāṇa* fifteen thousand four hundred, the

***Bhaviṣya Purāṇa* fourteen thousand five hundred, the *Brahmavaivarta Purāṇa* eighteen thousand and the *Liṅga Purāṇa* eleven thousand. The *Varāha Purāṇa* contains twenty-four thousand verses, the *Skanda Purāṇa* eighty-one thousand one hundred, the *Vāmana Purāṇa* ten thousand, the *Kūrma Purāṇa* seventeen thousand, the *Matsya Purāṇa* fourteen thousand, the *Garuḍa Purāṇa* nineteen thousand and the *Brahmāṇḍa Purāṇa* twelve thousand. Thus the total number of verses in all the *Purāṇas* is four hundred thousand. Eighteen thousand of these, once again, belong to the beautiful *Bhāgavatam*.**

PURPORT

Śrīla Jīva Gosvāmī has quoted from the *Matsya Purāṇa* as follows:

aṣṭādaśa purāṇāni
kṛtvā satyavatī-sutaḥ
bhāratākhyānam akhilaṁ
cakre tad-upabṛṁhitam

lakṣaṇaikena tat proktaṁ
vedārtha-paribṛṁhitam
vālmīkināpi yat proktaṁ
rāmopakhyānam uttamam

brahmaṇābhihitaṁ tac ca
śata-koṭi-pravistarāt
āhṛtya nāradenaiva
vālmīkāya punaḥ punaḥ

vālmīkinā ca lokeṣu
dharma-kāmārtha-sādhanam
evaṁ sa-pādāḥ pañcaite
lakṣās teṣu prakīrtitāḥ

"After compiling the eighteen *Purāṇas*, Vyāsadeva, the son of Satyavatī, composed the entire *Mahābhārata*, which contains the essence of all the *Purāṇas*. It consists of over one hundred thousand verses and is filled with all the ideas of the *Vedas*. There is also the account of the pastimes of Lord Rāmacandra, spoken by Vālmīki—an account originally related by Lord Brahmā in one billion verses. That *Rāmāyaṇa* was later summarized by Nārada and related to Vālmīki, who further presented it to mankind so that human beings could attain the goals of religiosity, sense gratification and economic development. The total number of verses in all the *Purāṇas* and *itihāsas* (histories) is thus known in human society to amount to 525,000."

Śrīla Viśvanātha Cakravartī Ṭhākura points out that in the First Canto, Third Chapter, of this work, after Sūta Gosvāmī lists the incarnations of Godhead, he adds the special phrase *kṛṣṇas tu bhagavān svayam:* "But Kṛṣṇa is the original Personality of Godhead." Similarly, after mentioning all of the *Purāṇas*, Śrī Sūta Gosvāmī again mentions the *Śrīmad-Bhāgavatam* to emphasize that it is the chief of all Purāṇic literatures.

TEXT 10

इदं भगवता पूर्वं ब्रह्मणे नाभिपंकजे ।
स्थिताय भवभीताय कारुण्यात्सम्प्रकाशितम् ॥१०॥

idaṁ bhagavatā pūrvaṁ
brahmaṇe nābhi-paṅkaje
sthitāya bhava-bhītāya
kāruṇyāt samprakāśitam

idam—this; *bhagavatā*—by the Supreme Personality of Godhead; *pūrvam*—first; *brahmaṇe*—to Brahmā; *nābhi-paṅkaje*—upon the lotus growing from the navel; *sthitāya*—who was situated; *bhava*—of material existence; *bhītāya*—who was fearful; *kāruṇyāt*—out of mercy; *samprakāśitam*—was fully revealed.

TRANSLATION

It was to Lord Brahmā that the Supreme Personality of Godhead first revealed the *Śrīmad-Bhāgavatam* in full. At the time, Brahmā, frightened by material existence, was sitting on the lotus flower that had grown from the Lord's navel.

PURPORT

Lord Kṛṣṇa enlightened Brahmā with the knowledge of *Śrīmad-Bhāgavatam* before the creation of this universe, as indicated here by the word *pūrvam*. Also, the first verse of the *Bhāgavatam* states, *tene brahma hṛdā ya ādi-kavaye:* "Lord Kṛṣṇa expanded perfect knowledge into the heart of Lord Brahmā." Because conditioned souls can experience only temporary objects, which are created, maintained and destroyed, they cannot readily understand that *Śrīmad-Bhāgavatam* is an eternal, transcendental literature nondifferent from the Absolute Truth.

As stated in the *Muṇḍaka Upaniṣad* (1.1.1):

brahmā devānāṁ prathamaḥ sambabhūva
viśvasya kartā bhuvanasya goptā
sa brahma-vidyāṁ sarva-vidyā-pratiṣṭhām
atharvāya jyeṣṭha-putrāya prāha

"Among all the demigods, Brahmā was the first to take birth. He is the creator of this universe and also its protector. To his eldest son, Atharvā, He instructed the spiritual science of the self, which is the basis of all other branches of knowledge." Despite his exalted position, however, Brahmā still fears the influence of the Lord's illusory potency. Thus this energy seems virtually insurmountable. But Lord Caitanya is so kind that during His missionary activities in eastern and southern India, He freely distributed Kṛṣṇa consciousness to everyone, urging them to become teachers of *Bhagavad-gītā*. Lord Caitanya, who is Kṛṣṇa Himself, encouraged the people by saying, "By My order just become a teacher of Lord Kṛṣṇa's message and save this country. I assure you that the waves of *māyā* will never stop your progress." (Cc. *Madhya* 7.128)

If we give up all sinful activities and engage constantly in the *saṅkīrtana* movement of Caitanya Mahāprabhu, victory is assured in our personal lives and also in our missionary efforts.

TEXTS 11–12

आदिमध्यावसानेषु वैराग्याख्यानसंयुतम् ।
हरिलीलाकथाव्राताममृतानन्दितसत्सुरम् ॥११॥
सर्ववेदान्तसारं यद् ब्रह्मात्मैकत्वलक्षणम् ।
वस्त्वद्वितीयं तन्निष्ठं कैवल्यैकप्रयोजनम् ॥१२॥

ādi-madhyāvasāneṣu
vairāgyākhyāna-saṁyutam
hari-līlā-kathā-vrātā-
mṛtānandita-sat-suram

sarva-vedānta-sāraṁ yad
brahmātmaikatva-lakṣaṇam
vastv advitīyaṁ tan-niṣṭhaṁ
kaivalyaika-prayojanam

ādi—in the beginning; *madhya*—the middle; *avasāneṣu*—and the end; *vairāgya*—concerning renunciation of material things; *ākhyāna*—with narrations; *saṁyutam*—full; *hari-līlā*—of the pastimes of Lord Hari; *kathā-vrāta*—of the many discussions; *amṛta*—by the nectar; *ānandita*—in which are made ecstatic; *sat-suram*—the saintly devotees and demigods; *sarva-vedānta*—of all the *Vedānta; sāram*—the essence; *yat*—which; *brahma*—the Absolute Truth; *ātma-ekatva*—in terms of nondifference from the spirit soul; *lakṣaṇam*—characterized; *vastu*—the reality; *advitīyam*—one without a second; *tat-niṣṭham*—having that as its prime subject matter; *kaivalya*—exclusive devotional service; *eka*—the only; *prayojanam*—ultimate goal.

TRANSLATION

From beginning to end, the *Śrīmad-Bhāgavatam* is full of narrations that encourage renunciation of material life, as well as nectarean accounts of Lord Hari's transcendental pastimes, which give ecstasy to the saintly devotees and demigods. This *Bhāgavatam* is the essence of all *Vedānta* philosophy because its subject matter is the Absolute Truth, which, while nondifferent from the spirit soul, is the ultimate reality, one without a second. The goal of this literature is exclusive devotional service unto that Supreme Truth.

PURPORT

Vairāgya, renunciation, means giving up everything that has no relation with the Absolute Truth. Saintly devotees and demigods are enthused by the nectar of the Lord's spiritual pastimes, which are the essence of all Vedic knowledge. Vedic knowledge elaborately negates the ultimate reality of material things by emphasizing their temporary, fleeting existence. The ultimate goal is *vastu,* the factual substance, which is *advitīyam,* one without a second. That unique Absolute Truth is a transcendental person far beyond the mundane categories and characteristics of personality found in our pale material world. Thus the ultimate goal of *Śrīmad-Bhāgavatam* is to train the sincere reader in love of Godhead. Lord Kṛṣṇa is supremely lovable because of His eternal, transcendental qualities. The beauty of this world is a dim reflection of the unlimited beauty of the Lord. Without compromise, *Śrīmad-Bhāgavatam* persistently declares the glories of the Absolute Truth and is therefore the supreme spiritual literature, awarding a full taste of the nectar of love of Kṛṣṇa in full Kṛṣṇa consciousness.

TEXT 13

प्रौष्ठपद्यां पौर्णमास्यां हेमसिंहसमन्वितम् ।
ददाति यो भागवतं स याति परमां गतिम् ॥१३॥

prauṣṭhapadyāṁ paurṇamāsyāṁ
hema-siṁha-samanvitam
dadāti yo bhāgavataṁ
sa yāti paramāṁ gatim

prauṣṭhapadyām—in the month of Bhādra; *paurṇamāsyām*—on the full-moon day; *hema-siṁha*—upon a golden throne; *samanvitam*—seated; *dadāti*—gives as a gift; *yaḥ*—who; *bhāgavatam*—*Śrīmad-Bhāgavatam;* *saḥ*—he; *yāti*—goes; *paramām*—to the supreme; *gatim*—destination.

TRANSLATION

If on the full moon day of the month of Bhādra one places *Śrīmad-Bhāgavatam* on a golden throne and gives it as a gift, he will attain the supreme transcendental destination.

PURPORT

One should place *Śrīmad-Bhāgavatam* on a golden throne because it is the king of all literature. On the full-moon day of the month of Bhādra, the sun, which is compared to this king of literatures, is present in the constellation Leo and looks as if raised up on a royal throne. (According to astrology, the sun is said to be exalted in the sign of Leo). Thus one may unreservedly worship *Śrīmad-Bhāgavatam*, the supreme divine scripture.

TEXT 14

राजन्ते तावदन्यानि पुराणानि सतां गणे ।
यावद् भागवतं नैव श्रूयतेऽमृतसागरम् ॥१४॥

rājante tāvad anyāni
purāṇāni satāṁ gaṇe
yāvad bhāgavataṁ naiva
śrūyate 'mṛta-sāgaram

rājante—they shine forth; *tāvat*—that long; *anyāni*—the other; *purāṇāni*—*Purāṇas; satām*—of saintly persons; *gaṇe*—in the assembly; *yāvat*—as long as; *bhāgavatam*—*Śrīmad-Bhāgavatam; na*—not; *eva*—indeed; *śrūyate*—is heard; *amṛta-sāgaram*—the great ocean of nectar.

TRANSLATION

All other Purāṇic scriptures shine forth in the assembly of saintly devotees only as long as that great ocean of nectar, *Śrīmad-Bhāgavatam,* is not heard.

PURPORT

Other Vedic literatures and other scriptures of the world remain prominent until the *Śrīmad-Bhāgavatam* is duly heard and understood. *Śrīmad-Bhāgavatam* is the ocean of nectar and the supreme literature. By faithful hearing, recitation and distribution of *Śrīmad-Bhāgavatam,* the world will be sanctified and other, inferior literatures will fade to minor status.

TEXT 15

सर्ववेदान्तसारं हि श्रीभागवतमिष्यते ।
तद्रसामृततृप्तस्य नान्यत्र स्याद् रतिः क्वचित् ॥१५॥

sarva-vedānta-sāraṁ hi
śrī-bhāgavatam iṣyate
tad-rasāmṛta-tṛptasya
nānyatra syād ratiḥ kvacit

sarva-vedānta—of all *Vedānta* philosophy; *sāram*—the essence; *hi*—indeed; *śrī-bhāgavatam*—*Śrīmad-Bhāgavatam; iṣyate*—is said to be; *tat*—of it; *rasa-amṛta*—by the nectarean taste; *tṛptasya*—for one who is satisfied; *na*—not; *anyatra*—elsewhere; *syāt*—there is; *ratiḥ*—attraction; *kvacit*—ever.

TRANSLATION

Śrīmad-Bhāgavatam is declared to be the essence of all *Vedānta* philosophy. One who has felt satisfaction from its nectarean mellow will never be attracted to any other literature.

TEXT 16

निम्नगानां यथा गंगा देवानामच्युतो यथा ।
वैष्णवानां यथा शम्भुः पुराणानामिदं तथा ॥१६॥

nimna-gānāṁ yathā gaṅgā
devānām acyuto yathā
vaiṣṇavānāṁ yathā śambhuḥ
purāṇānām idaṁ tathā

nimna-gānām—of rivers flowing down to the sea; *yathā*—as; *gaṅgā*—the Ganges; *devānām*—of all deities; *acyutaḥ*—the infallible Supreme Personality of Godhead; *yathā*—as; *vaiṣṇavānām*—of devotees of Lord Viṣṇu; *yathā*—as; *śambhuḥ*—Śiva; *purāṇānām*—of *Purāṇas; idam*—this; *tathā*—similarly.

TRANSLATION

Just as the Gaṅgā is the greatest of all rivers, Lord Acyuta the supreme among deities and Lord Śambhu [Śiva] the greatest of Vaiṣṇavas, so *Śrīmad-Bhāgavatam* is the greatest of all *Purāṇas*.

TEXT 17

क्षेत्राणां चैव सर्वेषां यथा काशी ह्यनुत्तमा ।
तथा पुराणव्रातानां श्रीमद्भागवतं द्विजाः ॥१७॥

kṣetrāṇāṁ caiva sarveṣāṁ
yathā kāśī hy anuttamā
tathā purāṇa-vrātānāṁ
śrīmad-bhāgavataṁ dvijāḥ

kṣetrāṇām—of holy places; *ca*—and; *eva*—indeed; *sarveṣām*—of all; *yathā*—as; *kāśī*—Benares; *hi*—indeed; *anuttamā*—unexcelled; *tathā*—thus; *purāṇa-vrātānām*—of all the *Purāṇas; śrīmat-bhāgavatam*—*Śrīmad-Bhāgavatam; dvijāḥ*—O *brāhmaṇas.*

TRANSLATION

O *brāhmaṇas*, in the same way that the city of Kāśī is unexcelled among holy places, *Śrīmad-Bhāgavatam* is supreme among all the *Purāṇas*.

TEXT 18

श्रीमद्भागवतं पुराणममलं यद्वैष्णवानां प्रियं
यस्मिन् पारमहंस्यमेकममलं ज्ञानं परं गीयते ।
तत्र ज्ञानविरागभक्तिसहितं नैष्कर्म्यमाविष्कृतं
तच्छृण्वन् सुपठन् विचारणपरो भक्त्या विमुच्येन्नरः ॥१८॥

śrīmad-bhāgavataṁ purāṇam amalaṁ yad vaiṣṇavānāṁ priyaṁ
yasmin pāramahaṁsyam ekam amalaṁ jñānaṁ paraṁ gīyate
tatra jñāna-virāga-bhakti-sahitaṁ naiṣkarmyam āviṣkṛtaṁ
tac chṛṇvan su-paṭhan vicāraṇa-paro bhaktyā vimucyen naraḥ

śrīmat-bhāgavatam—*Śrīmad-Bhāgavatam; purāṇam*—the *Purāṇa; amalam*—perfectly pure; *yat*—which; *vaiṣṇavānām*—to the Vaiṣṇavas; *priyam*—most dear; *yasmin*—in which; *pāramahaṁsyam*—attainable by the topmost devotees; *ekam*—exclusive; *amalam*—perfectly pure; *jñānam*—knowledge; *param*—supreme; *gīyate*—is sung; *tatra*—there; *jñāna-virāga-bhakti-sahitam*—together with knowledge, renunciation and devotion; *naiṣkarmyam*—freedom from all material work; *āviṣkṛtam*—is revealed; *tat*—that; *śṛṇvan*—hearing; *su-paṭhan*—properly chanting; *vicāraṇa-paraḥ*—who is serious about understanding; *vimucyet*—becomes totally liberated; *naraḥ*—a person.

TRANSLATION

***Śrīmad-Bhāgavatam* is the spotless *Purāṇa*. It is most dear to the Vaiṣṇavas because it describes the pure and supreme knowledge of the *paramahaṁsas*. This *Bhāgavatam* reveals the means for becoming free from all material work, together with the processes of transcendental knowledge, renunciation and devotion. Anyone who seriously tries to understand *Śrīmad-Bhāgavatam*, who properly hears and chants it with devotion, becomes completely liberated.**

PURPORT

Because *Śrīmad-Bhāgavatam* is completely free of contamination by the modes of nature, it is endowed with extraordinary spiritual beauty and is therefore dear to the pure devotees of the Lord. The word *pāramahaṁsyam* indicates that even completely liberated souls are eager to hear and narrate *Śrīmad-Bhāgavatam*. Those who are trying to be liberated should faithfully serve this literature by hearing and reciting it with faith and devotion.

TEXT 19

कस्मै येन विभासितोऽयमतुलो ज्ञानप्रदीपः पुरा
तद्रूपेण च नारदाय मुनये कृष्णाय तद्रूपिणा ।
योगीन्द्राय तदात्मनाथ भगवद्राताय कारुण्यतस्
तच्छुद्धं विमलं विशोकममृतं सत्यं परं धीमहि ॥१९॥

kasmai yena vibhāsito 'yam atulo jñāna-pradīpaḥ purā
tad-rūpeṇa ca nāradāya munaye kṛṣṇāya tad-rūpiṇā
yogīndrāya tad-ātmanātha bhagavad-rātāya kāruṇyatas
tac chuddhaṁ vimalaṁ viśokam amṛtaṁ satyaṁ paraṁ dhīmahi

kasmai—unto Brahmā; *yena*—by whom; *vibhāsitaḥ*—thoroughly revealed; *ayam*—this; *atulaḥ*—incomparable; *jñāna*—of transcendental knowledge; *pradīpaḥ*—the torchlight; *purā*—long ago; *tat-rūpeṇa*—in the form of Brahmā; *ca*—and; *nāradāya*—to Nārada; *munaye*—the great sage; *kṛṣṇāya*—to Kṛṣṇa-dvaipāyana Vyāsa; *tat-rūpiṇā*—in the form of Nārada; *yogi-indrāya*—to the best of *yogīs*, Śukadeva; *tat-ātmanā*—as Nārada; *atha*—then; *bhagavat-rātāya*—to Parīkṣit Mahārāja; *kāruṇyataḥ*—out of mercy; *tat*—that; *śuddham*—pure; *vimalam*—uncontaminated; *viśokam*—free from misery; *amṛtam*—immortal; *satyam*—upon the truth; *param*—supreme; *dhīmahi*—I meditate.

TRANSLATION

I meditate upon that pure and spotless Supreme Absolute Truth, who is free from suffering and death and who in the beginning personally revealed this incomparable torchlight of knowledge to Brahmā. Brahmā then spoke it to the sage Nārada, who narrated it to Kṛṣṇa-dvaipāyana Vyāsa. Śrīla Vyāsa revealed this *Bhāgavatam* to the greatest of sages, Śukadeva Gosvāmī, and Śukadeva mercifully spoke it to Mahārāja Parīkṣit.

PURPORT

The first verse of *Śrīmad-Bhāgavatam* states, *satyaṁ paraṁ dhīmahi*—"I meditate upon the Supreme Truth"—and now at the conclusion of this magnificent transcendental literature, the same auspicious sounds are vibrated. The words *tad-rūpeṇa, tad-rūpiṇā* and *tad-ātmanā* in this verse clearly indicate that Lord Kṛṣṇa Himself originally spoke *Śrīmad-Bhāgavatam* to Brahmā and then continued to speak this literature through the agency of Nārada Muni, Dvaipāyana Vyāsa, Śukadeva Gosvāmī and other great sages. In other words, whenever saintly devotees vibrate *Śrīmad-Bhāgavatam,* it is to be understood that Lord Kṛṣṇa Himself is speaking the Absolute Truth through the agency of His pure representatives. Anyone who submissively hears this literature from the

Lord's bona fide devotees transcends his conditioned state and becomes qualified to meditate upon the Absolute Truth and serve Him.

TEXT 20

नमस्तस्मै भगवते वासुदेवाय साक्षिणे ।
य इदं कृपया कस्मै व्याचचक्षे मुमुक्षवे ॥२०॥

namas tasmai bhagavate
vāsudevāya sākṣiṇe
ya idaṁ kṛpayā kasmai
vyācacakṣe mumukṣave

namaḥ—obeisances; *tasmai*—to Him; *bhagavate*—the Supreme Personality of Godhead; *vāsudevāya*—Lord Vāsudeva; *sākṣiṇe*—the supreme witness; *yaḥ*—who; *idam*—this; *kṛpayā*—out of mercy; *kasmai*—to Brahmā; *vyācacakṣe*—explained; *mumukṣave*—who was desiring liberation.

TRANSLATION

We offer our obeisances to the Supreme Personality of Godhead, Lord Vāsudeva, the all-pervading witness, who mercifully explained this science to Brahmā when he anxiously desired salvation.

TEXT 21

योगीन्द्राय नमस्तस्मै शुकाय ब्रह्मरूपिणे ।
संसारसर्पदष्टं यो विष्णुरातममूमुचत् ॥२१॥

yogīndrāya namas tasmai
śukāya brahma-rūpiṇe
saṁsāra-sarpa-daṣṭaṁ yo
viṣṇu-rātam amūmucat

yogi-indrāya—to the king of mystics; *namaḥ*—obeisances; *tasmai*—to him; *śukaya*—Śukadeva Gosvāmī; *brahma-rūpiṇe*—who is a personal manifestation of the Absolute Truth; *saṁsāra-sarpa*—by the snake of material existence; *daṣṭam*—bitten; *yaḥ*—who; *viṣṇu-rātam*—Parīkṣit Mahārāja; *amūmucat*—freed.

TRANSLATION

I offer my humble obeisances to Śrī Śukadeva Gosvāmī, the best of mystic sages and a personal manifestation of the Absolute Truth. He saved Mahārāja Parīkṣit, who was bitten by the snake of material existence.

PURPORT

Sūta Gosvāmī now offers obeisances to his own spiritual master, Śukadeva Gosvāmī. Śrīla Viśvanātha Cakravartī Ṭhākura clarifies that just as Arjuna was placed into material confusion so that *Bhagavad-gītā* might be spoken, so King Parīkṣit, a pure, liberated devotee of the Lord, was cursed to die so that *Śrīmad-Bhāgavatam* might be spoken. Actually, King Parīkṣit is *viṣṇu-rāta,* eternally under the protection of the Lord. Śukadeva Gosvāmī liberated the king from his so-called illusion to exhibit the merciful nature of a pure devotee and the enlightening effect of his association.

TEXT 22

भवे भवे यथा भक्तिः पादयोस्तव जायते ।
तथा कुरुष्व देवेश नाथस्त्वं नो यतः प्रभो ॥२२॥

bhave bhave yathā bhaktiḥ
pādayos tava jāyate
tathā kuruṣva deveśa
nāthas tvaṁ no yataḥ prabho

bhave bhave—in life after life; *yathā*—so that; *bhaktiḥ*—devotional service; *pādayoḥ*—at the lotus feet; *tava*—of You; *jāyate*—arises; *tathā*—so; *kuruṣva*—please do; *deva-īśa*—O Lord of lords; *nāthaḥ*—the master; *tvam*—You; *naḥ*—our; *yataḥ*—because; *prabho*—O Lord.

TRANSLATION

O Lord of lords, O master, please grant us pure devotional service at Your lotus feet, life after life.

TEXT 23

नामसंकीर्तनं यस्य सर्वपापप्रणाशनम् ।
प्रणामो दुःखशमनस्तं नमामि हरिं परम् ॥२३॥

nāma-saṅkīrtanaṁ yasya
sarva-pāpa-praṇāśanam
praṇāmo duḥkha-śamanas
taṁ namāmi hariṁ param

nāma-saṅkīrtanam—the congregational chanting of the holy name; *yasya*—of whom; *sarva-pāpa*—all sins; *praṇāśanam*—which destroys; *praṇāmaḥ*—the bowing down; *duḥkha*—misery; *śamanaḥ*—which subdues; *tam*—to Him; *namāmi*—I offer my obeisances; *harim*—to Lord Hari; *param*—the Supreme.

TRANSLATION

The congregational chanting of the Lord's holy names destroys all sinful reactions, and the offering of obeisances unto the Lord relieves all material suffering. Therefore I offer my respectful obeisances unto the Supreme Lord Hari.

Thus end the purports of the humble servant of His Divine Grace A. C. Bhaktivedanta Swami Prabhupāda to the Twelfth Canto, Thirteenth Chapter, of the Śrīmad-Bhāgavatam, *entitled "The Glories of* Śrīmad-Bhāgavatam."

The Twelfth Canto was completed at Gainesville, Florida, on Sunday, July 18, 1982.

END OF THE TWELFTH CANTO

CONCLUSION

We offer our most respectful obeisances at the lotus feet of His Divine Grace Oṁ Viṣṇupāda Paramahaṁsa Parivrājakācārya Aṣṭottara-śata Śrī Śrīmad Bhaktivedanta Swami Prabhupāda and, by his mercy, to the six Gosvāmīs of Vṛndāvana, to Lord Caitanya and His eternal associates, to

Śrī Śrī Rādhā-Kṛṣṇa and to the supreme transcendental literature, *Śrīmad-Bhāgavatam*. By the causeless mercy of Śrīla Prabhupāda we have been able to approach the lotus feet of Śrīla Bhaktisiddhānta Sarasvatī Ṭhākura, Śrīla Jīva Gosvāmī, Śrīla Viśvanātha Cakravartī Ṭhākura, Śrīla Śrīdhara Svāmī and other great Vaiṣṇava *ācāryas*, and by carefully studying their liberated commentaries we have humbly tried to complete the *Śrīmad-Bhāgavatam*.

I also offer my obeisances to my Godbrother Śrīmad Gopīparāṇadhana dāsa Adhikārī, who has so nicely assisted me in this task. We are the insignificant servants of our spiritual master, Śrīla Prabhupāda, and by his mercy we are being allowed to serve him through the presentation of *Śrīmad-Bhāgavatam*.

Appendixes

The Author

His Divine Grace Śrīla Hridayananda dāsa Goswami Ācāryadeva is one of the foremost spiritual leaders of the International Society for Krishna Consciousness. He enjoys the unique status of being among the first Western-born members of the authorized chain of disciplic succession descending from the Supreme Lord, Kṛṣṇa. In modern times, the most essential task of Kṛṣṇa conscious spiritual masters has been to translate the Vedic scriptures of ancient India into modern languages and distribute them widely throughout the world. Śrīla Ācāryadeva has made this mission his life and soul.

Śrīla Ācāryadeva appeared in this world on November 5, 1948, in Los Angeles, California. As an academically gifted student at the University of California, Berkeley, he attended a talk given by His Divine Grace A. C. Bhaktivedanta Swami Prabhupāda, the founder and spiritual master of the Kṛṣṇa consciousness movement. Impressed by Śrīla Prabhupāda's scholarship and saintliness, Śrīla Ācāryadeva became a member of the Kṛṣṇa consciousness community in Berkeley and, shortly thereafter, on February 8, 1970, was initiated as Śrīla Prabhupāda's disciple.

From the beginning, Śrīla Ācāryadeva distinguished himself by his oratorical skills, his spiritual dedication and his devotion to studying the writings of his spiritual master, through which he acquired a deep knowledge of Sanskrit. He quickly gained recognition from Śrīla Prabhupāda himself, who marked him as "a literary man" and in 1970 sent him to Boston to accept responsibilities with ISKCON's publishing activities there. Later, Śrīla Ācāryadeva served as president in ISKCON's centers in Gainesville, Florida, and Houston, Texas, and made a significant contribution to the rapid expansion of the Kṛṣṇa consciousness movement there in the early 1970s. In 1972, he adopted the renounced order (*sannyāsa*) in order to fully dedicate himself to serving the mission of his spiritual master: the propagation of the Kṛṣṇa consciousness movement throughout the world. For the next two years he traveled widely, speaking at colleges and universities throughout the United States.

In 1974, Śrīla Ācāryadeva was appointed to the Governing Body Commission of ISKCON and entrusted with the development of the Kṛṣṇa consciousness movement in Latin America. Over the following three years, he established twenty-five centers of the Society and attracted thousands of Latin Americans to the movement, as predicted by Śrīla Prabhupāda himself. In the course of his travels he met with numerous heads of state, government ministers and high religious leaders, conversing with them in fluent Spanish and Portuguese. He also founded the Spanish- and Portuguese-language divisions of the Bhaktivedanta Book Trust for the translation and publication of Śrīla Prabhupāda's books. At present, more than 20 million books in these two languages have been distributed throughout Latin America and abroad.

Shortly before his departure from this world in November, 1977, His Divine Grace Śrīla Prabhupāda chose Śrīla Ācāryadeva, along with ten other senior disciples, to accept the role of spiritual master and to initiate disciples. Currently, Śrīla Ācāryadeva serves as the Governing Body Commissioner for Brazil and the state of Florida and as one of the initiating spiritual masters for Latin America and the southern United States. His most challenging assignment came, however, in 1979, when the leaders of ISKCON, in recognition of his devotional scholarship, commissioned him to complete Śrīla Prabhupāda's monumental translation of and commentary on the *Śrīmad-Bhāgavatam*. For thousands of years in India, great spiritual masters have presented commentaries on the *Bhāgavatam* to make its urgent message clear to the people of their times. Śrīla Ācāryadeva is the first Westerner to be entrusted with this demanding task, and his success in communicating the essence of India's spiritual heritage to modern readers has already been noted by scholars and religionists around the world.

His Divine Grace
A. C. Bhaktivedanta Swami Prabhupada

His Divine Grace A.C. Bhaktivedanta Swami Prabhupāda appeared in this world in 1896 in Calcutta, India. He first met his spiritual master, Śrīla Bhaktisiddhānta Sarasvatī Gosvāmī, in Calcutta in 1922. Bhaktisiddhānta Sarasvatī, a prominent religious scholar and the founder of sixty-four Gauḍīya Maṭhas (Vedic institutes), liked this educated young man and convinced him to dedicate his life to teaching Vedic knowledge. Śrīla Prabhupāda became his student, and eleven years later (1933) at Allahabad he became his formally initiated disciple.

At their first meeting, in 1922, Śrīla Bhaktisiddhānta Sarasvatī Ṭhākura requested Śrīla Prabhupāda to broadcast Vedic knowledge through the English language. In the years that followed, Śrīla Prabhupāda wrote a commentary on the *Bhagavad-gītā*, assisted the Gauḍīya Maṭha in its work and, in 1944, started *Back to Godhead*, an English fortnightly magazine. Maintaining the publication was a struggle. Singlehandedly, Śrīla Prabhupāda edited it, typed the manuscripts, checked the galley proofs, and even distributed the individual copies. Once begun, the magazine never stopped; it is now being continued by his disciples in the West and is published in over thirty languages.

Recognizing Śrīla Prabhupāda's philosophical learning and devotion, the Gauḍīya Vaiṣṇava Society honored him in 1947 with the title "Bhaktivedanta." In 1950, at the age of fifty-four, Śrīla Prabhupāda retired from married life, adopting the *vānaprastha* (retired) order to devote more time to his studies and writing. Śrīla Prabhupāda traveled to the holy city of Vṛndāvana, where he lived in very humble circumstances in the historic medieval temple of Rādhā-Dāmodara. There he engaged for several years in deep study and writing. He accepted the renounced order of life (*sannyāsa*) in 1959. At Rādhā-Dāmodara, Śrīla Prabhupāda began work on his life's masterpiece: a multivolume translation of and commentary on the eighteen-thousand-verse *Śrīmad-Bhāgavatam* (*Bhāgavata Purāṇa*). He also wrote *Easy Journey to Other Planets*.

After publishing three volumes of the *Bhāgavatam*, Śrīla Prabhupāda came to the United States, in September 1965, to fulfill the mission of his spiritual master. Subsequently, His Divine Grace wrote more than sixty volumes of authoritative translations, commentaries and summary studies of the philosophical and religious classics of India.

When he first arrived by freighter in New York City, Śrīla Prabhupāda was practically penniless. Only after almost a year of great difficulty did he establish the International Society for Krishna Consciousness, in July of 1966. Before his passing away on November 14, 1977, he guided the Society and saw it grow to a worldwide confederation of more than one hundred *āśramas*, schools, temples, institutes and farm communities.

In 1968, Śrīla Prabhupāda created New Vrindaban, an experimental Vedic community in the hills of West Virginia. Inspired by the success of New Vrindaban, now a thriving farm community of more than two thousand acres, his students have since founded several similar communities in the United States and abroad.

In 1972, His Divine Grace introduced the Vedic system of primary and secondary education in the West by founding the Gurukula school in Dallas, Texas. Since then, under his supervision, his disciples have established children's schools throughout the United States and the rest of the world, with the principal educational center now located in Vṛndāvana, India.

Śrīla Prabhupāda also inspired the construction of several large international cultural centers in India. The center at Śrīdhāma Māyāpur in West Bengal is the site for a planned spiritual city, an ambitious project for which construction will extend over the next decade. In Vṛndāvana, India, are the magnificent Kṛṣṇa-Balarāma Temple and International Guesthouse, and Śrīla Prabhupāda Memorial and Museum. There is also a major cultural and educational center in Bombay. Other centers are planned in a dozen important locations on the Indian subcontinent.

Śrīla Prabhupāda's most significant contribution, however, is his books. Highly respected by the academic community for their authority, depth and clarity, they are used as standard textbooks in numerous college courses. His writings have been translated into over fifty languages. The Bhaktivedanta Book Trust, established in 1972 to publish the works of His

Divine Grace, has thus become the world's largest publisher of books in the field of Indian religion and philosophy.

In just twelve years, in spite of his advanced age, Śrīla Prabhupāda circled the globe fourteen times on lecture tours that took him to six continents. In spite of such a vigorous schedule, Śrīla Prabhupāda continued to write prolifically. His writings constitute a veritable library of Vedic philosophy, religion, literature and culture.

References

The purports of *Śrīmad-Bhāgavatam* are all confirmed by standard Vedic authorities. The following authentic scriptures are specifically cited in this volume. For specific page references, consult the general index.

Viṣṇu Purāṇa

Śrīmad-Bhāgavatam

Śrī Hayaśīrṣa Pañcarātra

Skanda Purāṇa

Padma Purāṇa

Matsya Purāṇa

Muṇḍaka Upaniṣad

Glossary

A

Ārati—a ceremony for greeting the Lord with offerings of food, lamps, fans, flowers, incense and other sanctified articles.

Arghya—the ceremonious offering of water and other auspicious items in a conchshell.

Atharva Veda—*See Vedas.*

B

Brahmā—the first created being in the universe, and its secondary creator (after Lord Kṛṣṇa).

Brahmacārī—a celibate student of a spiritual master.

Brahmaloka—the planet ruled by Lord Brahmā. It is the highest planet in the material universe.

Brāhmaṇa—a person wise in Vedic knowledge, fixed in goodness, and knowledgeable of Brahman, the Absolute Truth; a member of the first Vedic social order.

C

Cedirāja—the king of Cedi; also known as Śiśupāla. Lord Kṛṣṇa killed him because of his blasphemy.

D

Dhenukāsaura—a demon who assumed the form of an ass and was killed by Lord Balarāma.

Dhruva—a saintly king. As a child, he worshiped Lord Viṣṇu to achieve a kingdom greater than Lord Brahmā's.

Diti—the mother of the demons.

G

Gajendra—the king of the elephants. He was saved from a crocodile by Lord Viṣṇu and awarded liberation.

Gandharvas—demigod singers and dancers.

Garbhodaka Ocean—the body of water that fills the bottom part of each material universe.

Garbhodakaśāyī Viṣṇu—the second expansion of Lord Viṣṇu for creating the universes. He lies down on the Garbhodaka Ocean in each universe, and then Lord Brahmā takes birth on the lotus that grows from His navel.

Garuḍa—a huge eagle who serves as Lord Viṣṇu's carrier.

Gopīs—Lord Kṛṣṇa's cowherd girlfriends in Vṛndāvana. They are His most confidential devotees.

Govardhana—a large hill dear to Lord Kṛṣṇa and His devotees. Kṛṣṇa held it up for seven days to protect His devotees in Vṛndāvana from a devastating storm sent by Indra.

H

Hayaśīrṣā—the horse-headed incarnation of Lord Kṛṣṇa. He spoke the *Vedas* to Lord Brahmā.

Hiraṇyakaśipu—the demonic father of the devotee Prahlāda. He was killed by Lord Nṛsiṁhadeva (Narasiṁha).

Hiraṇyākṣa—the demonic younger brother of Hiraṇyakaśipu. He was killed by the Lord's boar incarnation.

I

Ikṣvāku—the son of Vaivasvata Manu, who imparted the teachings of *Bhagavad-gītā* to him.

Indra—the king of the heavenly planets and chief of the administrative demigods.

K

Kāliya—the many-headed serpent chastised by Lord Kṛṣṇa for poisoning a section of the Yamunā River.

Kapila, Lord—an incarnation of Kṛṣṇa who appeared as the son of Devahūti and Kardama to propound the Sāṅkhya philosophy.

Keśī—a demon who assumed the form of a huge horse and was killed by Lord Kṛṣṇa.

Khaṭvāṅga—a saintly king who is famous for attaining unalloyed Kṛṣṇa consciousness just moments before his death.

Kūrma, Lord—Lord Kṛṣṇa's tortoise incarnation. He provided a pivot for Mount Mandara when the demigods and demons used it to churn nectar from the Milk Ocean.

M

Mahat-tattva—the total material energy in its original, undifferentiated form. From it is manifested the entire material world.

Manus—the original forefathers of the human race.

Mathurā—the area surrounding Vṛndāvana. There Lord Kṛṣṇa took birth and enacted His pastimes as a young prince.

Matsya, Lord—the Lord's incarnation as a fish. He preserved the *Vedas* during the flood at the time of partial annihilation.

N

Nābhi—the saintly king who was the father of Lord Ṛṣabhadeva.

Nāgas—a race of serpents who live on the subterranean heavenly planets.

Nanda Mahārāja—the devotee who takes the role of Lord Kṛṣṇa's father in His Vṛndāvana pastimes; the king of the cowherds.

Nārada Muni—a great devotee of Kṛṣṇa's who spreads His glories throughout the universe. He is one of the twelve *mahājanas*, great authorities on devotional service.

Narasiṁha, Lord (Nṛsiṁhadeva)—the incarnation of the Lord as a half man, half lion. He killed the demon Hiraṇyakaśipu to save His devotee Prahlāda.

Nṛga—a king who was cursed to become a snake because of a slight discrepancy in his service to *brāhmaṇas*. He was delivered by Lord Kṛṣṇa.

P

Pañcarātra—supplementary Vedic literatures describing the process of Deity worship for devotees in the present age.

Parīkṣit Mahārāja—a great, saintly king of Vedic times; the grandson of Arjuna. He heard the *Śrīmad-Bhāgavatam* from Śukadeva Gosvāmī.

Pauṇḍraka—a demon who attempted to imitate Lord Kṛṣṇa and was killed by Him.

Pracetās—the ten sons of King Pracīnabarhi. They satisfied the Lord with their cooperative spirit and extreme austerities.

Pracīnabarhi—a great king who was advised against material attachment by Nārada Muni.

Prahlāda Mahārāja—a devotee who was persecuted by his demoniac father Hiraṇyakaśipu but who was protected by the Lord and ultimately saved by Him in His incarnation as Lord Nṛsiṁhadeva.

Prakṛti—one of two energies of the Supreme Lord: either the inferior, material energy or the superior, spiritual energy.

Priyavrata—the younger son of Svāyambhuva Manu. At the request of Lord Brahmā, he gave up his renounced life and took charge of his father's kingdom.

Pṛthu Mahārāja—a great king of Vedic times. He was an incarnation of the Lord's ruling power.

Purāṇas—the Vedic histories of the universe, in relation to the Supreme Lord and His devotees.

Pūtanā—a demoness who took the form of a beautiful young woman and was killed by infant Kṛṣṇa.

Rākṣasa—a man-eating demon.

Rāmacandra, Lord—Lord Kṛṣṇa's incarnation as a perfect king. His glories are recorded by Vālmīki in the *Rāmāyaṇa.*

Ṛg Veda—See: *Vedas.*

Ṛṣabhadeva—an incarnation of Lord Kṛṣṇa who ruled the earth as a king. He is known for his extreme renunciation and austerity.

Rukmiṇī—Lord Kṛṣṇa's foremost queen in Dvārakā.

S

Sāma Veda—*See: Vedas.*

Sāṅkhya—the philosophical process of realizing the Absolute Truth by analyzing matter into its different aspects to distinguish it from spirit.

Śatarūpā—the wife of Svāyambhuva Manu.

Saubhari Muni—a powerful mystic who temporarily fell down from his position on account of sex attraction.

Śiva, Lord—the chief demigod. He presides over the mode of ignorance and the destruction of the material manifestation.

Supersoul—the direct expansion of the Supreme Lord who dwells within the heart of every living being and within every atom.

Sūtra—the intermediate manifestation of the *mahat-tattva*, when it is predominated by the mode of passion.

Svāyambhuva Manu—one of the administrative demigods who are the fathers and lawgivers of mankind.

T

Tārā—the wife of Bṛhaspati. She was kidnapped by the moon-god.

Tṛṇāvarta—the demon who assumed the form of a whirlwind and was killed by infant Kṛṣṇa.

U

Uddhava—an intimate devotee of Lord Kṛṣṇa's. Kṛṣṇa gave him elaborate instructions just before His disappearance.

V

Vāmanadeva, Lord—the dwarf incarnation of Lord Kṛṣṇa.

Vatsāsura—the demon who took the form of a calf and was killed by Lord Kṛṣṇa.

Vedas—the original revealed scriptures, first spoken by Lord Kṛṣṇa. They consist of the *Ṛg*, *Yajur*, *Sāma* and *Atharva Vedas*.

Vyāsadeva—the literary incarnation of Viṣṇu. He compiled the *Vedas*, *Purāṇas*, *Mahābhārata*, *Vedanta-sūtra* and other scriptures.

Y

Yadu dynasty—the dynasty in which Lord Kṛṣṇa appeared.

Yajur Veda—*See: Vedas.*

Yakṣas—a race of demons.

Yoga—any one of several processes for linking one's consciousness with the Supreme.

Yogī—one who practices *yoga*.

Sanskrit Pronunciation Guide

Vowels

अ a आ ā इ i ई ī उ u ऊ ū ऋ ṛ ॠ ṝ

ऌ ḷ ए e ऐ ai ओ o औ au

ं ṁ (*anusvāra*) ः ḥ (*visarga*)

Consonants

Gutturals:	क ka	ख kha	ग ga	घ gha	ङ ṅa
Palatals:	च ca	छ cha	ज ja	झ jha	ञ ña
Cerebrals:	ट ṭa	ठ ṭha	ड ḍa	ढ ḍha	ण ṇa
Dentals:	त ta	थ tha	द da	ध dha	न na
Labials:	प pa	फ pha	ब ba	भ bha	म ma
Semivowels:	य ya	र ra	ल la	व va	
Sibilants:	श śa	ष ṣa	स sa		
Aspirate:	ह ha	ऽ ' (*avagraha*) – the apostrophe			

The numerals are: ० -0 १-1 २-2 ३-3 ४-4 ५-5 ६-6 ७-7 ८-8 ९-9

The vowels above should be pronounced as follows:

a – like the *a* in org*a*n or the *u* in b*u*t
ā – like the *a* in f*a*r but held twice as long as short *a*
i – like the *i* in p*i*n
ī – like the *i* in p*i*que but held twice as long as short *i*

u – like the *u* in p*u*sh.
ū – like the *u* in r*u*le but held twice as long as short *u*.
ṛ – like the *ri* in *ri*m.
ṝ – like *ree* in *ree*d.
ḷ – like *l* followed by *r* (*lr*).
e – like the *e* in th*e*y.
ai – like the *ai* in *ai*sle.
o – like the *o* in g*o*.
au – like the *ow* in h*ow*.
ṁ (*anusvāra*) – a resonant nasal like the *n* in the French word *bon*.
ḥ (*visarga*) – a final *h*-sound: *aḥ* is pronounced like *aha*; *iḥ* like *ihi*.

The vowels are written as follows after a consonant:

ा ā ि i ी ī ु u ू ū ृ ṛ ॄ ṝ े e ै ai ो o ौ au

For example: क ka का kā कि ki की kī कु ku कू kū

कृ kṛ कॄ kṝ के ke कै kai को ko कौ kau

The vowel "a" is implied after a consonant with no vowel symbol.

The symbol virāma (्) indicates that there is no final vowel: क्

The consonants are pronounced as follows:

k – as in *k*ite
kh – as in Ec*kh*art
g – as in *g*ive
gh – as in di*g-h*ard
ṅ – as in si*ng*
c – as in *ch*air
ch – as in staun*ch-h*eart
j – as in *j*oy
jh – as in he*dgeh*og
ñ – as in ca*ny*on
ṭ – as in *t*ub
ṭh – as in ligh*t-h*eart
ḍ – as in *d*ove
ḍha- as in re*d-h*ot
ṇ – as r*na* (prepare to say the *r* and say *na*).

t – as in *t*ub but with tongue against teeth.
th – as in ligh*t-h*eart but with tongue against teeth.

d – as in *d*ove but with tongue against teeth
dh – as in re*d-h*ot but with tongue against teeth
n – as in *n*ut but with tongue between teeth
p – as in *p*ine
ph – as in u*ph*ill (not *f*)
b – as in *b*ird
bh – as in ru*b-h*ard
m – as in *m*other
y – as in *y*es
r – as in *r*un

l – as in *l*ight
v – as in *v*ine
ś (palatal) – as in the *s* in the German word *sprechen*
ṣ (cerebral) – as the *sh* in *sh*ine
s – as in *s*un
h – as in *h*ome

Generally two or more consonants in conjunction are written together in a special form, as for example: क्ष kṣa त्र tra

There is no strong accentuation of syllables in Sanskrit, or pausing between words in a line, only a flowing of short and long (twice as long as the short) syllables. A long syllable is one whose vowel is long (ā, ī, ū, e, ai, o, au), or whose short vowel is followed by more than one consonant (including anusvāra and visarga). Aspirated consonants (such as kha and gha) count as only single consonants.

Index of Sanskrit Verses

This index constitutes a complete listing of the first and third lines of each of the Sanskrit poetry verses of this volume of *Śrīmad-Bhāgavatam*, arranged in English alphabetical order. The first column gives the Sanskrit transliteration, and the second and third columns, respectively, list the chapter-verse reference and page number for each verse.

A

abhyayād ati-saṅkliṣṭaḥ 9.32 76
ācaranty anumodante 10.29 97
ādānaṁ pārijātasya 12.38 168
adhīmahi vyāsa-śiṣyāc 7.7 5
adhīyanta vyāsa-śiṣyāt 7.6 5

adhīyetāṁ saṁhite dve 7.3 3
ādi-madhyāvasāneṣu 13.11 200
adṛśyatātta-cāpeṣuḥ 8.22 34
aghāsura-vadho dhātrā 12.29 163
agny-arka-guru-viprātmasv 8.9 26

ahaṁ ca bhagavān brahmā 10.21 91
ahaṁ ca saṁsmārita ātma-tattvam 12.57 181
āha tv ātmānubhāvena 10.16 89
aho īśvara-līleyam 10.28 97
āhuś cirāyuṣam ṛṣim 8.2 23

ailasya soma-vaṁśasya 12.25 161
ā-kalpāntād yaśaḥ puṇyam 10.36 102
akrūrāgamanaṁ paścāt 12.34 165
akṣa-mālā-ḍamaruka- 10.12 86
akṣa-sthaviṣṭhā mumucus taḍidbhiḥ 9.11 63

amoghaṁ darśanaṁ yeṣām 10.19 90
anādy-āvartitaṁ nṝṇām 10.41 105
anādy-avidyayā viṣṇor 11.29 129
anapāyinī bhagavatī 11.20 121
aṅgopāṅgāyudhākalpair 11.23 125

aṅgopāṅgāyudhākalpam 11.2 110
aniruddha iti brahman 11.21 123
atharva-vit sumantuś ca 7.1 1
antar bahiś cādbhir ati-dyubhiḥ kharaiḥ 9.13 64
antardadha ṛṣeḥ sadyo 9.33 77

anubhūtaṁ bhagavato 10.40 105
anugrahāyāvirāsīn 8.32 39
anumlocā śaṅkhapālo 11.38 135
anuvarṇitam etat te 10.40 105
anvīyamāno gandharvair 8.22 34

apāṁ tattvaṁ dara-varam 11.14 117
āpūryamāṇo varaṣadbhir ambudaiḥ 9.14 65
ārādhayan hṛṣīkeśam 8.11 26
ardha-nārī-narasyātha 12.11 153
arhaṇenānulepena 8.38 43

arthāṁśuḥ kaśyapas tārkṣya 11.41 137
arthendriyāśaya-jñānair 11.22 124
aryamā pulaho 'thaujāḥ 11.34 133
ātapatraṁ tu vaikuṇṭham 11.19 120
athāpi saṁvadiṣyāmo 10.7 84

athāpy ambuja-patrākṣa 9.6 59
atha taṁ bālakaṁ vīkṣya 9.32 76
athemam arthaṁ pṛcchāmo 11.1 109
athomā tam ṛṣiṁ vīkṣya 10.4 82
ātmany api śivaṁ prāptam 10.11 86

atra brahma paraṁ guhyam 12.4 148
atra saṅkīrtitaḥ sākṣāt 12.3 147
avatārānugītaṁ ca 12.7 150
avatāro bhagavataḥ 12.13 154
āviśat tad-guhākāśam 10.10 85

avismṛtiḥ kṛṣṇa-padāravindayoḥ 12.55 180
avismṛtiḥ śrīdhara-pāda-padmayor 12.54 179
avyākṛta-guṇa-kṣobhān 7.11 9
avyākṛtam anantākhyam 11.13 117
ayaṁ hi paramo lābho 10.7 84
ayutāyuta-varṣāṇām 9.19 68

B

babhruḥ śiṣyo 'thāṅgirasaḥ	7.3	3
bhagaḥ sphūrjo 'riṣṭanemir	11.42	137
bhagavāṁs tad abhijñāya	10.10	85
bhagavān bhaga-śabdārtham	11.18	120
bhagavata upalabdhi-mātra-dhāmne	12.68	188
bhagavaty acyutāṁ bhaktim	10.34	101
bhaktiṁ parāṁ bhagavati	10.6	83
bhakti-yogaḥ samākhyāto	12.5	149
bhārāvataraṇaṁ bhūmer	12.41	169
bhavadbhir yad ahaṁ pṛṣṭo	12.2	147
bhave bhave yathā bhaktiḥ	13.22	208
bhaviṣyaṁ brahma-vaivartam	7.24	18
bho bho brahmarṣi-varyo 'si	9.2	56
bhṛśam udvigna-madhyāyāḥ	8.26	36
bhūta-sūkṣmendriyārthānām	7.11	9
bhuva uddharaṇe 'mbhodher	12.10	152
bibharti sāṅkhyaṁ yogaṁ ca	11.12	116
bibharti sma catur-mūrtir	11.23	125
bibhrāṇaṁ sahasā bhātam	10.13	86
bibhrat kamaṇḍaluṁ daṇḍam	8.8	26
bibhraty ātma-samādhāna-	10.24	93
bījādi-pañcatāntāsu	7.20	15
brahmā bhṛgur bhavo dakṣo	8.12	28
brahmā bibhety alam ato dvi-	8.43	47
brāhmaṁ daśa-sahasrāṇi	13.4	195
brāhmaṁ pādmaṁ vaiṣṇavaṁ ca	7.23	17
brāhmaṇāḥ sādhavaḥ śāntā	10.20	91
brāhmaṇebhyo namaskṛtya	12.1	146
brāhmaṇebhyo namasyāmo	10.24	93
brahmann idaṁ samākhyātam	7.25	18
brahmāpeto 'tha śatajid	11.43	138
brahma-varcasvino bhūyāt	10.37	103
bṛhad-vrata-dharaḥ śānto	8.8	26
brūhi naḥ śraddadhānānām	11.28	128
bubhuje gurv-anujñātaḥ	8.10	26

C

caidya-pauṇḍraka-śālvānām	12.40	169
caran samantāt tanute	11.46	141
cārv-aṅgulibhyāṁ pāṇibhyām	9.25	70
catur-daśa bhaviṣyaṁ syāt	13.6	195
catur-vidhaṁ vīkṣya sahātmanā munir	9.13	64
catur-vidhaś ca pralaya	12.44	171
catur-viṁśati vārāham	13.7	195
chandāṁsy adhītya dharmeṇa	8.7	26
codayanti rathaṁ pṛṣṭhe	11.48	142

D

dadāti yo bhāgavatam	13.13	201
dadhyāv adhokṣajaṁ yogī	8.13	29
dahyamānā nivavṛtuḥ	8.29	37
daityeśvarasya caritam	12.18	157
dakṣa-janma pracetobhyas	12.17	156
damanaṁ kāliyasyāher	12.31	164
dānaṁ dānasya māhātmyam	13.3	194
daśabhir lakṣaṇair yuktam	7.10	7
daśāṣṭau brahma-vaivartam	13.6	195
daśāṣṭau śrī-bhāgavatam	13.5	195
dauṣmanter bharatasyāpi	12.26	161
dehādy apārtham asad antyam	8.44	48
deha-tyāgaś ca rājarṣer	12.45	171
devahūtyāś ca saṁvādaḥ	12.13	154
devāsura-mahā-yuddham	12.21	158
devatā munayaḥ siddhāḥ	12.62	184
devyai tat-karma kathayann	10.38	104
dharma-jñānādibhir yuktam	11.13	117
dharmaṁ grāhayituṁ prāyaḥ	10.29	97
dharmaṁ yaśaś ca bhagavāṁś	11.18	120
dhātā kṛtasthalī hetir	11.33	132
dhenukasya saha-bhrātuḥ	12.30	163
dhruvasya caritaṁ paścāt	12.14	155
dhyānāvasthita-tad-gatena manasā	13.1	192
dhyāyan sarvatra ca harim	9.9	61
drakṣye māyāṁ yayā lokaḥ	9.6	59
dravyaṁ phalam iti brahman	11.31	131
dṛṣṭvā nistejasaṁ kāmam	8.31	39
dṛṣṭvotthāyādareṇoccair	8.35	41
dvādaśasv api māseṣu	11.46	141
dvādaśyāṁ ekādaśyāṁ vā	12.60	183
dvija-ṛṣabha sa eṣa brahma-yoniḥ	11.24	125
dvīpa-varṣa-samudrāṇām	12.16	156
dyu-patibhir aja-śakra-śaṅkarādyair	12.67	188

E

eka eva hi lokānām 11.30 130
eka evārṇave bhrāmyan 8.4 23
ekaikām aham eteṣām 7.6 5
ekānta-bhaktā asmāsu 10.20 91
ekona-viṁśat sauparṇam 13.8 195

eṣa naḥ saṁśayo bhūyān 8.5 23
etā bhagavato viṣṇor 11.45 140
etad vaḥ kathitaṁ viprā 12.2 147
etad vaḥ kathitaṁ viprāḥ 12.58 182
etad vai pauruṣaṁ rūpam 11.6 113

etat kecid avidvāṁso 10.41 105
etat purandaro jñātvā 8.15 30
ete ātharvaṇācāryāḥ 7.4 4
evaṁ hy anādi-nidhano 11.50 143
evaṁ lakṣaṇa-lakṣyāṇi 7.22 17

evaṁ purāṇa-sandohaś 13.9 196
evaṁ stutaḥ sa bhagavān 10.18 90
evaṁ tapaḥ-svādhyāya-paro 8.11 26
evaṁ varān sa munaye 10.38 104

G

gaja-muṣṭika-cāṇūra- 12.35 166
gandharvāpsarasaḥ kāmam 8.16 31
gandharvās taṁ pragāyanti 11.47 142
ghātanaṁ yavanendrasya 12.37 167
ghṛtācī gautamaś ceti 11.39 135

gopa-druma-latā-jālais 8.21 33
gopānāṁ ca paritrāṇam 12.30 163
govardhanoddhāraṇaṁ ca 12.32 164
govinda gopa-vanitā-vraja-bhṛtya-gīta- 11.25 127
gṛhītvājādayo yasya 9.5 58
guṇaiḥ kurvadbhir ābhāti 10.31 99

H

harasya jṛmbhaṇaṁ yuddhe 12.39 168
haraye nama ity uccair 12.47 173
hari-līlā-kathā-vrātā- 13.11 200
hetur jīvo 'sya sargāder 7.18 13

himālayaṁ puṣpavahāṁ ca tāṁ nadīm 9.30 75
hṛṣṭa-romāśru-pūrṇākṣo 8.36 42
hutvāgniṁ samupāsīnam 8.23 34

I

idaṁ bhagavatā pūrvam 13.10 198
iha tu punar bhagavān aśeṣa-mūrtiḥ 12.66 187
ikṣvāku-janma tad-vaṁśaḥ 12.21 158
ilopākhyānam atroktam 12.22 159
indriyāṇi śarān āhur 11.16 118

indro viśvāvasuḥ śrotā 11.37 134
īśānaḥ sarva-vidyānām 10.8 84
itas tato bhramad-dṛṣṭeś 8.27 36
iti candra-lalāmasya 10.26 95
iti coktaṁ dvija-śreṣṭhā 12.46 172

itīḍito 'rcitaḥ kāmam 9.7 60
itīndrānucarair brahman 8.30 38
itthaṁ bṛhad-vrata-dharas 8.13 29
ity arcito 'bhiṣṭutaś ca 10.35 102
ity uktvā tam upeyāya 10.8 84

J

jarāsandha-samānīta- 12.37 167
jitaṁ te deva-deveśa 9.4 58
jñānaṁ ca tad-upākhyānam 12.4 148
jñānaṁ trai-kālikaṁ brahman 10.37 103
jyotiś-cakrasya saṁsthānam 12.16 156

K

kāla-rūpaṁ dhanuḥ śārṅgam 11.15 117
kālasya sthūla-sūkṣmasya 12.10 152
kali-mala-saṁhati-kālano 'khileśo 12.66 187
kālo deśaḥ kriyā kartā 11.31 131
kalpe kalpe svam ātmānam 11.50 143

kambu-grīvaṁ mahoraskam 9.22 70
kāmo maharṣe sarvo 'yam 10.36 102
kaṁ vṛṇe nu paraṁ bhūman 10.33 100
karavāma kim īśāna 10.16 89
karkoṭakaḥ pūrvacittiḥ 11.42 137

kasmai yena vibhāsito 'yam atulo 13.19 206
kaśyapo 'haṁ ca sāvarṇī 7.7 5
kaurmaṁ mātsyaṁ nārasiṁham 12.20 158
kaurmaṁ sapta-daśākhyātam 13.8 195
kaustubha-vyapadeśena 11.10 115

kecit pañca-vidhaṁ brahman 7.10 7
kevalāyādvitīyāya 10.32 99
khaṁ rodasī bhā-gaṇān adri-sāgarān 9.28 74
khaṭvāṅgasya ca māndhātuḥ 12.23 160
kim idaṁ kuta eveti 10.13 86

kiṁ varṇaye tava vibho yad-udīrito 'suḥ 8.40 44
krīḍantyāḥ puñjikasthalyāḥ 8.26 36
kṛṣṇājinaṁ sākṣa-sūtram 8.9 26
kṛtam uddhava-rāmābhyām 12.36 166
kṛtā svena nṛṇāṁ tatra 7.13 10

kṣetrāṇāṁ caiva sarveṣām 13.17 204
kṣiroda-mathanaṁ tadvad 12.20 158
kṣut-tṛṭ-parīto makarais timiṅgilair 9.16 67
kumudaḥ śunako brahman 7.2 2
kurv asya tapasaḥ sākṣāt 10.5 82

kutaḥ punaḥ śaśvad abhadram īśvare 12.53 178
kvacic chokaṁ kvacin moham 9.18 67
kvacin magno mahāvarte 9.17 67
kvacin mṛtyum avāpnoti 9.18 67
kvacit pūjāṁ visasmāra 9.9 61

L

lajjottaro 'dharo lobho 11.8 113
līlā dhṛtā yad api sattva-mayī 8.45 49
līlāvatāra-karmāṇi 12.46 172
loka-tantrāya carati 11.32 131

M

madhu-kulyā ghṛta-kulyāḥ 12.63 185
madhur mano rajas-toka 8.25 35
madhv-ādiṣu dvādaśasu 11.32 131
mahā-marakata-śyāmam 9.22 70
mahānti bhūtāny atha bhautikāny asau 9.29 74

mahā-puruṣa-vinyāsaḥ 12.45 171
māhātmyaṁ ca vadhas teṣām 12.41 169
māhātmyaṁ vāsudevasya 12.58 182
manasā yoga-pakvena 9.5 58
maṇḍalaṁ deva-yajanam 11.17 119

manvantaraṁ manur devā 7.15 12
manv-antarānukathanam 12.19 157
manv-antarāvatārāś ca 12.19 157
mārkaṇḍaṁ nava vāhnaṁ ca 13.5 195
mathurāyāṁ nivasatā 12.36 166

matta-barhi-naṭāṭopam 8.19 32
matta-bhramara-saṅgītam 8.19 32
mauliṁ padaṁ pārameṣṭhyam 11.12 116
māyādyair navabhis tattvaiḥ 11.5 112
māyā-mayeṣu tad brahma 7.19 14

mayi bhaktyānapāyinyā 9.2 56
mīlitākṣaṁ durādharṣam 8.23 34
mitro 'triḥ pauruṣeyo 'tha 11.35 133
mṛdaṅga-vīṇā-paṇavair 8.24 35
mṛṣā giras tā hy asatīr asat-kathā 12.49 175

mṛtasyānayanaṁ sūnoḥ 12.35 166
mukhe nidhāya viprendro 9.25 70
munaye preṣayām āsa 8.16 31
munayo 'ṣṭādaśa prāhuḥ 7.22 17
mūrtī ime bhagavato bhagavaṁs 8.41 45

N

nābhes tato 'nucaritam 12.15 155
nābhiḥ sūryo 'kṣiṇī nāse 11.6 113
nabho-nibhaṁ nabhas-tattvam 11.15 117
na duṣyetānubhāvas tair 10.30 98
na hy am-mayāni tīrthāni 10.23 93

naimittikaḥ prākṛtiko 7.17 13
naiṣkarmyam apy acyuta-bhāva- 12.53 178
naitāvatā bhagavataḥ 10.30 98
naivādhunāpi bhūtānām 8.3 23
naivecchaty āśiṣaḥ kvāpi 10.6 83

nakṣatrakalpaḥ śāntiś ca 7.4 4
namaḥ śivāya śāntāya 10.17 89
nāmāny anantasya yaśo 'ṅkitāni yat 12.52 177
nāma-saṅkīrtanaṁ yasya 13.23 209
namaskṛtya gurūn vakṣye 11.4 111

namas tasmai bhagavate 13.20 207
namo dharmāya mahate 12.1 146
namo nama itīśānau 8.37 42
nānā bibharṣy avitum anya-tanūr 8.41 45
nandādayo 'ṣṭau dvāḥ-sthāś ca 11.20 121

nanṛtus tasya purataḥ 8.24 35
nānyaṁ tavāṅghry-upanayād 8.43 47
nāradaḥ kacchanīraś ca 11.34 133
nāradasya ca saṁvādas 12.15 155
nāradīyaṁ bhāgavatam 7.23 17

nārāyaṇa-kathā yatra 8.6 25
nārāyaṇaṁ devam adevam īśam 12.56 181
nārāyaṇāya ṛṣaye ca narottamāya 8.47 51
nārāyaṇo hṛṣīkeśo 12.3 147
nārāyaṇo nara-sakhaḥ 9.1 56

na te mayy acyute 'je ca 10.22 92
nātmanaś ca janasyāpi 10.22 92
nava-brahma-samutpattir 12.14 155
na veda ruddha-dhī-vṛttir 10.9 85
na yad vacaś citra-padaṁ harer yaśo 12.51 176

netre unmīlya dadṛśe 10.14 87
nibhṛtoda-jhaṣa-vrāto 10.5 82
nimer aṅga-parityāgo 12.24 160
nimna-gānāṁ yathā gaṅgā 13.16 203

nirmito dṛśyate yatra 11.5 112
nirmito loka-tantro 'yam 11.29 129
nṛ-deva-pitṛ-bhūtāni 8.12 28
nyāgrodha-potaṁ dadṛśe 9.20 69

O

ojaḥ-saho-bala-yutam 11.14 117

P

padārtheṣu yathā dravyam 7.20 15
padma-garbhāruṇāpāṅgam 9.24 70
padmākṣa-mālām uta jantu-mārjanam 8.34 40
paricaryā bhagavata 11.17 119
pārīkṣitam upākhyānam 12.5 149

parituṣṭaḥ prasannātmā 10.18 90
paśyemaṁ bhagavan vipram 10.4 82
paṭhaty anaśnan prayataḥ 12.60 183
patitaḥ skhalitaś cārtaḥ 12.47 173
pavitra-pāṇī upavītakaṁ tri-vṛt 8.33 40

prāgjyotiṣa-patiṁ hatvā 12.39 168
prāg-uttarasyāṁ śākhāyām 9.21 69

prahṛṣṭa-romādbhuta-bhāva-śaṅkitaḥ 9.26 72
prajāpatiḥ prajananam 11.7 113
pramlocā rākṣaso varyo 11.37 134

praṇāmo duḥkha-śamanas 13.23 209
prapanno 'smy aṅghri-mūlaṁ te 10.2 80
prāpta-dvi-jāti-saṁskāro 8.7 26
prasādo yajña-patnībhyo 12.32 164
praśnas tvayā maharṣe 'yam 8.6 25

prauṣṭhapadyāṁ paurṇamāsyām 13.13 201
praviśya cittaṁ vidhunoty aśeṣam 12.48 174
prāyopaveśe nṛpateḥ parīkṣitaḥ 12.57 181
prāyopaveśo rājarṣer 12.6 149
proktaṁ bhagavatā yat tu 12.64 186

pṛṣṭhe bhrāmyad amanda-mandara- 13.2 193
pulastyas tumburur iti 11.33 132
punar ānamya pādābhyām 8.39 44
puṇya-dvija-kulākīrṇam 8.18 32
purāṇa-lakṣaṇaṁ brahman 7.8 6

purāṇa-saṁhitām etām 12.64 186
purāṇa-saṁhitā-praśno 12.8 151
purāṇa-saṅkhyā-sambhūtim 13.3 194
purato 'bhimukhaṁ yānti 11.49 143
puruṣānugṛhītānām 7.12 9

pūṣā dhanañjayo vātaḥ 11.39 135
puṣkare mathurāyāṁ ca 12.61 184
puṣpabhadrā nadī yatra 8.17 31
pūtanāsu-payaḥ-pānam 12.28 162

R

rājante tāvad anyāni 13.14 202
rājñāṁ brahma-prasūtānām 7.16 12
rajo-juṣe 'tha ghorāya 10.17 89
rakṣācyutāvatārehā 7.14 11
rāmasya bhārgavendrasya 12.25 161

rāmasya kośalendrasya 12.24 160
rathasvana iti hy ete 11.35 133
ṛco yajūṁṣi sāmāni 12.63 185
romāṇi bhūruhā bhūmno 11.8 113
ṛṣayo 'ṁśāvatārāś ca 7.15 12

ṛtur varcā bharadvājaḥ	11.40	136
rudraṁ tri-lokaika-gurum	10.14	87
rudrāṇyā bhagavān rudro	10.3	81
rukmiṇyā haraṇaṁ yuddhe	12.38	168

S

sa ciraṁ māyayā viṣṇor	10.27	96
sa eka evorvarito mahā-munir	9.15	66
sa evam anubhūyedam	10.1	79
sa kadācid bhramaṁs tasmin	9.20	69
śākhā-praṇayanaṁ ṛṣer	12.45	171
sa-kṣmāntarikṣaṁ sa-divaṁ	9.15	66
sa-lokā loka-pālās tān	10.21	91
sāmarg-yajurbhis tal-liṅgair	11.47	142
samasta-tantra-rāddhānte	11.1	109
śambaro dvividaḥ pīṭho	12.40	169
saṁhitāṁ so 'pi pathyāya	7.1	1
samīra-vegormibhir ugra-nakra-	9.12	64
saṁsāra-sarpa-daṣṭaṁ yo	13.21	207
saṁśrāvayet saṁśṛṇuyād u tāv ubhau	10.42	106
saṁstheti kavibhiḥ proktaś	7.17	13
saṁstuto bhagavān ittham	9.1	56
sandadhe 'straṁ sva-dhanuṣi	8.25	35
śaṅkhacūḍasya durbuddher	12.33	164
saṅkīrtyamāno bhagavān anantaḥ	12.48	174
santāno dharma-patnīnām	12.12	153
sargo 'syātha visargaś ca	7.9	7
sarvaṁ tatrābhavan mogham	8.28	37
sarva-veda-kriyā-mūlam	11.30	130
sarva-vedānta-sāraṁ hi	13.15	203
sarva-vedānta-sāraṁ yad	13.12	200
śatarūpā ca yā strīṇām	12.12	153
sa tat-sandarśanānanda-	8.36	42
sattvaṁ rajas tama itīśa	8.45	49
sattvasya śuddhiṁ paramātma-bhaktim	12.55	180
saukanyaṁ cātha śaryāteḥ	12.23	160
śauklāyanir brahmabalir	7.2	2
sauro gaṇo māsi māsi	11.27	128
sa vā asmat-kulotpannaḥ	8.3	23
sa viśvas taijasaḥ prājñas	11.22	124
sāyaṁ prātaḥ sa gurave	8.10	26
śayānaṁ parṇa-puṭake	9.21	69
śiṣya-śiṣya-praśiṣyāṇām	7.25	18
śiva-vāg-amṛta-dhvasta-	10.27	96
skāndaṁ śataṁ tathā caikam	13.7	195
ślokam ekaṁ tad-ardhaṁ vā	12.59	183
smaratāṁ sandhyayor nṛṇām	11.45	140
so 'py avāpta-mahā-yoga-	10.39	104
spandanti vai tanu-bhṛtām aja-	8.40	44
śraddhāvān yo 'nuśṛṇuyāt	12.59	183
śravaṇād darśanād vāpi	10.25	94
śrī-kṛṣṇa kṛṣṇa-sakha vṛṣṇy-	11.25	127
śrīmad-bhāgavataṁ purāṇam amalaṁ	13.18	204
śrī-vaiṣṇavaṁ trayo-viṁśac	13.4	195
sṛjati harati pātīty ākhyayānāvṛtākṣo	11.24	125
śṛṇuṣva buddhim āśritya	7.8	6
sṛṣṭvedaṁ manasā viśvam	10.31	99
śrutvānubhāvaṁ brahmarṣer	8.31	39
sthitāya bhava-bhītāya	13.10	198
śudhyerann antya-jāś cāpi	10.25	94
śukasya brahmarṣabhasya	12.6	149
sukham āsanam āsīnau	8.39	44
śuko yad āha bhagavān	11.27	128
śukraś citrasvanaś caiva	11.36	134
sumanobhiḥ pariṣvakto	8.20	32
sūrya-vaṁśānukathanam	12.22	159
sūta jīva ciraṁ sādho	8.1	22
svāgatāsana-pādyārghya-	10.15	88
sva-māyāṁ vana-mālākhyām	11.11	116
śvāsaijad-alakābhātam	9.23	70
śvāsaijad-vali-saṁvigna-	9.24	70
sva-sukha-nibhṛta-cetās	12.69	189

T

tac-cittaḥ prayato japtvā	11.26	127
tad-āśrama-padaṁ puṇyam	8.18	32
tad-bāhavo loka-pālā	11.7	113
tad-darśanād vīta-pariśramo mudā	9.26	72
tad dhvāṅkṣa-tīrthaṁ na tu haṁsa-	12.51	176
tad eva ramyaṁ ruciraṁ navaṁ navam	12.50	176
tad eva satyaṁ tad u haiva maṅgalam	12.49	175
tad eva śokārṇava-śoṣaṇaṁ nṛṇām	12.50	176

tad-rasāmṛta-tṛptasya 13.15 203
tad vāg-visargo janatāgha-samplavo 12.52 177

tad vai bhajāmy ṛta-dhiyas tava 8.44 48
ta ittham apakurvanto 8.29 37
tam āha bhagavāñ charvaḥ 10.35 102
tam aham ajam anantam ātma-tattvam 12.67 188
tam anv atha vaṭo brahman 9.34 77

tamasy apāre bhramatām 8.1 22
tamasy apāre patito bhraman diśo 9.16 67
taṁ caṇḍa-śabdaṁ samudīrayantam 9.11 63
tam eva cintayann artham 9.8 61
tam evaṁ nibhṛtātmānam 10.3 81

taṁ naś chindhi mahā-yogin 8.5 23
taṁ sarva-vāda-viṣaya-pratirūpa-śīlam 8.49 53
tan-mātrāṇy asyābhivyaktim 11.16 118
tan-māyayāvṛta-matiḥ sa u eva sākṣād 8.48 52
tan no varṇaya bhadraṁ te 11.3 110

tāntrikāḥ paricaryāyām 11.2 110
tapat-taḍid-varṇa-piśaṅga-rociṣā 8.34 40
tapo-viśaṅkito brahmann 8.15 30
tasmai namo bhagavate 10.32 99
tasmai namo bhagavate puruṣāya 8.47 51

tasmai saparyāṁ vyadadhāt 10.15 88
tasmāt taveha bhagavann atha 8.46 50
tasmin pṛthivyāḥ kakudi prarūḍham 9.31 76
tasyaikadā bhṛgu-śreṣṭha 9.10 62
tasyaivam udvīkṣata ūrmi-bhīṣaṇaḥ 9.14 65

tasyaivaṁ yuñjataś cittam 8.14 29
tasyaivaṁ yuñjataś cittam 8.32 39
tasya karmāṇy apārāṇi 12.28 162
tasyāvituḥ sthira-careśitur 8.42 46
tataḥ prākṛtikaḥ sargaḥ 12.9 152

tathā kuruṣva deveśa 13.22 208
tathā purāṇa-vrātānām 13.17 204
tatheti sa smayan prāgād 9.7 60
tato brahmāṇḍa-sambhūtir 12.9 152
tato martya-parityāga 12.43 170

tato vyadṛśyanta catuḥ samudrāḥ 9.12 64
tat-prabhā vyāpinī sākṣāt 11.10 115
tatra jñāna-virāga-bhakti-sahitaṁ 13.18 204

tatrāpy ado nyastam acaṣṭa kṛtsnaśo 9.27 73
tatrāṣṭa-daśa-sāhasram 13.9 196

tau śukla-kṛṣṇau nava-kañja-locanau 8.33 40
tāvac chiśor vai śvasitena bhārgavaḥ 9.27 73
tāvān asāv api mahā- 11.9 114
tāvat sa bhagavān sākṣād 9.33 77
tayor āgamanaṁ sākṣād 10.9 85

tayor āsanam ādāya 8.38 43
te punanty uru-kālena 10.23 93
teṣāṁ nāmāni karmāṇi 11.28 128
te vai bhagavato rūpe 8.35 41
te vai tad-āśramaṁ jagmur 8.17 31

tirodhāyi-kṣaṇād asya 9.34 77
tiryaṅ-martyarṣi-deveṣu 7.14 11
tokaṁ ca tat prema-sudhā-smitena 9.31 76
trayyāruṇiḥ kaśyapaś ca 7.5 4
tri-vṛd vedaḥ suparṇākhyo 11.19 120

tṛṇāvartasya niṣpeṣas 12.29 163
try-akṣaṁ daśa-bhujaṁ prāṁśum 10.11 86
tvaṣṭā ṛcīka-tanayaḥ 11.43 138
tvāṣṭrasya janma-nidhanam 12.18 157

U

uddhavasya ca saṁvādo 12.42 170
udyac-candra-niśā-vaktraḥ 8.21 33
unnahyanti rathaṁ nāgā 11.48 142
upacita-nava-śaktibhiḥ sva ātmany 12.68 188

upāsīnasya sandhyāyām 9.10 62
upoṣya saṁhitām etām 12.61 184
ūrdhva-tiryag-avāk-sargo 12.11 153
utthāya prāñjaliḥ prahva 8.37 42

V

vaco 'mṛtāyanam ṛṣir 10.26 95
vaibhavaṁ yoga-māyāyās 10.1 79
vaiśampāyana-hārītau 7.5 4
vaiṣṇavānāṁ yathā śambhuḥ 13.16 203
vaiśyo nidhi-patitvaṁ ca 12.65 186

vālakhilyāḥ sahasrāṇi 11.49 143
vaṁśānucaritaṁ teṣām 7.16 12
vaṁśo vaṁśānucaritam 7.9 7
vanāni deśān saritaḥ purākarān 9.28 74
vārāhaṁ mātsyaṁ kaurmaṁ ca 7.24 18

varam ekaṁ vṛṇe 'thāpi 10.34 101
varaṁ pratīccha bhadraṁ te 9.3 57
varaṁ vṛṇīṣva naḥ kāmam 10.19 90
vareṇaitāvatālaṁ no 9.4 58
vasann agny-arka-somāmbu- 9.8 61

vāsaś chando-mayaṁ pītam 11.11 116
vasiṣṭho varuṇo rambhā 11.36 134
vastv advitīyaṁ tan-niṣṭham 13.12 200
vasudeva-gṛhe janma 12.27 162
vāsudevaḥ saṅkarṣaṇaḥ 11.21 123

vaṭa-patra-puṭe tokam 8.4 23
vayaṁ te parituṣṭāḥ sma 9.3 57
vāyuḥ praviṣṭa ādāya 8.20 32
vāyur jahāra tad-vāsaḥ 8.27 36
vedadarśasya śiṣyās te 7.2 2

vicaraty adhunāpy addhā 10.39 104
vidrumādhara-bhāseṣac- 9.23 70
viduroddhava-saṁvādaḥ 12.8 151
vidyucchatrur mahāśaṅkhaḥ 11.41 137
vipra-śāpāpadeśena 12.42 170

vipro 'dhītyāpnuyāt prajñām 12.65 186
virameta yadā cittam 7.21 16
visargo 'yaṁ samāhāro 7.12 9
visasarja tadā bāṇam 8.28 37
viṣṇur aśvataro rambhā 11.44 138

viśva airāvataś caiva 11.40 136
viṣvaksenas tantra-mūrtir 11.20 121
viśvāmitro makhāpeta 11.44 138
viśvaṁ vipaśyañ chvasitāc chiśor vai 9.30 75
vivasvān ugrasenaś ca 11.38 135

vraja-strīṇāṁ vilāpaś ca 12.34 165
vrata-caryā tu kanyānām 12.31 164
vṛttir bhūtāni bhūtānām 7.13 10
vyāghra-carmāmbaraṁ śūla- 10.12 86

vyatanuta kṛpayā yas tattva-dīpaṁ 12.69 189
vyatirekānvayo yasya 7.19 14
vyatīyāya mahān kālo 8.14 29
vyatīyur bhramatas tasmin 9.19 68

Y

yacchanti kāmān gṛṇataḥ 12.62 184
yad-darśanaṁ nigama ātma-rahaḥ- 8.49 53
yad-darśanāt pūrṇa-kāmaḥ 10.33 100
yādobhir bhakṣyate kvāpi 9.17 67
yad vai stuvanti ninamanti yajanty 8.42 46

ya etat śrāvayen nityam 12.59 182
ya evam etad bhṛgu-varya varṇitam 10.42 106
yaḥ kalpānte hy urvarito 8.2 23
yāḥ proktā veda-tantrābhyām 11.4 111
ya idaṁ kalya utthāya 11.26 127

ya idaṁ kṛpayā kasmai 13.20 207
yajñābhiṣekaṁ kṛṣṇasya 12.33 164
yaṁ brahmā varuṇendra-rudra- 13.1 192
yaṁ cānuśāyinaṁ prāhur 7.18 13
yaṁ vai na veda vitathākṣa-pathair 8.48 52

yan-māyayāpi vibudhā 10.2 80
yan nāgād ahamo bhāvam 8.30 38
yan namantīśitavyāni 10.28 97
yaśaḥ-śriyām eva pariśramaḥ paro 12.54 179
yat kiñcid anyad vyavahāra-kāraṇam 9.29 74

yato devāsura-narās 12.17 156
yatrātma-vidyā hy akhilā 12.43 170
yatrāvatīrṇo bhagavān 12.27 162
yat-saṁskāra-kalānuvartana-vaśād 13.2 193
yat sātvatāḥ puruṣa-rūpam uśanti 8.46 50

yāvad bhāgavataṁ naiva 13.14 202
yāvān ayaṁ vai puruṣo 11.9 114
yayāter jyeṣṭha-putrasya 12.26 161
yena kriyā-naipuṇena 11.3 110
yoga-dhāraṇayotkrāntiḥ 12.7 150

yogena vā tadātmānam 7.21 16
yogīndrāya namas tasmai 13.21 207
yogīndrāya tad-ātmanātha 13.19 206
yuga-lakṣaṇa-vṛttiś ca 12.44 171
yūyaṁ dvijāgryā bata bhūri-bhāgā 12.56 180

General Index

Numerals in boldface type indicate references to translations of the verses of *Śrīmad-Bhāgavatam*.

A

Absolute Truth
as free from suffering & death, **206**
Personality of, 201
pervasiveness of, **15**
as ultimate reality, **200**
See also: Kṛṣṇa; Supreme Lord
Āṅgirasa, **4**
Acyuta, Lord. *See:* Kṛṣṇa; Supreme Lord
Adhokṣaja, Lord. *See:* Kṛṣṇa; Supreme Lord
Age, present. *See:* Kali-yuga
Aghāsura, **163**
Aila, King, **161**
Airāvata, **136**
Akṛtavraṇa, **5, 6**
Akrūra, **166**
Aṁśu as sun, **137**
Analogies
calm water & Mārkaṇḍeya, **82**
clay & Lord, 16
darkness & misfortune, **174**
dreamer & Lord, **99**
fire of digestion & devotional service, 16–17
Kāśī & *Bhāgavatam*, **204**
king & *Śrīmad-Bhāgavatam*, 194
magician & Lord, **98**
seed & activities, **10**
seed & desire, **10**
Śiva & *Bhāgavatam*, **203**
sun & Kṛṣṇa, **174**
wind & Śiva, **86**
Ananta, Lord, **117**
See also: Balarāma, Lord
Aṅgirā, **135**
Aniruddha, **124**
Annihilation
causes of, **14**
four types of, **13**
living entity &, **14**
Mārkaṇḍeya wandering in, **63–68**
Annihilation (*continued*)
as potency of Kṛṣṇa, **13**
as topic of *Bhāgavatam*, **151, 171**
as topic of *Purāṇas*, **7**
Anumlocā, **135**
Apsarā, Puñjikasthalī, **36–37**
Apsarās, 129
Ariṣṭa demon, **165**
Arjuna, 208
Aryamā as sun, **133**
Āsāraṇa, **135**
Aśvatara, **139**
Atharvā, 199
Atharva Veda, **4**
Athaujā, **133**
Atri, **133**

B

Babhru, **3**
Badarikāśrama, **60,** 61
Bakāsura, **163**
Balarāma, Lord
Dhenukāsura &, **164**
Dvivida gorilla &, **169**
See also: Ananta, Lord
Bāṇāsura, **169**
Benediction(s)
via giving *Bhāgavatam* as gift, **201–**202
via hearing Kṛṣṇa's pastimes, **182–83**
via hearing *Bhāgavatam*, **182–86**
via narration about *Purāṇa*, **19**
Bhadra, 123
Bhaga as sun, **137**
Bhagavān, Lord. *See:* Kṛṣṇa; Supreme Lord
Bhaktisiddhānta Sarasvatī Ṭhākura
cited
on Caitanya chanting, **173**
on Supreme Lord's breathing, **193**
commentary on *Bhāgavatam* by, 210

Bhaktivedanta Swami Prabhupāda, 210
Bharadvāja, **136**
Bharata, **161**
Bharata, King, **155**
Bhavānī. *See:* Umā
Bhīṣma, **161**
Bhṛgu, **135**
  Mārkaṇḍeya &, **28**
  Mārkaṇḍeya descendant of, **24, 56, 105**
  Paraśurāma descendant of, **161**
Birth, four sources of, 65
Body, material, Kṛṣṇa &, **15,** 16
Body, subtle, 16-17
Brahmā, Lord
  Atharvā son of, 199
  as benediction giver, **91**
  calves & cowherd boys hidden by, **163**
  day of, measurement of, 24
  glories of Kṛṣṇa fathomless to, **188**
  Kṛṣṇa speaks *Bhāgavatam* to, **198–99,** 206
  as manifestation of Kṛṣṇa's potency, 92-93
  Nārada's conversation with, **150**
  passion mode represented by, 51
  planet of, **116**
  position of, attainment of, 59
  Rāmāyaṇa &, 198
  spiritual science instructed by, 199
  as *Śrīmad-Bhāgavatam's* first recipient, 199, **198, 206**
  Śrīmad-Bhāgavatam spoken by, **206**
  time's passage &, **47**
Brahmaloka, **116**
Brahmāpeta, **138**

C

Caitanya Mahāprabhu
  Kṛṣṇa consciousness distributed by, 199
  Śrīvāsa Ṭhākura &, **173**
Cāmara fans, **120**
Caṇḍa, 123
Cāṇūra, **166**
Cedi, King of, **169**
Celestial sphere as topic of *Bhāgavatam,* **156**
Celibacy, Mārkaṇḍeya &, **27, 29**
Chanting of Kṛṣṇa's holy names, **209**
Chariot of sun-god, **142, 143**
Citrā Mountain, **31**
Citrasvana, **134**
Civilization (modern), & transcendental literature, **178**
Conditioned soul(s)
  birth of, four sources of, 65
  as causes of universal functions, 14
  control desired by, 97
  knowledge cultivated by, 81
  perceptions by, limited, 14, 60
  satisfied via Lord, **193**
  understanding by, limitations on, 199
Consciousness, stages of, **15, 16, 124**
Cowherd boys
  Brahmā hides, **163**
  Kṛṣṇa saves from forest fire, **164**
Creation of universe(s)
  causes of, **14**
  elements of, 112
  living entity &, **14**
  nine elements of, 112
  secondary, **10**
  Supreme Lord source of, **99–100**
  as topic of *Bhāgavatam,* **150, 152, 171**
  as topic of *Purāṇas,* **7,** 8
Creation, the
  defined, **9**
  See also: Material world
Cupid, **34, 36, 37, 38**

D

Dakṣa
  destruction of sacrifice of, **155**
  Mārkaṇḍeya &, **28**
  Pracetās &, **156**
Dantavakra, **169**
Death
  Absolute Truth free of, **206**
  Mārkaṇḍeya Ṛṣi &, **28**
Demigod(s)
  churning of milk ocean by, **158**
  vs. demons, **159**

Demigods (*continued*)
incarnation of Kṛṣṇa as, **12**
worship to, 51
Demon(s)
vs. demigods, **159**
Kṛṣṇa kills, **163–65,** 166, 167, 168–69
as topic of *Bhāgavatam,* **153, 157, 159**
Desire, material, **10**
Devahūti, **154**
Devī. *See:* Umā
Devotee(s) of Supreme Lord
assocation with, **84**
mundane topics neglected by, **177**
pure. *See:* Pure devotee(s)
purification via seeing, **93, 95**
sinful reactions removed from, **148**
Śiva greatest of, **203**
Śiva's praise for, **84, 92–95**
understanding of life via, 101
Devotional service to Supreme Lord
vs. false ego, 17
intelligence in, via *Bhāgavatam,* **186**
prayers for, **208**
sinful reactions eradicated via, **119**
as *Śrīmad-Bhāgavatam's* goal, **200**
as supreme religious principle, **146**
as topic of *Bhāgavatam,* **149**
Dhanañjaya, **136**
Dhātā as sun, 123, **132**
Dhenukāsura, **164**
Dhṛtarāṣṭra, **138**
Dhruva Mahārāja, **155**
Diti, descendants of, **157**
Doorkeepers of Lord, **121,** 123
Duṣmanta, **161**
Dvādaśī, **184**
Dvārakā City, **167**
Dvivida, **169**
Dynasty defined, **13**

E

Earth planet
as manifestation of Lord, 126
saved from Garbhodaka Ocean, **153**
as topic of *Bhāgavatam,* **156**
Ekādaśī, **184**
Elāpatra, **135**
Elements of creation listed, 112
Energies of Lord
arrangement of, **189**
inferior. *See:* Illusory energy
internal, **121**
universal functions &, **188**
Evolution, **152**
Existence
Kṛṣṇa Soul of, **181**
maintenance of, by Lord, **125**
as topic of *Bhāgavatam,* **156**
See also: Material world; Universe(s)

F

False ego
devotional service vs., 17
division of, threefold, **9**
as element of creation, 112
via *mahat-tattva,* **9**
Fasting & hearing *Bhāgavatam,* **184**
Fear, **49**
Fire & Sudarśana disc, **118**
Fruitive activities
nature of, **178**
renunciation of, **16**
threefold division of, **9**

G

Gajendra, **158**
Gandharvas, 129
Ganges River, **203**
Garbhodaka Ocean, **153**
Garbhodakaśāyī Viṣṇu, **152–53**
Garuḍa, **121**
Ghṛtācī, **136**
Giriśa, Lord. *See:* Śiva, Lord
Goddess of fortune, **121–**23
Godhead, returning to
via pure goodness, **50**
via studying *Bhāgavatam,* **186**

Gokula, Kṛṣṇa in, **162**
Goodness, mode of
  liberation via **49, 50**
  pure, **51**
  throne of Kṛṣṇa &, **117**
Gopīparāṇadhana dāsa, 210
Govardhana Hill, **165**

H

Hāhā, **133**
Hari, Lord. *See:* Kṛṣṇa; Supreme Lord
Hārīta, **5**
Hayaśīrṣā, Lord
  as topic of *Bhāgavatam*, **158**
  See also: Kṛṣṇa, Lord; Supreme Lord
Hearing & chanting about Kṛṣṇa
  auspiciousness via **127**
  benedictions via, **182–86**
  compared with *varṇāśrama* & hearing *Vedas*, **179**
  Kali-yuga purified —via, **25**
  misfortune ended via, **174**
  realization of Lord via, **128**
  remembering Kṛṣṇa via, **179**
  sinful reaction ended via, **174**
  as suitable engagement for human being, **147**
Hell, **156**
Heti, **132**
Hiraṇyākṣa, **153–57**
Hṛṣīkeśa, Lord *See:* Kṛṣṇa; Supreme Lord
Hūhū, **134**
Human form of life
  civilized, compared with animalistic, 175
  suitable engagement in, **147**

I

Ignorance, mode of
  result of, **49**
  shield of Kṛṣṇa &, **118**
  Śiva represents, 51
Ikṣvāku, **159**
Ilā, **159**
Illusory energy
  Brahmā &, 199
  demigods bewildered by, **80**
  hearing & chanting about Kṛṣṇa ends influence of, **174**
  Mārkaṇḍeya curious about, **60,** 61
  Mārkaṇḍeya wandering in, **63–68, 96**
Incarnation(s) of Supreme Lord. *See:* Kṛṣṇa, incarnation(s) of
Indra, Lord
  glories of Kṛṣṇa fathomless to, **188**
  incarnation of Kṛṣṇa as, **12**
  Kṛṣṇa &, **165**
  Mārkaṇḍeya attacked by, **31–39**
  as sun-god, **135**
Initiation, spiritual
  of Mārkaṇḍeya, **27**
  purification via, **119**
Intelligence, conceptions of Lord in terms of, **124**
Internal potency of Lord, **121**–23
Iṣa, month of, **138**

J

Jājali, **3**
Jamadagni, **138**
Janaka, King, **160**
Jarāsandha, **167**
Jaya, 123
Jīva Gosvāmī, cited
  on *Purāṇas'* topics, 8
  on list of *Purāṇas*, 18
  on Śaunaka & Sūta, 22
  on goddess of fortune, 122
  on *Mahābhārata* & *Rāmāyaṇa*, 197-98
Jīva Gosvāmī, commentary on *Bhāgavatam* by, 210

K

Kabandha, **1,** 2
Kacchanīra, **133**

Kakutstha, **160**
Kālayavana, King, **167**
Kali-yuga
  purification of, **25**
  as topic of *Bhāgavatam*, **171**
Kambalāśva, **138**
Kaṁsa, **166**
Kapila, Lord, **154**
Kardama Muni, **154**
Kāśī, city of, **204**
Kaśyapa Muni, **4–6, 137**
Kaustubha gem, **115**
Keśī demon, **165**
King(s)
  study of *Bhāgavatam* recommended for, **186**
  See also: specific kings & Mahārājas
Knowledge
  conception of Lord needed with, **178**
  conditioned souls cultivation of, 81
  Kṛṣṇa as highest, 54
  about Kṛṣṇa, satisfaction for soul via, 54
  pure, **126**
  via remembering Kṛṣṇa, **180**
  transcendental, 54, **149**
Kośala, King of. *See:* Rāmacandra, Lord
Kṛṣṇa, Lord
  as abode of moving & nonmoving creatures, **189**
  advent of, in Vasudeva's home, **162**
  Aghāsura &, **163**
  as all-pervading witness, **207**
  arrows of, **118**
  associates & paraphernalia of, 125
  Brahmā enlightened by, **198–**99
  vs. Cāṇūra, **166**
  vs. Cedi's king, **169**
  conchshell of, **118**
  cowherd boys saved from fire by, **164**
  demons killed by, **163–69**
  disappearance of, from mortal world, **170**
  disturbing elements destroyed by, **127**
  earrings of, **116**
  emphasis on, as original Personality of Godhead, 198
  energies of. *See:* Energies of Lord
Kṛṣṇa, Lord (*continued*)
  forest fire &, **164**
  form of
    described, **115, 116**
    as pure goodness, **51**
  gestures of hands of, **119**
  glories of, as fathomless, **188**
  glorification of
    benefits of, **173, 174, 176, 177–78**
    See also: Hearing & chanting about Kṛṣṇa
  in Gokula, **162**
  gopīs &, **165**
  Govardhana Hill lifted by, **165**
  highest benediction given by, 57–58
  illusory energy of. *See:* Illusory Energy
  incarnation(s) of
    as Kūrma **193**
    in *manv-antaras*, **158**
    as Nara-Nārāyaṇa, **40**
    partial, six kinds of, **112**
    as topic of *Bhāgavatam*, **148–50, 158, 162–70**
    in various species, **11**
  internal potency of, **121,** 122
  vs. Kālayavana, **167**
  vs. Kāliya serpent, **165**
  vs. Keśī demon, **165**
  as leader of all deities, **189**
  as Lord of Sātvatas, **148**
  lotus feet of, 71–72
  love for. *See:* Love for Kṛṣṇa
  Mārkaṇḍeya sees, on island, **70–73, 76**
  as master of Yadu dynasty, 148
  in Mathurā, **166–67**
  vs. Mura demon, **169**
  Nanda rescued from snake by, **165**
  obeisances to, **173**
  paraphernalia & associates of, **114–24**
  pārijāta tree &, **168**
  Parīkṣit protected by, 208
  pastimes of
    auspiciousness via hearing, **127**
    benedictions for hearing, **182–83**
    encouragement for devotees via, **200**
    inauspiciousness ended via hearing, **182**
    as Kūrma, **193**

Kṛṣṇa, Lord
pastimes of (*continued*)
Śukadeva attracted to, **190**
for Yadu dynasty's satisfaction, **167**
pervasiveness of, **52**
prayers to, for devotional service, **208**
vs. Pūtanā, **163**
quiver of, **118**
Rāma &, **163**
remembering, via hearing & chanting, **179**
representative of, protocol to, 101
Rukmiṇī kidnapped by, **168**
vs. Śālva, **169**
vs. Śambara, **169**
Sāndipani Muni's son recovered by, **166**
vs. Śaṅkhacūḍa, **165**
as senses' controller, 148
shield of, **118**
sins of Kali-yuga annihilated by, **187**
vs. Śiva, **168**
as Soul of all existence, **181**
Śrīmad-Bhāgavatam spoken by, **198,** 199, **206, 207**
Sudharmā assembly hall &, **168**
as supreme among Deities, **203**
as supreme creator, **146**
Surabhi cow &, **165**
surrender to, 54
sword of, **118**
vs. Tṛṇāvarta, **163**
Uddhava's conversation with, **170**
umbrella of, **121**
understanding, via Vedic knowledge, **53**
Vārāṇasi City &, **169**
vs. wrestlers, **166**
Yadu dynasty withdrawn by, **170**
yawning weapon of, **168**
yellow garment of, **116**
See also: Supreme Lord
Kṛṣṇa consciousness. *See:* Devotional service; Love for Kṛṣṇa
Kṛṣṇa-dvaipāyana Vyāsa. *See:* Vyāsadeva
Kṛtasthalī, **132**
Kumuda, **3**, 123
Kūrma, Lord, **158, 193**
Kurukṣetra battle, **169**

L

Leo, constellation of, 202
Liberation
via mode of goodness, **49**
as topic of *Bhāgavatam,* **150**
as topic of *Purāṇas,* 8
via *Śrīmad-Bhāgavatam,* **205**
Life forms, human. *See:* Human form of life
Literature, materialistic, **175,** 202, **203**
Living entities
attitude toward, proper, 126
causes of universal activities &, **14**
Love for Kṛṣṇa
as goal of *Bhāgavatam,* 201
See also: Devotional service

M

Madhu, month of, **132**
Mahāpuruṣa
benediction via hearing & chanting about, **128**
See also: Universal form of Lord
Mahārāja Bharata, **155**
Mahārāja Parīkṣit. *See:* Parīkṣit Mahārāja
Mahārāja Prācīnabarhi, **155**
Mahārāja Priyavrata, **155**
Mahāśaṅkha, **137**
Maitreya & Vidura, **151**
Makaras, **67**
Makhāpeta, **139**
Māndhātā, **160**
Manus & incarnations of Kṛṣṇa, **12**
Manu(s). *See: specific Manus*
Mārkaṇḍeya Ṛṣi
benediction requested from Śiva by, **101**
benediction via hearing pastimes of, **107**
as Bhṛgu's descendant, **24, 56, 105**
celibacy practiced by, **27, 29**
Cupid &, **34, 36, 37, 38**
as curious to witness Māyā, **62**
death conquered by, **28**
description of, **27–28**
father of, **24, 27**

Mārkaṇḍeya Ṛṣi (*continued*)
hermitage of, location of, **31**
illusory energy wandered in by, **63–68, 75–76, 96**
Kṛṣṇa seen by, on island, **70–73, 76**
liberation not desired by, **83**
life span of, **103**
meditation by
extent of, **85**, 88
Indra's attempt to ruin, **31–39**
Nara-Nārāyaṇa sages &, **40–53**
in ocean of dissolution, **63–68, 75–76, 96**
praised by Lord, **57**
prayers by
to Kṛṣṇa, **58–60, 99–100**
to Nara-Nārāyaṇa, **45–53, 58–60**
quoted
on lords of universe, **97–98**
on Śiva, **89**–90, **100**
on Supreme Lord as creator of world, **99–100**
on universal controllers, **97–98**
Śiva appears to, **86–87**
Śiva's benediction for, **103**
Śiva's words appreciated by, **95**
story about, as historical narration, 106
tolerance of, **38**
as topic of *Bhāgavatam*, **172**
Umā &, 57, **82**
universe viewed by, before annihilation, **73, 75**
wandering in inundation, **63–68, 75–76, 96**
Maruts, **192**
Material body, Kṛṣṇa &, **15,** 16
Materialists' perceptions, **52–53**
Material life
renunciation of, **200**
transcended via *Bhāgavatam*, 206
Material nature
Ananta as unmanifest phase of, **117**
Mahā-māyā controls, 122
universal functions via, **126**
Material work. *See:* Fruitive activities
Material world
beauty of, 201
Material world (*continued*)
perception of, by conditioned soul, 60
purpose of, 14
three ruling deities of, 92–93
universal form's corollaries in, **114**
Matsya, Lord, **158**
Māyā. See: Illusory energy
Meditation
by Mārkaṇḍeya Ṛṣi, **62**
sun object of, 119
Menakā, **133**
Mental speculators, **193**
Milk Ocean, **158**
Mind
conceptions of Lord in terms of, **124**
material platform transcended by, **16**
Mitra, **133**
Moon-god, dynasty of, **161**
Mṛkaṇḍu, **24**
Mundane literature, 175
Mura demon, **169**
Muṣṭika, **166**

N

Nabhas, month of, **135**
Nābhi, King, **155**
Nāgas, 129
Nahuṣa, King, **161**
Nakṣatrakalpa, **4**
Nanda (Lord's doorkeeper), **121,** 123
Nanda Mahārāja, **165**
Nara-Nārāyaṇa sages
Badarikāśrama hermitage of, **60–**61
description of, **41**
Mārkaṇḍeya Ṛṣi &, **40–53, 57**
Nārada Muni
Brahmā's conversation with, **150**
Prācīnabarhi &, **155**
Śrīmad-Bhāgavatam spoken by, **206**
universal form &, **133**
Vālmiki &, 198
Vasudeva's conversation with, **170**
Narasiṁha, Lord, **158**
Nārāyaṇa, Lord
name of, explained, 148
See also: Kṛṣṇa; Supreme Lord

Nature, material. *See:* Material nature; Material world
Nimi, King, **160**
Nṛga, King, **159**

O

Obeisances, **209**
Ocean tides, **193**
Ocean of dissolution, **63–68**
Oṁ syllable, **116**

P

Pañcajana demon, **169**
Pāṇḍavas, **169**
Paraśurāma, Lord, **161**
Pārijāta tree, **168**
Parīkṣit Mahārāja
  curse by *brāhmaṇa's* son, **150**
  disappearance of, **172**
  protected by Kṛṣṇa, 208
  Śrīmad-Bhāgavatam recitation facilitated by, 208
  Śukadeva &, **206, 208**
  as *viṣṇu-rāta*, 208
Passion, mode of
  Brahmā represents, 51
  result of, **49**
Pathya, **1**, 2, **3**
Pauṇḍraka, **169**
Pauruṣeya, **133**
Philosopher(s), understandings by, various, **53**, 54
Pīṭha demon, **169**
Planets
  sun-god &, **130**
  sun &, **132**
Prabhupāda, Śrīla, 210
Pracaṇḍa, 123
Pracetās & Dakṣa, **156**
Pradyumna, **124**
Prāgjyotiṣa-pura city, **169**
Praheti, **133**
Prahlāda Mahārāja, **157**
Prajāpati Dakṣa, **28, 156**
Pralambāsura, **164**
Pramlocā, **135**
Prayers
  to Kṛṣṇa, **58–60, 99–100**
  by Mārkaṇḍeya. *See:* Mārkaṇḍeya, prayers by
  to Śiva, **89–90**
  to sun-god, **142, 143**
Priyavrata Mahārāja, **155**
Pṛthu Mahārāja, **155**
Pulaha, **133**
Pulastya, **132**
Puṇḍarīkākṣa, 123
Puñjikasthalī, **36–37**
Purāṇa(s)
  Bhāgavata. See: Śrīmad-Bhāgavatam
  Śrīmad-Bhāgavatam compared with others, 194, **202–204**
  Śrīmad-Bhāgavatam compilation of, **186**
Pure devotee(s)
  as most elevated *brāhmaṇas*, 94
  qualifications of, 54
  See also: specific pure devotees
Pure goodness
  Godhead returned to via, **50**
  Kṛṣṇa's form composed of, **51**
Purification
  via devotees, **93**
  via hearing *Bhāgavatam*, **182–84**, 202
  via initiation, **119**
  via remembering Kṛṣṇa, **180**
  of world via *Bhāgavatam*, 202
Pūṣā, **136**
Puṣpabhadrā River, **31, 63**
Puṣya, month of, **137**
Pūtanā demon, **163**

R

Rākṣasas, 129
Rāma, **6**
Rāmacandra, Lord
  pastimes of, in *Rāmāyaṇa*, 198
  as topic of *Bhāgavatam*, **160**

Rambhā, **134, 139**
Rathakṛt, **132**
Rathasvana, **133**
Religion, supreme principle of. *See:* Devotional service
Renunciation
  defined, 200
  Śrīmad-Bhāgavatam encourages, **200**
  as topic of *Bhāgavatam,* **149**
Romaharṣaṇa
  Sūta Gosvāmī son of, **5**
  as Vyāsadeva's disciple, **5, 6**
Ṛṣabha, Lord, **155**
Ṛtasena, **137**
Ṛtu, **136**
Rudra, Lord. *See:* Śiva, Lord
Rukmiṇī kidnapped by Kṛṣṇa, **168**

S

Sahajanya, **134**
Sahas, month of, **137**
Saindhavāyana, **3**
Śālva, **169**
Sāndīpani Muni, **166**
Śaṅkara, Lord
  glories of Kṛṣṇa fathomless to, **188**
  See also: Śiva, Lord
Saṅkarṣaṇa, Lord, **124**
Śaṅkhacūḍa, **165**
Śaṅkhapāla, **135**
Sāṅkhya, **116**
Śaṅkukarṇa, 123
Śāntanu, **161**
Śāntikalpa, **4**
Śārṅga sword, **118**
Śarva, Lord. *See:* Śiva, Lord
Śaryāti, **160**
Śaśāda, **159**
Śatajit, **138**
Śatarūpā, **154**
Satyavatī, 197
Saubhari, **160**
Śaunaka Ṛṣi
  questions by
    about advent & description of Lord, **111**
    about *tantra* scriptures' conclusion, **110**
  quoted
    on Mārkaṇḍeya Ṛṣi, **24**
    on sun-god's associates, **129**
    on worship to Lord, immortality via, **111**
Sāvarṇi, **5, 6**
Senajit, **136**
Senses
  arrows of Kṛṣṇa as, **116**
  false ego's development &, **9**
Sinful activities, renunciation of, 199
Sinful reactions
  devotees' removed, **148**
  devotional service ends, **119**
  freedom from
    via chanting of Kṛṣṇa's names, **209**
    via hearing & chanting about Kṛṣṇa, **173**
    via obeisances to Lord, **173**
    via study of *Bhāgavatam,* **186**
Śiva, Lord
  benefits of seeing, **100**
  bull carrier of, **81**
  as greatest devotee, **203**
  vs. Kṛṣṇa, **168**
  as manifestation of Lord's potency, 92–93
  Mārkaṇḍeya &, **28**
  Mārkaṇḍeya offered benediction by, **91, 103**
  Mārkaṇḍeya welcomes, **87–90**
  in Mārkaṇḍeya's heart, **86–87**
  Mārkaṇḍeya's suffering ended by, **96**
  mode of ignorance represented by, 51
  quoted
    on benedictions, givers of, **91**
    on devotees, **84, 92–94**
    on immortality, **91**
  as servant of Lord, **101**
  as shelter of pure souls, **84**
  as topic of *Bhāgavatam,* **153**
  Umā &, **82–84**
Sky, **118**
Sleep, **124**

Soul(s)
  Kaustubha gem representative of, **115**
  as nondifferent from Absolute Truth, **200**
Species of life, creation of various, **153–156**
Spiritual knowledge, 54, **149**
Śrīdhara Svāmī
  cited on Vedadarśa's edition of *Atharva Veda*, 3
  commentary on *Bhāgavatam* by, 210
Śrī, goddess of fortune, **121–23**
Śrīmad-Bhāgavatam
  See also: *Śrīmad-Bhāgavatam*, quotation(s) from
  benedictions for giving, **201–202**
  benedictions for hearing & studying, **182–86**
  Brahmā first recipient of, **198**, 199, **206**
  Brahmā speaks, **206**
  commentaries on, 210
  compared with *Purāṇas*, 194, **202–204**
  as compilation of *Purāṇas*, **186**
  contents of. *See: Śrīmad-Bhagavatam*, topic(s) of
  devotional service goal of, **200**
  as essence of *Vedānta* philosophy, **200, 203**
  first verse of, content of, 199, 206
  goal of
    devotional service as, **200**
    love for Kṛṣṇa as, 201
  as greatest of *Purāṇas*, **203–204**
  hearing
    benedictions for, **182–86**
    compared with studying *Vedas*, **185**
    during fasting, **184**
    See also: Hearing & chanting about Kṛṣṇa
  intelligence in devotional service via, **186**
  Kṛṣṇa speaks, **198–**199, **206**
  length of, **196**
  liberation via, **205**
  Parīkṣit facilitates recitation of, 208
  Parīkṣit hears recitation of, **182**
  presentation of, via Prabhupāda's mercy, 210
  purification of world via, 202
Śrīmad-Bhāgavatam (*continued*)
  purity of, **205**
  renunciation of material life encouraged by, **200**
  study of
    for kings, **186**
    for *śūdras*, **186**
    for *vaiśyas*, **186**
    liberation via, **205**
    sinful reactions ended via, **186**
  Sūta hears narration of, **182**
  topics of
    Absolute Truth as, **149**, 201
    Aila as, **161**
    annihilation of universe as, **151**
    Bharata as, **155, 161**
    Bhīṣma as, **161**
    celestial sphere as, **156**
    characteristics of people in various ages as, **171**
    conversation between Kardama & Devahūti as, **154**
    creation of universe as, **150, 152**
    creation of various species as, **153**
    Dakṣa as, **156**
    Dakṣa's sacrifice as, **155**
    demigods churning milk ocean as, **158**
    demigods' creation as, **153**
    demons' death as, **163–65,** 166, 167, 168–69
    devotional service as, **149**
    Dhruva Mahārāja as, **155**
    disappearance of Kṛṣṇa from mortal world as, **170**
    dissemination of *Vedas* as, **172**
    Dvārakā as, **167**
    earth as, **153,156**
    evolution via elemental transformation as, **152**
    freedom from material life as, **205**
    Gajendra as, **158**
    Garbhodakaśāyī Viṣṇu & lotus as, **152–53**
    glories of Absolute Truth as, 201
    Hayaśīrṣā as, **158**
    hell as, **156**
    Hiraṇyakaśipu as, **157**

Śrīmad-Bhāgavatam
topics of (*continued*)
Hiraṇyākṣa as, **153, 157**
history of Absolute Truth as, **149**
Ikṣvāku as, **159**
Ilā as, **159**
incarnations of Lord as, **150**
inquiries about *Bhāgavatam* as, **151**
Janaka's descendants as, **160**
Kakutstha as, **160**
Kali-yuga as, **171**
Kapila as, **154**
Khaṭvāṅga as, **160**
kings as, **155–161**
knowledge about Lord as, **149**
knowledge of *paramahaṁsas* as, **205**
Kṛṣṇa's pastimes as, **150, 162–70, 187, 190, 200**
liberation as, **150**
list of ten, 8
lotus & Garbhodakaśāyī Viṣṇu as, **152–153**
Māndhātā as, **160**
Mārkaṇḍeya Ṛṣi as, **172**
Nābhi as, **155**
Nahuṣa as, **161**
Nārada & Brahmā's conversation as, **150**
Nārada & Vasudeva's conversation as, **170**
Nārada's history as, **149**
Nṛga as, **159**
Parīkṣit & Śukadeva's conversation as, **150**
Parīkṣit's disappearance as, **172**
Parīkṣit's history as, **149**
Paraśurāma as, **161**
pastimes of Kṛṣṇa as, **150, 162–70, 187, 190, 200**
Prācīnabarhi as, **155**
Prahlāda as, **157**
Priyavrata as, **155**
progeny of Dakṣa's daughters as, **156**
Rāmacandra as, **160**
renunciation as, **149**
Ṛṣabha as, **155**
Sagara as, **160**

Śrīmad-Bhāgavatam
topics of (*continued*)
Śāntanu as, **161**
Śaryāti as, **160**
Śaśāda as, **159**
Śatarūpā as, **154**
Saubhari as, **160**
Śiva's birth as, **153**
subterranean regions as, **156**
Sudyumna as, **159**
Śukadeva & Parīkṣit's conversation as, **150**
Sukanyā as, **160**
sun as, **172**
sun-god's descendants as, **159**
Svāyambhuva Manu as, **153**
Tārā as, **159**
ten, listed, 8
time as, **152**
topics of *Bhāgavatam* as, **151**
Uddhava & Kṛṣṇa's conversation as, **170**
universe's annihilation as, **151**
universe's creation as, **150, 152**
universe's structure as, **152**
universal form as, **172**
Vedas' dissemination as, **172**
Vidura's conversations with Uddhava & Maitreya as, **151**
Vṛtrāsura as, **157**
Yadu dynasty as, **161, 170**
Yayāti as, **161**
yoga as, **150**
transcending material life via, 206
understanding, obeisances to Śukadeva necessary for, **190**
Śrīmad-Bhāgavatam, quotations from
on devotional service
on Kṛṣṇa enlightening Brahmā, 199
on *Purāṇas'* subject matter, 8
Śrīvāsa Ṭhākura, **173**
Śrotā, **135**
Subhadra, 123
Subterranean regions, **156**
Subtle body, 16–17
Śuci, month of, **134**
Sudharmā assembly hall, **168**

Sudyumna, **159**
Suffering
 Absolute Truth free of, **206**
 freedom from, via obeisances to Kṛṣṇa, **209**
Śukadeva Gosvāmī
 obeisances to
  importance of, **190**
  by Sūta Gosvāmī, **208**
 Parīkṣit instructed by. *See: specific subject matter*
 Parīkṣit saved by, **208**
 pastimes of Kṛṣṇa attract, **190**
 Sūta disciple of, 208
 Vyāsadeva father of, **190**
 Vyāsadeva speaks *Bhāgavatam* to, **206**
Śukra, **134**
Śukra, month of, **133**
Sumantu Ṛṣi, **1**, 2
Sumukha, 123
Sun
 as creation of Lord, **130**
 as expansion of Lord, **129**
 in Leo constellation, 201-202
 planets regulated by, **132**
 as soul of universe, **172**
 worship of Lord on, **119**
 See also: Sun-god(s)
Śunaka, **3**
Sunanda, 123
Sun-god(s)
 associates of, **132–39**
 descendants of, as topic of *Bhāgavatam*, **159**
 description of, in nine aspects, **131**
 as expansions of Lord, **130, 141**
 glorification of, **142**
 list of various, **132–39**
 as nondifferent from Lord, **130**
 prayers to, by Vālakhilya *brāhmaṇas*, **142**
 sinful reactions ended via remembering, **141**
 source of ritualistic activities, **130**
 travels of, purpose of, **132, 141**
 See also: specific sun-gods
Supreme Lord
 as abode of moving & nonmoving creatures, **189**
 as Adhokṣaja, **103**
 associates & paraphernalia of, **114–24**
Supreme Lord (*continued*)
 Brahmā manifestation of creating potency of, 92
 breathing by, ocean tides &, **193**
 conceptions of, via consciousness' stages, **124**
 conditioned souls satisfied by, **193**
 creation effected by, **99–100**
 doorkeepers for, **121**
 earth manifestation of, 126
 energies of. *See:* Energies of Lord
 existence maintained by, **125**
 forms of
  description of, **115, 116**
  as Nara-Nārāyaṇa. *See:* Nara-Nārāyaṇa sages
  See also: Kṛṣṇa, Lord, incarnation(s) of
 four personal expansions of, **124, 125**
 glorification of
  benefits of, **173, 174, 176, 177–78**
  See also: Chanting holy names of Kṛṣṇa; Hearing & chanting about Kṛṣṇa
 goddess of fortune &, **122–**123
 illusory potency of. *See:* Illusory energy
 incarnations of. *See:* Kṛṣṇa, incarnation(s) of
 lotus flower from navel of, **198**
 Mārkaṇḍeya praised by, **57**
 Māyā potency of. *See:* Illusory energy
 mental speculators satisfied by, **193**
 mercy of
  activities in material world performed via, **10**
  pastimes of Lord as, **98**
 mystic perfections of, **121**
 obeisances to, by Sūta Gosvāmī, **192**
 paraphernalia associates of, 125
 Parīkṣit under protection of, 208
 pastimes of. *See:* Kṛṣṇa, pastimes of
 as performer of material functions, **126**
 personal expansions of, four, **124**
 philosophers' understandings of, various, **53,** 54
 potencies of
  annihilation enacted by inherent, **13**
  Brahmā manifestation of, 92
  goddess of fortune representation of internal, **121**
  See also: Energies of Lord

Supreme Lord (*continued*)
realization about, via hearing & chanting, **128**
representative of, protocol to, 101
as Supersoul, **99**
as topic of *Bhāgavatam*, **148–50, 158, 162–70**
transcendental hymns praising, **192**
universal functions enacted by, **188**
Viṣṇu manifestation of, 93
See also: Kṛṣṇa, Lord
Surabhi cow, **165**
Surrender to Kṛṣṇa, 54
Sūryavarcā, **139**
Suṣeṇa, **136**
Sūta Gosvāmī
blessing to audience by, **193**
Kṛṣṇa's status described by, 198
obeisances by
to Kṛṣṇa, **207, 209**
to Śukadeva, **208**
Purāṇas studied by, **5**
quoted. *See: specific subject matter*
Romaharṣaṇa father of, **5**
Śaunaka requests Mārkaṇḍeya story from, **22–24**
Śrīmad-Bhāgavatam narration heard by, **182**
Śukadeva heard by, **182**
Śukadeva spiritual master of, **190**

T

Takṣaka, **133**
Tapas, month of, **136**
Tārā, **159**
Tārkṣya, **137**
Tilottamā, **138**
Time
sword of Kṛṣṇa &, **118**
as topic of *Bhāgavatam*, **152**
Timiṅgila fish, **67**
Transcendental literature
compared with mundane literature, **175**
See also: Śrīmad-Bhāgavatam
Tṛṇāvarta demon, **163**
Tumburu, **132**
Tvaṣṭā, **138**

U

Uddhava, **151**
Ugrasena, **135**
Umā
Mārkaṇḍeya observed by, **81–82**
as pleased with Mārkaṇḍeya, 57
quoted on Mārkaṇḍeya, **82**
Universal form of Lord
composed of nine creative elements, **112**
corollaries of, in material world, **114**
description of, **115–20**
as topic of *Bhāgavatam*, **152, 172**
Universe
annihilation of. *See:* Annihilation
causes of creation, maintenance & destruction of, **14**
creation of. *See:* Creation of universe(s)
functions of, **126, 188**
goddess of fortune mother of, 122
lords of
purpose of pastimes of, **98**
See also: Brahmā; Demigod(s); Śiva; Viṣṇu structure of, **152**
Ūrja, month of, **139**
Urvaśī, **137**

V

Vaikuṇṭha, **121**
Vaiśampāyana, **5**
Vaiṣṇava(s). *See:* Devotee(s); *specific Vaiṣṇavas*
Vālakhilya *brāhmaṇas*, **142**
Vālmīki, 198
Vāmana, Lord, 123, **158**
Vārāṇasī city, **169**
Varcā, **136**
Varuṇa, Lord, **134**
Varya, **135**
Vasiṣṭha, **134**
Vasudeva & Kṛṣṇa, **162**
Vāsudeva, Lord
as direct expansion of Lord, **124**
See also: Kṛṣṇa; Supreme Lord

Vāsuki, **132**
Vāta, **136**
Vatsāsura, **163**
Vedadarśa, **1**, 2
Vedic scriptures. *See: Purāṇas; Śrīmad-Bhāgavatam*
Vidhātā, 123
Vidura, **151**
Vidyucchatru, **137**
Vijaya, 123
Vivasvān, Lord, **135**
Viṣṇu, Lord
  as benediction giver, **91**
  incarnation of. *See:* Kṛṣṇa, incarnations of
  as manifestation of Lord's potency, 93
  as ruling Deity of material world, **92–**93
  as sun, **139**
  See also: Kṛṣṇa; Supreme Lord
Viṣṇu-rāta defined, 208
Viṣṇurāta, King. *See:* Parīkṣit Mahārāja
Viśva, **136**
Viṣvaksena, **121**
Viśvāmitra, **139**
Viśvanātha Cakravartī Ṭhākura cited
  on Arjuna's confusion, 208
  on Kṛṣṇa's lotus feet, 71-72
  on Nārāyaṇa speaking to Mārkaṇḍeya, 57-58
  on Parīkṣit cursed to die, 208
  on perceiving Lord, 126
  on *Śrīmad-Bhāgavatam* compared with other *Purāṇas*, 194
  on *Śrīmad-Bhāgavatam's* topics listed, 151
Viśvanātha Cakravartī Ṭhākura's commentary on *Bhāgavatam*, 210
Viśvāvasu, **135**
Vṛṣṇi, **127**
Vṛtrāsura, **157**
Vyāghra, **135**
Vyāsadeva
  branches of *Vedas* disseminated by, **172**
  Nārada speaks *Bhāgavatam* to, **206**
  Purāṇas compiled by, 197
  Romaharṣaṇa disciple of, **5**
  as Satyavatī's son, 197
  Śrīmad-Bhāgavatam spoken by, **206**
Vyāsadeva (*continued*)
  Śukadeva Gosvāmī son of, **190**
  as topic of *Bhāgavatam*, **172**

W

Water & conchshell of Lord, **118**
Worship
  to demigods, 51
  to Kṛṣṇa
    as Nara-Nārāyaṇa sages, **43**
    immortality via, **111**
Wrestlers & Kṛṣṇa, **166**

Y

Yadu dynasty
  brāhmaṇas' curse &, **170**
  Kṛṣṇa master of, 148
  Kṛṣṇa performs pastimes for, **167**
  Kṛṣṇa withdraws, **170**
  as topic of *Bhāgavatam*, **161**
Yakṣas, 129
Yayāti, King, **161**